Mastering Flutter

Mastering Flutter helps the reader master the popular Flutter framework for rapid cross-platform app development.

Mobile applications grow in popularity every year, and developers keep looking for new tools to help them design them. A Google-backed, free and open-source mobile user interface framework, Flutter, stands out among these products.

Flutter enables developers to construct a native mobile app using just a single line of code. It implies that one could design two different applications using the same programming language and codebase (iOS and Android).

Flutter comprises two main components: a Framework and a Software Development Kit (SDK). You will use the Dart programming language to create Flutter apps. Dart is an object-oriented programming language with data types and its own paradigm.

The best part about Flutter is that you can use it to create apps for iOS, Android, desktop, and the web, all with the same codebase. Flutter comes with a widget-based UI library, a collection of UI elements (text boxes, picture blocks, buttons, and so on) that can be used to customize and construct apps. Consider Flutter to be the app's frontend user interface and Dart to be the backend code that is generated automatically.

Flutter is considerably easier to understand and use, perfect for creating MVPs. It is also supported by a variety of Integrated Development Environments.

Long story short, Flutter is paving the way for the future. Several companies have already begun using Flutter for cross-platform development. In fact, even Ubuntu Linux supports Flutter-based desktop apps. As such, learning Flutter can be a career-defining move for any coder.

With *Mastering Flutter*, learning Flutter becomes straightforward, which will help readers undoubtedly advance their careers.

The *Mastering Computer Science* series is edited by Sufyan bin Uzayr, a writer and educator with over a decade of experience in the computing field.

Mastering Computer Science
Series Editor: Sufyan bin Uzayr

Mastering Flutter: A Beginner's Guide
Divya Sachdeva, NT Ozman, and Reza Nafim

Mastering Vue.js: A Beginner's Guide
Lokesh Pancha, Divya Sachdeva, and Faruq KC

Mastering GoLang: A Beginner's Guide
Divya Sachdeva, D Nikitenko, and Aruqqa Khateib

Mastering KDE: A Beginner's Guide
Jaskiran Kaur, Mathew Rooney, and Shahryar Raz

Mastering Kotlin: A Beginner's Guide
Divya Sachdeva, Faruq KC, and Aruqqa Khateib

Mastering Visual Studio Code: A Beginner's Guide
Jaskiran Kaur, D Nikitenko, and Mathew Rooney

For more information about this series, please visit: https://www.routledge
.com/Mastering-Computer-Science/book-series/MCS

*The "Mastering Computer Science" series of books are authored by the
Zeba Academy team members, led by Sufyan bin Uzayr.*

*Zeba Academy is an EdTech venture that develops courses and content
for learners primarily in STEM fields, and offers education consulting
to Universities and Institutions worldwide. For more info, please visit
https://zeba.academy*

Mastering Flutter
A Beginner's Guide

Edited by
Sufyan bin Uzayr

CRC Press
Taylor & Francis Group
Boca Raton London New York

CRC Press is an imprint of the
Taylor & Francis Group, an **informa** business

First Edition published 2023
by CRC Press
6000 Broken Sound Parkway NW, Suite 300, Boca Raton, FL 33487-2742

and by CRC Press
2 Park Square, Milton Park, Abingdon, Oxon, OX14 4RN

CRC Press is an imprint of Taylor & Francis Group, LLC

Library of Congress Cataloging-in-Publication Data

Names: Bin Uzayr, Sufyan, editor.
Title: Mastering Flutter : a beginner's guide / edited by Sufyan bin Uzayr.
Description: First edition. | Boca Raton : CRC Press, 2023. | Includes
bibliographical references and index.
Identifiers: LCCN 2022020956 (print) | LCCN 2022020957 (ebook) |
ISBN 9781032289687 (hbk) | ISBN 9781032289489 (pbk) |
ISBN 9781003299363 (ebk)
Subjects: LCSH: Dart (Computer program language) | Flutter. |
Smartphones--Programming. | Application software--Development. |
Programming languages (Electronic computers) | Software frameworks. |
Cross-platform software development.
Classification: LCC QA76.73.D23 M37 2023 (print) | LCC QA76.73.D23
(ebook) | DDC 005.13/3--dc23/eng/20220714
LC record available at https://lccn.loc.gov/2022020956
LC ebook record available at https://lccn.loc.gov/2022020957

ISBN: 9781032289687 (hbk)
ISBN: 9781032289489 (pbk)
ISBN: 9781003299363 (ebk)

DOI: 10.1201/9781003299363

Typeset in Minion
by KnowledgeWorks Global Ltd.

Contents

Preface

The *Mastering Computer Science* covers a wide range of topics, spanning programming languages as well as modern-day technologies and frameworks. The series has a special focus on beginner-level content, and is presented in an easy-to-understand manner, comprising:

- Crystal-clear text, spanning various topics sorted by relevance.

- A special focus on practical exercises, with numerous code samples and programs.

- A guided approach to programming, with step-by-step tutorials for the absolute beginners.

- Keen emphasis on real-world utility of skills, thereby cutting the redundant and seldom-used concepts and focusing instead of industry-prevalent coding paradigm.

- A wide range of references and resources to help both beginner and intermediate-level developers gain the most out of the books.

The *Mastering Computer Science* series of books start from the core concepts, and then quickly move on to industry-standard coding practices, to help learners gain efficient and crucial skills in as little time as possible. The books assume no prior knowledge of coding, so even the absolute newbie coders can benefit from this series.

The *Mastering Computer Science* series is edited by Sufyan bin Uzayr, a writer and educator with more than a decade of experience in the computing field.

About the Author

Sufyan bin Uzayr is a writer, coder, and entrepreneur with over a decade of experience in the industry. He has authored several books in the past, pertaining to a diverse range of topics, ranging from History to Computers/IT.

Sufyan is the Director of Parakozm, a multinational IT company specializing in EdTech solutions. He also runs Zeba Academy, an online learning and teaching vertical with a focus on STEM fields.

Sufyan specializes in a wide variety of technologies such as JavaScript, Dart, WordPress, Drupal, Linux, and Python. He holds multiple degrees, including ones in Management, IT, Literature, and Political Science.

Sufyan is a digital nomad, dividing his time between four countries. He has lived and taught in universities and educational institutions around the globe. Sufyan takes a keen interest in technology, politics, literature, history, and sports, and in his spare time, he enjoys teaching coding and English to young students.

Learn more at sufyanism.com

CHAPTER 1

Getting Started with Flutter and Dart

IN THIS CHAPTER

> *Introduction to Fart*

> *Introduction to Flutter*

> Variables and data types

> Nullable and Non-nullable types

> Data type operators

Only by making a place in our mobile device can mobile app development emphasize our brand name. The more it reaches out to the public, the better our reputation will be.

Creating a profitable application now necessitates the selection of the appropriate app development framework. A framework that allows for rapid app development while not making it too expensive to invest in.

Flutter and Dart are two app development technologies that can meet your requirements. We may compare the features and benefits of both frameworks and then make an informed decision on which framework would best suit our app concept.

DOI: 10.1201/9781003299363-1

WHAT EXACTLY IS FLUTTER?

In definition, creating a mobile application is a time-consuming and difficult task. There are several frameworks available that offer great functionality for developing mobile applications. For developing mobile apps, Android offers a native framework based on Java and Kotlin, whereas iOS offers a framework based on Objective-C/Swift. As a result, we require two distinct languages and frameworks to create apps for both operating systems. Numerous frameworks have been designed to solve this difficulty that enables both operating system and desktop programs. These frameworks are referred to as cross-platform development tools.

The cross-platform development framework allows for creating a single piece of code that can deploy across several platforms (Android, iOS, and Desktop). It saves developers a considerable amount of time and effort. Web-based tools such as Ionic from Drifty Co. in 2013, Phonegap from Adobe, Xamarin from Microsoft, and React Native from Facebook are examples of cross-platform development tools. Each of these frameworks has had varying degrees of success in the mobile business. Flutter, a new framework developed by Google, has been released in the cross-platform development family.

Flutter is a user interface (UI) toolkit that allows us to create fast, attractive, natively built applications for mobile, web, and desktop using a single programming language and codebase. It is open-source and free. It was created by Google and is currently managed under an ECMA standard. The Dart programming language is used to create Flutter applications. Dart programming is similar to other programming languages, such as Kotlin and Swift, and it may be trans-compiled into JavaScript code.

Flutter is primarily designed for 2D mobile apps that run on Android and iOS platforms. We can also use it to create full-featured apps with the camera, storage, geolocation, network, third-party SDKs, and other features.

What Distinguishes Flutter

Flutter differs from other frameworks in that it does not use WebView or the OEM widgets that come with the device. Instead, it draws widgets using its high-performance rendering engine. It also implements most of its features, such as animation, gesture, and widgets, in the Dart programming language, enabling developers to read, edit, replace, or delete items. It provides comprehensive system control to developers.

Flutter's Features

It is a simple technique for creating gorgeous mobile and desktop apps with a complete collection of material designs and widgets. This section will go over its primary features for constructing the mobile framework.

- **Open-source:** Flutter is a free and open-source mobile application development framework.

- **Cross-platform:** This capability enables Flutter to write code once, maintain it, and execute it on several platforms. It saves developers' time, effort, and money.

- **Hot Reload:** When the developer changes the code, the changes are visible instantly, thanks to Hot Reload. It implies that the modifications are immediately displayed in the app. It is a highly useful feature that helps the developer to correct errors immediately.

- **Accessible Native Features and SDKs:** This feature makes app creation simple and enjoyable by utilizing Flutter's native code, third-party integration, and platform APIs. As a result, we have simple access to both systems' SDKs.

- **Minimal Code:** The Flutter app is written in the Dart programming language, which employs JIT (Just-in-Time) and AOT (Ahead-of-Time) compilation to increase total start-up time, functionality, and speed. JIT improves the development system and refreshes the UI without requiring additional work to create a new one.

- **Widgets:** The Flutter framework includes widgets, which may use to create unique, customizable designs. Most notably, Flutter has two sets of widgets: Material Design widgets and Cupertino widgets, which aid in providing a bug-free experience across all platforms.

Flutter Advantages

Flutter's advantage is that it meets the specific demands and criteria for designing mobile applications. It also has several benefits, which are stated as follows:

- Because of the hot-reload functionality, it speeds up the app development process significantly. This functionality allows us to edit or update the code, and the changes are reflected as soon as they are made.

- It enables smoother and more fluid app scrolling experiences with fewer hangs or cuts, allowing apps to run faster in contrast to competing mobile app development frameworks.

- Flutter minimizes testing time and effort. Because flutter apps are cross-platform, testers do not necessarily need to conduct the same set of tests on multiple platforms for the same app.

- It offers a fantastic user experience using a design-centric widget, powerful APIs, and many other features.

- It is comparable to a reactive framework in that developers do not need to change the UI content manually.

- Because of its quick development time and cross-platform nature, it is ideal for MVP apps.

Flutter's History

Google's Flutter is a free and open-source UI software development kit. It's used to develop apps for Android, iOS, Windows, and the web. The initial version of Flutter was revealed at the Dart Developer Summit in 2015. It was initially known as the "Sky" codename and is compatible with the Android operating system. In May 2017, the first Flutter Alpha version (v-0.06) was published after the launch of Flutter.

Later, in September 2018, at the keynote of Google Developer Days in Shanghai, Google published the second preview of Flutter, which was the last major release before the Flutter 1.0 version. At the Flutter Live event on December 4, 2018, the first stable version of the Flutter framework, denoted as Flutter 1.0, was published. On October 24, 2019, the framework's current stable release was Flutter v1.9.1+hotfix.6.

Prerequisites

Before diving into Flutter, you should have a solid grasp of Dart programming, Android Studio, and web scripting languages like HTML, JavaScript, and CSS.

Audience

We created this lesson for both novices and pros that wish to establish a career around Flutter or understand the fundamentals of Flutter quickly. There are several topics accessible to assist you master Flutter technology quickly.

Problems

We guarantee that our Flutter lesson will not cause us any problems. However, please let us know if we discover an error in the comments area.

INSTALLATION OF FLUTTER

This part describes about how to set up an environment for effective Flutter application development.

Windows System Requirements

To install and execute Flutter on a Windows PC, we must first fulfill the development environment requirements.

Operating System	Windows 7 or Later (I have Windows 10. You can also use Mac or Linux OS).
Disk Space	400 MB (Not including disk space for IDE/tools).
Tools	1. Windows PowerShell 2. Git for Windows 2.x (Here, Use Git from Windows Command Prompt option).
SDK	Flutter SDK for Windows
IDE	Android Studio (Official)

Install Git

- **Step 1:** Go to https://git-scm.com/download/win to get Git.

- **Step 2:** To complete the installation, run the.exe file. Ensure that you have picked the preferred option during installation.

Install the Flutter SDK

- **Step 1:** Download the Flutter Software Development Kit for Windows installation package. To download Flutter SDK, go to its official website https://docs.flutter.dev/get-started/install and click on the Get started button. The following page will appear.

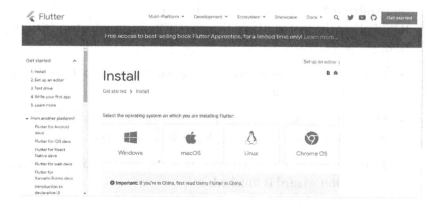

- **Step 2:** Next, click on the Windows button to download the most recent Flutter SDK. The SDK download link is available here.

- **Step 3:** Once your download is finished, unzip the zip file and store it in the selected installation folder or location such as D: /Flutter.

- **Step 4:** In order to run the Flutter command from the standard Windows console, you must alter the system path to include the flutter bin directory. To do this, the following actions must take:

  - **Step 4.1:** Navigate to MyComputer Properties > Advanced > Environment Variables. The screen will appear.

  - **Step 4.2:** Next, choose the path and then click on modify. The screen appears.

  - **Step 4.3:** In the preceding window, click New->write path of Flutter bin folder in variable value -> ok -> ok -> ok -> ok.

- **Step 5:** Finally, execute the $ flutter doctor command. This tool checks for all Flutter app development prerequisites and reports on the state of our Flutter installation.
  ```
  $ flutter doctor
  ```

- **Step 6:** When we run the above command, the system will analyze, and a report will display, as seen in the image below. Here we will discover information on all missing tools needed to execute Flutter and development tools that are available but not linked to the device.

- **Step 7:** Download and install the Android SDK https://developer.android.com/studio. If the flutter doctor command fails to locate the Android SDK tool, we must first install the Android Studio IDE. Follow the instructions given below to install Android Studio IDE.

  - **Step 7.1:** Get the most recent Android Studio executable or zip file from the official site.

  - **Step 7.2:** Double-click the.exe file to launch it once the download is complete. The following dialogue box will appear.

  - **Step 7.3:** Follow the installation wizard's instructions, when the installation wizard is finished.

- **Step 7.4:** On the previous screen, select Next-> Finish. After clicking the Finish button, select the "Don't import Settings" option and click OK. It will launch Android Studio.

- **Step 8:** Next, you must install an Android emulator. It's in charge of executing and testing the Flutter application.

  - **Step 8.1:** To create an Android emulator, navigate Android Studio > Tools > Android > AVD Manager and select Create Virtual Device. Alternatively, go to Help->Find Action->Enter Emulator in the search box. The screen will appear.

  - **Step 8.2:** Select our device definition and press the Next button.

  - **Step 8.3:** Click next after selecting the system image for the most recent Android version.

  - **Step 8.4:** Now, double-check the entire AVD setup. If everything is correct, click Finish. The screen appears.

  - **Step 8.5:** Finally, click on the icon pointing inside the red rectangle. The Android emulator was shown.

- **Step 9:** Install the Flutter and Dart plugins to construct a Flutter application in Android Studio. These plugins provide a template for creating a Flutter application and executing and debugging Flutter applications within Android Studio. To install these plugins, follow the steps given below.

  - **Step 9.1:** Launch Android Studio, then navigate to File-> Settings->Plugins.

  - **Step 9.2:** Now, look for the Flutter plugin. If the Flutter plugin is discovered, pick it and click Install. When we click on install, we will be prompt to install the Dart plugin, as seen in the screenshot below. To proceed, click Yes.

  - **Step 9.3:** Restart Android Studio.

macOS System Requirements

To install and execute Flutter on a macOS machine, we must first fulfill the following development environment requirements.

Operating System	macOS (64-bit)
Disk Space	2.8 GB (Not including disk space for IDE/tools).
Tools	bash
	curl
	git 2.x
	mkdir
	rm
	unzip
	which
IDE	Xcode (Official)

Download the Flutter SDK

- **Step 1:** Download the Flutter Software Development Kit for the macOS installation package. Go to the Flutter SDK's official website to download it from https://docs.flutter.dev/get-started/install.

- **Step 2:** Once our download is complete, unpack the zip file and store it in the installation folder or location of your choice.

- **Step 3:** In order to launch the Flutter command, you must change the system path to include the flutter bin directory.

```
$ export PATH="$PATH:'pwd'/flutter/bin"
```

- **Step 4:** Next, use the following command to enable the updated path in the current terminal window, and then check it.

```
source ~/.bashrc
source $HOME/.bash_profile
echo $PATH
```

- **Step 5:** Finally, execute the $ flutter doctor command. This tool checks for all Flutter app development prerequisites and reports on the state of our Flutter installation.

```
$ flutter doctor
```

- **Step 6:** When we execute the command mentioned above, it will assess the system and provide data on any missing tools necessary to run Flutter and any development tools that are present but not linked to the device.

- **Step 7:** If the Flutter doctor tool indicates that we need to update our Xcode tools, do so.

- **Step 8:** If the Flutter doctor tool indicates that you need to update our Android Studio and SDK, do so.

- **Step 9:** To design an iOS application, we must either set up an iOS emulator or connect an iPhone device to the system.

- **Step 10:** Install an android emulator or connect an android device to the system once more to construct an android application.

- **Step 11:** Install the Flutter and Dart plugins to construct a Flutter application in Android Studio. These plugins provide a template for creating a Flutter application and executing and debugging Flutter applications within Android Studio.

WHAT EXACTLY IS DART PROGRAMMING?

Dart is a general-purpose, object-oriented programming language with C-style syntax created by Google in 2011. Dart programming is used to construct frontend UIs for online and mobile apps. It is actively developed, compiled to native machine code for mobile apps, and strongly typed. It is influenced by the other programming languages such as Java, JavaScript, and C#. Because Dart is a compiled language, we cannot directly run our code; instead, the compiler parses it and converts it to machine code.

Unlike other programming languages, it supports most standard programming language features such as classes, interfaces, and functions. Dart does not directly support arrays. It has collection support, which is used to reproduce data structures like arrays, generics, and optional type.

The following example demonstrates basic Dart programming:

```
void main() {
  for (int x = 0; x < 5; x++) {
    print('helloo ${x + 1}');
  }
}
```

Dart is a client-optimized programming language for creating quick apps on any platform. Its purpose is to provide the most productive programming language for cross-platform development and a flexible execution runtime platform for app frameworks.

Languages are characterized by their technical envelope, the decisions made during development that form a language's capabilities and strengths. Dart is built for a technical envelope ideal for client development, focusing on development (sub-second stateful Hot Reload) and high-quality production experiences across a wide range of compilation targets (web, mobile, and desktop).

Dart is also the basis for Flutter. Dart offers the language and runtimes that power Flutter apps, but it also helps with many essential development responsibilities, including code formatting, analysis, and testing.

Dart: Language

Dart is type safe; it employs static-type checking to verify that a variable's value always matches the static type of the variable. This is sometimes referred to as sound typing. Although types are required, type annotations are not required due to type inference. Dart's typing system is very versatile, enabling the usage of a dynamic type in conjunction with runtime checks, which can be beneficial during experimentation or for work that requires a high degree of dynamicity.

Dart has good null safety, which means that values can't be null until we explicitly state they can. Dart's sound null safety protects us from null exceptions at runtime via static code inspection. Unlike many other null-safe languages, when Dart concludes that a variable is non-nullable, it stays that way. If we examine our running code in the debugger, we'll notice that non-nullability is preserved at runtime.

The following code example demonstrates numerous Dart language capabilities, including libraries, async calls, nullable and non-nullable types, arrow syntax, generators, streams, and getters. See the samples page for examples of how to use other Dart capabilities.

```
import 'dart:math' show Random;
void main() async {
  print('Compute π using Monte Carlo method.');
  await for (final estimate in computePi().take(110)) {
    print('π ≅ $estimate');
  }
}
```

```dart
/// Generates stream of increasingly accurate
estimates of π.
Stream<double> computePi({int batch = 120000}) async* {
  var totals = 0; // Inferred to be of type int
  var counts = 0;
  while (true) {
    final points = generateRandom().take(batch);
    final inside = points.where((p) =>
p.isInsideUnitCircle);
    totals += batch;
    counts += inside.length;
    final ratio = counts / totals;
    // Area of circle is A = π·r², therefore π = A/r².
    // So, when given the random points with x ∈
<0,1>,
    // y ∈ <0,1>, the ratio of those inside a unit
circle
    // should approach π / 4. Therefore, value of π
    // should be:
    yield ratio * 4;
  }
}
Iterable<Point> generateRandom([int? seed]) sync* {
  final random = Random(seed);
  while (true) {
    yield Point(random.nextDouble(), random.
nextDouble());
  }
}
class Point {
  final double a;
  final double b;
  const Point(this.a, this.b);
  bool get isInsideUnitCircle => a * a + b * b <= 1;
}
```

Characteristics of Dart

Dart is a powerful object-oriented, open-source programming language with many helpful features. It is a new programming language that includes various programming utilities such as interfaces, collections, classes, dynamic, and optional typing. It is designed for both the server and the browser. The following is a list of the essential Dart features.

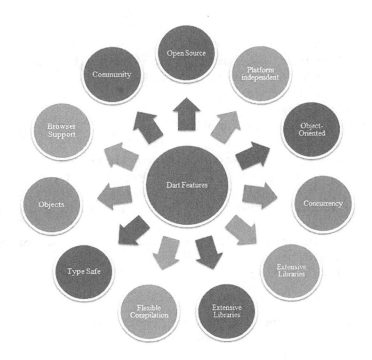

Features of Dart.

Open Source
Dart is an open source programming language, which is free to use. Google created it, is compliant with the ECMA standard, and is licensed under the BSD license.

Platform Independent
Dart is platform-independent, supporting all major operating systems such as Windows, Linux, and Macintosh. Dart has its Virtual Machine (VM), known as the Dart VM, which allows us to run Dart code on any operating system.

Object-Oriented
Dart is an object oriented programming language that supports all oops concepts, including classes, inheritance, interfaces, and optional typing.

It also supports advanced ideas such as mixin, abstract, classes, reified generic, and a robust type system.

Concurrency

Dart is an asynchronous programming language that allows multi-threading through Isolates. Isolates are independent entities tied to threads but do not share memory and communicate across processes via message passing. To ensure successful communication, the message should be serialized. The message is serialized by utilizing a snapshot created by the provided object and then transmitted to isolation for destabilization.

Extensive Libraries

Dart has numerous important inbuilt libraries such as SDK (Software Development Kit), core, math, async, convert, html, IO, and so on. It also allows us to structure our Dart code into libraries with correct namespacing. The import statement will enable it to be reused.

Easy to Learn

As we established in the last part, learning Dart is not a Hercules task because its syntax is similar to Java, C#, JavaScript, kotlin, and other programming languages. If we know any of these languages, we can learn Dart quickly.

Flexible Compilation

Dart allows us to compile code in various ways that are both flexible and quick. It supports two compilation processes: AOT and JIT. The Dart code is sent in another language that contemporary web-brewers can execute.

Type Safe

Dart is a type-safe language, which implies that it utilizes both static type checking and runtime checks to ensure that a variable's value always matches the variable's static type, also known as sound typing.

Type annotations are optional due to type interference, even if types are necessary. This improves the readability of the code. Another advantage of using a type-safe language is that when we alter a code section, the system alerts us about the previous update.

Objects

The Dart considers everything to be an item. An object is a value that is assigned to the variable. Dart also considers functions, integers, and texts to be objects. All objects derive from the Object class.

Browser Support

The Dart supports all recent web browsers. It includes the dart2js compiler, which translates Dart code into efficient JavaScript code suited for all types of web browsers.

Community

Dart has a sizable global community. So, if we have difficulty when coding, we may efficiently locate assistance. The devoted development team is working hard to improve its functioning.

Dart's Libraries

Dart includes a robust set of core libraries that provide the foundation for many common programming tasks:

- Dart programs provide built-in types, collections, and other essential features (dart:core)

- Queues, linked lists, hashmaps, and binary trees are more complex collection types (dart:collection)

- Encoders and decoders for transforming data representations such as JSON and UTF-8 (dart:convert)

- Random number creation and mathematical constants and functions (dart:math)

- Non-web apps can use file, socket, HTTP, and other I/O methods (dart:io)

- Asynchronous programming is supported by classes such as Future and Stream (dart:async)

- Lists that handle fixed-sized data effectively (for example, unsigned 8-byte integers) and SIMD numeric types (dart:typed data)

- Foreign function interfaces are used to interoperate with other code that uses a C-style interface (dart:ffi)

- Concurrent programming using isolates – autonomous workers that are comparable to threads but do not share memory and communicate exclusively via messages (dart:isolate)

- HTML elements and other resources for web-based applications that must communicate with browsers and the Document Object Model (DOM) (dart:html)

Aside from the core libraries, many APIs are available through a diverse range of packages. Dart's team releases a plethora of useful supplemental packages, such as these:

- characters

- intl

- markdown

- http

- crypto

Furthermore, third-party publishers and the greater community publish thousands of packages with support for features like these.

- XML

- Windows integration

- compression

- SQLite

Dart: Platforms

Dart's compiler technology allows us to run code in a variety of ways:

- Dart contains a Dart VM with JIT compilation and an AOT compiler for creating machine code for programs targeting mobile and desktop platforms.

- Dart contains a development time compiler (dartdevc) and a production time compiler for web-targeted programs (dart2js). Dart is translated into JavaScript by both compilers.

The Flutter framework is a popular multi-platform UI toolkit driven by the Dart platform that provides tools and UI frameworks for creating UI experiences that operate on iOS, Android, macOS, Windows, Linux, and the web.

Native Dart (Machine Code JIT and AOT)

A quick developer cycle is essential for iteration throughout development. The Dart VM includes a JIT compiler with incremental recompilation (allowing Hot Reload), live metrics collectors (powering DevTools), and extensive debugging capabilities.

When apps are ready for production deployment, whether to an app store or a production backend, the Dart AOT compiler enables AOT compilation to native ARM or x64 machine code. Your AOT-compiled program starts up quickly and consistently.

The AOT-compiled code executes within a fast Dart runtime that enforces the sound Dart type system and manages memory with rapid object allocation and a generational garbage collector (GC).

Dart Web (JavaScript Dev and Prod)

Dart Web allows us to run Dart code on web platforms that use JavaScript. Dart Web compiles Dart code to JavaScript code, which runs in a browser such as V8 within Chrome.

Dart web has an incremental dev compiler that allows for a quick development cycle and an optimized production compiler, dart2js, that converts Dart code to fast, compact, deployable JavaScript utilizing methods like dead-code reduction.

Dart's Runtime

Regardless of the platform or how your code is compiled or running, it requires a Dart runtime. This runtime is in charge of the critical tasks listed as follows:

- Dart employs a managed memory model in which unused memory is recovered by a GC.

- **Enforcing the Dart type system:** While most Dart type tests are static (compile-time), others are dynamic (runtime). The Dart runtime, for example, enforces dynamic checks via type check and cast operators.

- **Managing isolates:** The Dart runtime is in charge of the primary isolate (where code generally executes) and any other isolates created by the app.

- The Dart runtime is automatically included into self-contained executables on native systems, and it is part of the Dart VM given via the dart run command.

A Fundamental Darts Program

Many of Dart's most fundamental features are used in the following code:

```
// Define function.
void printInteger(int aNumbers) {
  print('The number is $aNumbers.'); // Print to
console.
}
// This is where app starts executing.
void main() {
  var numbers = 52; // Declare and initialize
variable.
  printInteger(numbers); // Call function.
}
```

This application employs the following technique, which is applicable to all (or almost all) Dart apps:

- **// This is a comment:** A single-line comment. Dart also allows for multiline comments and document comments.

- **void:** A special type that represents a value that will never be utilized. The void return type is used by functions that do not explicitly return a value such as printInteger() and main().

- **int:** Another type that denotes an integer. String, List, and bool are among more built-in types (52).

- **A literal number:** Number literals function as a type of compile-time constant.

- **print():** It is a convenient method for displaying output.

- **'...' (or "..."):** A string literal.

- **$variableName (or $expression):** String interpolation: including the string equivalent of a variable or expression within a string literal.

- **main():** A unique, mandatory top-level function that initiates program execution.

- **var:** A variable declaration without identifying its type. The initial value of this variable (int) determines its type (int) (52).

Key Actions

Keep the following facts and concepts in mind while we study the Dart language:

- Everything we put in a variable is an object, and every object is a class instance. Objects include integers, functions, and null. All objects, with the exception of null (if sound null safety is enabled), derive from the Object class.

- Dart is tightly typed, yet type annotations are not required since Dart can infer types. The code above assumes that the number is of type int.

- If we activate null safety, variables cannot contain null unless you explicitly specify that they may. By appending question mark (?) to the end of a variable's type, it can be made nullable. A variable of type int ? , for example, might be an integer or null. If you know an expression never evaluates to null, but Dart disagrees, we may add ! to assert that it isn't null (and to throw an exception if it is). In this case, int a = nullableButNotNullInt.

- When we wish to explicitly declare that any type is acceptable, use the type Object? (if null safety is enabled), Object or type checking must be deferred until the special type dynamic runtime.

- Dart supports generic types such as Listint> (a list of integers) and ListObject> (a list of objects) (a list of objects of any type).

- Dart allows both top-level functions (such as main()) and functions that are attached to a class or object (static and instance methods, respectively). Functions within functions can also create (nested or local functions).

- Dart, too, provides top-level variables and variables associated with a class or object (static and instance variables). Instance variables are also referred to as fields or properties.

- Dart, unlike Java, lacks the keywords public, protected, and private. If an identifier begins with an underscore (_), it is reserved for its library.

- Identifiers can begin with a letter or an underscore (_), including any combination of those characters and numerals.

- Dart supports expressions (which contain runtime values) and statements (which do not). For instance, consider the conditional expression condition ? expr1: expr2 is either expr1 or expr2. In comparison, an if-else sentence has no utility. A statement frequently comprises one or more expressions, but an expression cannot contain a statement directly.

- Dart tools can provide two types of faults and warnings. Warnings are just signals that our code may not function properly, but they do not prohibit our application from running. Errors can occur at either the build or execution time. A compile-time error stops the code from running at all; a runtime problem causes an exception to be thrown while the code is running.

Variables

Here's an example of generating and initializing a variable:

```
var name = 'Bobby';
```

Variables keep track of references. The variable name has a reference to a String object with the value "Bobby."

The name variable's type is inferred to be String, but we can alter it by specifying it. Specify the Object type if an object is not bound to a single type (or dynamic if necessary).

```
Object name = 'Bobby';
```

Another method is to indicate the type that will infer explicitly:

```
String name = 'Bobby';
```

Default Value

Uninitialized variables of the nullable type have a null value as their default value. (If we haven't enabled null safety, each variable has a nullable type.) Because numbers, like everything else in Dart, are objects, variables with numeric types are initially null.

```
int? lineCounts;
assert(lineCounts == null);
```

If we enable null safety, we must first initialize the values of non-nullable variables:

```
int lineCounts = 0;
```

A local variable does not have to be initialized when it is declared, but it must be assigned a value before it may be used. For example, the following code is valid since Dart can detect that lineCounts is not null when it is supplied to print():

```
int lineCounts;
if (weLikeToCount) {
  lineCounts = countLines();
} else {
  lineCounts = 0;
}
print(lineCounts);
```

Top-level and class variables are initialized lazily; the initialization code is executed the first time the variable is used.

INSTALLATION OF DART

We must first install the Dart programming environment on our local system to study Dart. The following instructions describe installing the Dart SDK (Software Development Kit) on various operating systems.

Install the Dart SDK on Windows

To install Dark SDK in Windows, follow these steps:

- **Step 1:** Open a browser and navigate to the following URL to download the SDK.

  It will take us to the specified page. Please follow the link below.
  http://www.gekorm.com/dart-windows/

- **Step 2:** Launch the Dart installer (the.exe file we downloaded in the previous step) and select the Next button.

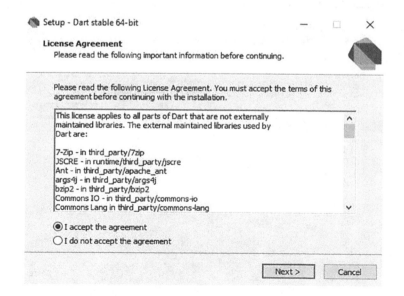

- **Step 3:** It gives us a choice to choose the Dart installation path. After we've decided on a path, click the Next button.

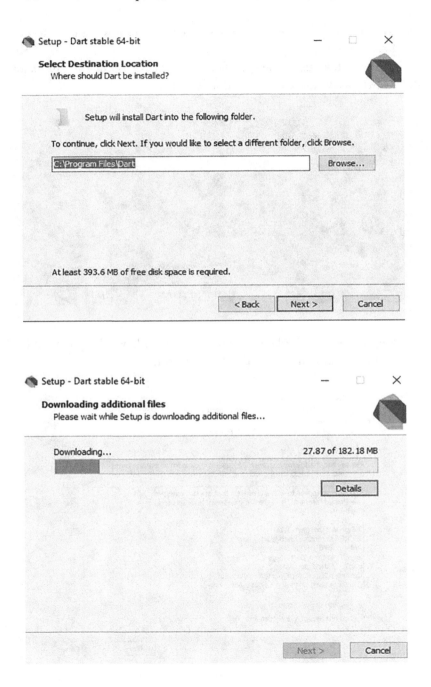

- **Step 4:** Once the download is complete, change the PATH environment variable in the system properties to "C:\Program Files\Dart\ dart-sdk\bin."

- **Step 5:** Now, open the terminal and type dart to confirm the Dart installation.

Install the Dart SDK on Linux

The procedures for installing Dart on Linux are shown below.

Before installing the Dart, if we are running Debian/Ubuntu on AMD64(64-bit Intel) on our local system, we can do it via one of the following methods:

- Install using apt-get

- Install a Debian package

Installation Using apt-get

- **Step 1:** For a one-time setup, enter the following commands:

```
$sudo apt-get update
$ sudo apt-get install apt-transport-https

$ sudo sh -c 'wget -qO- https://dl-ssl.google.com/
linux/linux_signing_key.pub | apt-key add -'
```

```
$ sudo sh -c 'wget -qO- https://storage.
googleapis.com/download.dartlang.org/linux/debian/
dart_stable.list > /etc/apt/sources.list.d/dart_
stable.list'
```

- **Step 2:** Type the following command to install the Dart SDK using the apt-get option in the terminal.

```
$sudo apt-get update
$ sudo apt-get install dart
```

The Dart SDK will download successfully.

Installation of a Debian Package

Dart SDK is available for download as a Debian package in .deb format. To make all Dart binaries available, modify the PATH using the following command:

```
export PATH="$PATH:/usr/lib/dart/bin"
```

To modify the PATH for upcoming terminal sessions, use the following command:

```
$ echo 'export PATH="$PATH:/usr/lib/dart/bin"'
>> ~/.profile
```

Installation of the Dark SDK on Mac

- **Step 1:** We should have the Homebrew package manager, but if we don't, install it and perform the following command. The Dart will download successfully on the Mac.

```
$brew tap dart-lang/dart
$ brew install dart
```

- **Step 2:** Run the following command to see which version we have installed.

```
$brew info dart
```

Editor of Online Dart

We have already addressed Dark installation on several operating systems, but if we do not want to install Dart, an online Dark editor (known as DartPad) is available to execute the Dark apps. DartPad is available online at https://dartpad.dev/. The DartPad allows us to run dart programs and view HTML and terminal output. The online DartPad looks like the image below.

Support of Dart IED

The IDEs from JetBrains that support Dart Programming include Eclipse, IntelliJ, and WebStorm; however, WebStorm is more popular than the others. It is available for download at https://www.jetbrains.com/webstorm/download/#section=windows-version.

The dart2js Tool

The Dark SDK includes the dart2js tool, which converts Dart code into JavaScript code that can execute. It is required since only a few web browsers support the Dart VM.

To compile the Dart code into JavaScript code, run the following command in the terminal.

```
dart2js - - out = <output_file>.js  <dart_script>.dart
```

The preceding command will generate a file containing the JavaScript code that corresponds to the Dart code.

First Program in Dart

Dart is simple to learn if you are familiar with Java, C++, JavaScript, and other programming languages. The simplest "Helloo World" program demonstrates the programming language's basic grammar. It's a method of testing the system and the working environment. In this course, we will cover the fundamentals of Dart syntax. The first program can be run in numerous ways, as shown below:

- Using Command Line

- Running on Browser

- Using IDE

Before launching the first application, we must confirm that the Dart SDK has been correctly installed. In our last session, we went over the whole installation method. Let's start with our first program.

Using Command Line

- **Step 1:** Type dart into the terminal; if it displays dart runtime, Dart has been successfully installed.

- **Step 2:** Open a text editor and save the file as "hellooword.dart." The file extension should be .dart to indicate a Dart program file.

```
//The first program
//This will execute on the command line
Main()
{
print("Helloo world");
}
```

  - **main():** The main() function signifies that we are starting our program. It is a crucial function that initiates the program's execution.

  - **print():** This function prints the output to the console. It's comparable to C, JavaScript, or any other programming language. Curly brackets and semicolons are required for proper usage.

- **Step 3:** Launch the command line and compile the program. By executing dart hellooworld.dart, we may launch the Dart program. The screen will display Helloo World.

Running on Browser

Dart includes an online editor known as DartPad, which may be found at https://dartpad.dartlang.org/. We may write the code on the left side of the screen, and the output appears on the right. With the Dart Code, we can add HTML and CSS. Dart also includes several sample programs that may use to learn the language.

Using IDE

Dart is supported by a number of IDEs, including Visual Studio Code, WebStorm, IntelliJ, and others. Download the dart extension and execute the code to get the visual studio code.

Basic Dart Syntax

Dart is a Google-created static programming language. According to the GitHub popularity index, it has surpassed Python as the most popular programming language since it supports the flutter toolkit. Flutter is a framework that generates quick cross-platform apps by utilizing Dart's native compilation capability. Dart allows for two forms of compilation: JIT and AOT. Its syntax is a hybrid of CPP, Python, Java, and JavaScript. We will look at the basic grammar of Dart and how to describe the language that the machine understands in this section.

Dart Identifiers

An identifier is a name used to declare variables, methods, classes, and functions, among other things. An identifier is a string of letters ([A to Z], [a to z]), digits ([0–9]), and underscore (_), with the first character not being a number. A few guidelines for defining IDs are as follows:

- A digit should not be used as the initial character.

- Special characters are not permitted except for the underscore (_) and the dollar symbol ($).

- Two underscores (__) in a row are not permitted.

- The initial character must be an alphabetic letter (uppercase or lowercase) or an underscore.

- Identifiers must be one-of-a-kind and cannot include any whitespace.

- They take instance into account. The variables Joseph and joseph will be handled differently.

The following table contains a list of valid and incorrect identifiers.

Valid Identifiers	Invalid Identifiers
Firstnames	__firstnames
firstNames	first names
vari1	V5ari
$counts	first-names
_firstnames	1results
First_names	@vari

String Interpolation and Dart Printing

The print() method sends output to the console, and $expression is used to interpolate string. Here's an example:

```
void main()
{
    var names = "Param";
    var roll_no = 25;
    print("My name ${names} My roll number is
${roll_no}");
}
```

Dart's Semicolon

The semicolon is used to conclude a sentence, indicating that the statement has concluded. A semicolon must use to end each statement (;). Using a semicolon as a delimiter, we may write many statements on a single line. If the compiler is not used correctly, it will issue an error. Here's an example:

```
var msg1 = "Helloo World!";
var msg2 = "How are you???"
```

Line Breaks and Dart Whitespace

The Dart compiler ignores whitespaces. Our application is used to indicate space, tab, and newline characters. It denotes the separation of one component of a statement from another part. We can also utilize space and tabs to specify indentation in our software and offer the necessary format. It makes code more understandable and readable.

Block in Dart

The block is a grouping of the statements enclosed by curly braces. Curly braces are used in Dart to gather all of the statements in a block. Consider the following syntax.

Syntax:

```
{ //start block
    //block of statement(s)
}// end block
```

Command-Line Options for Dart

The Dart command-line parameters are used to affect the execution of Dart script. The following are the normal command-line arguments.

Sr.	Command-line Options	Descriptions
1.	-c or –c	It supports assertions as well as type checks.
2.	--version	It displays information about the VM version.
3.	--package<path>	It specifies the location of the package resolution configuration file.
4.	-p <path>	It specifies where the libraries may be found.
5.	-h or –help	It is used to request help.

Enable Checked Mode

In general, the Dart program operates in two modes, which are described as follow:

- Checked Mode
- Production Mode

Checked Mode

The checked mode allows several Dart code checks such as type-checking. While developing processes, it alerts or throws errors. To activate the checked mode, type -c or – checked before the name of the dart script-file on the command prompt. The Dart VM operates in checked mode by default.

Production Mode

The Dart script is now in production mode. It ensures that performance will improve while the script is executing. Consider the following scenario.

```
void main() {
    int vari = "helloo";
    print(vari);
}
```

Now, type dart -c or – checked mode to enable the checked mode.

```
dart -c mode.dart
```

The Dart VM will display the following error message.

Unhandled exception:

```
type "String" is not a subtype of the type "int" of
"n" where
    String is from dart:core
    int is from dart:core
```

COMMENTS IN DART

The collection of statements disregarded by the Dart compiler during program execution is known as comments. It is used to make the source code more readable. In general, comments provide a concise overview of what is happening in the code. We can explain the operation of variables, functions, classes, or any other expression in the code. Programmers should make advantage of the comment to improve their practice. In the Dart, there are three categories of comments.

Comments Types

Dart supports three types of comments:

- Single-line comments

- Multi-line comments

- Documentation comments

Single-Line Comments

We may use the // to add comments to a single line (double-slash). The single-line comments can be used till there is a line break.

Example:

```
void main(){
    // This will print the given
    print("Welcome to Dart");
}
```

The Dart compiler entirely ignores the // (double-slash) command and retunes the result.

Multi-Line Comments

When we need to apply comments to many lines, we may use / *. . . .*/. The compiler ignores anything typed inside the / *...*/; however, it cannot be nested with multiline comments. Consider the following example:

```
void main(){
    /* This is example of multi-line comment
    This will print the given */
    print("Welcome to Dart");
}
```

Documentation Comments

Document comments are used to create documentation or reference a project/software package. It can be a single or multiline comment beginning with /// or /*. On successive lines, we may use ///, which is the same as a multiline comment. Except for those put inside the curly brackets, these lines are ignored by the Dart compiler. Classes, functions, parameters, and variables can all be defined. Consider the following scenario.

```
///This
///is a
///example of multi
/// line comment
```

Example:

```
void main(){
    ///This is
    ///the example of a
    ///multiline comment
    ///This will print the given
    print("Welcome to Dart");
}
```

KEYWORDS IN DART

Dart Keywords are reserved words with particular significance for the compiler. It can't be used as a variable, class, or function name. Keywords are case sensitive; therefore, they must type exactly as defined. The Dart language contains 61 keywords. Some are common, and we may be familiar with some of them, while others are unique. The following is a list of the Dart keywords.

abstract[2]	Else	import[2]	super
as[2]	Enum	In	switch
Assert	export[2]	interface[2]	sync[1]
async[1]	extends	Is	This
await[3]	extension[2]	library[2]	throw
Break	external[2]	mixin[2]	True
Case	factory	New	Try
Catch	False	Null	typedef[2]
Class	Final	on1	Var
Const	finally	operator[2]	void
Continue	For	part[2]	while
covarient[2]	Function[2]	Rethrow	with
Default	get[2]	Return	yield[3]
deffered[2]	hide[1]	set[2]	
Do	If	show[1]	
dynamic[2]	implements[2]	static[2]	

A few keywords are indicated with a superscript in the preceding list of keywords (1, 2, and 3). Following that, we will explain why superscript is used.

- **Subscript 1:** These are known as contextual keywords. They have a specific meaning and are utilized in certain areas.

- **Subscript 2:** These are known as built-in identifiers. These keywords are used to translate JavaScript code to Dart; they are considered legitimate identifiers but cannot be used in class names, function names, or import prefixes.

- **Subscript 3:** These are newly added asynchrony-related keywords.

DATA TYPES IN DART

The most significant fundamental characteristics of a programming language are its data types. The data type of a variable in Dart is specified by its value. Variables are used to store values and reserve memory space. The data-type indicates the sort of value that the variable will store. Each variable has a unique data type. Dart is a static language, which means that variables cannot change.

Dart has built-in support for the following data types:

- Number
- Strings
- Boolean
- Lists
- Maps
- Runes
- Symbols

Dart Number

The Darts Number is used to keep track of the numerical values. There are two sorts of numbers: integers and double.

- **Integer:** An integer value is a whole number or a non-fractional value. Integer data types provide 64-bit non-decimal values ranging from –263 to 263. An unsigned or signed integer value can store in a variable. The following is an example:

```
int marks = 98;
```

- **Double:** A double value represents 64 bits of information (double precision) for a floating number or a number with several decimal points. The double keyword is used to declare a variable of the double type.

```
double pi = 3.14;
```

Data String

A string is the character sequence. If we save data such as a name, address, special character, and so on. Either single or double quotation marks indicate it. A Dart string is a string made up of UTF-16 code units.

```
var msg = "Welcome to Dart";
```

Dart Boolean

The Boolean type represents true and false. The term bool is used to represent Boolean Type. The numeric numbers 1 and 0 cannot express whether a value is true or false.

```
bool isValid = true;
```

Dart Lists

The list in Dart is a collection of ordered things (value). A list is comparable to an array in concept. A collection of several elements in a single variable is defined as an array. The list's items are separated by a comma in a square bracket[]. The following is an example list:

```
var list = [14,21,32]
```

Dart Maps

The maps type is used to hold key-value pairs of values. Each key has a value associated with it. Any type of key and value can use. The key in Map must be unique, but the value can appear several times. Curly braces {} define the Map, and a comma separates each pair.

```
var students = {'names': 'Jose', 'age':22, 'Branch':
'Computer-Science'}
```

Dart Runes

Strings, as we know, are a sequence of Unicode UTF-16 code units. Unicode is a method for describing a unique numeric value for each digit, letter, and symbol. Dart Runes are a unique string of Unicode UTF-32 units. It's used to express the unique syntax.

The special heart character (♥), for example, is identical to Unicode code u2665, where u stands for Unicode, and the digits are hexadecimal integers. If the hex value is less than or more than four digits, it is enclosed in a curly braces {}.

Example:

```
void main(){
    var hearts_symbol = '\u2665';
    print(hearts_symbol);
}
```

Dart Symbols

Dart Symbols are objects used to refer to an operator or identifier declared in a Dart program. It is typical in APIs to refer to identifiers by name since identifier names can change but not identifier symbols.

Dart Dynamic Type

Dart is a language that may be typed or not. If the variable type is not explicitly provided, the variable type is dynamic. The dynamic keyword is used explicitly for type annotation.

VARIABLE IN DART

A variable is used to hold a value and refer to a computer's memory region. When we declare a variable, the Dart compiler allocates memory space. The kind of variable determines the size of the memory block. Specific guidelines must be followed while creating a variable. Here's an example of establishing a variable and assigning it a value:

```
var name = 'Devaan';
```

The variable name carries the string value "Devaan" here. Variables in Dart are used to hold references. The variable above has a reference to a String with the value Devaan.

Variable Creation Rule

Creating a variable with an appropriate name in any programming language is a necessary task. Dart has several rules for defining variables. These guidelines are outlined below:

- The variable does not allow whitespace, mathematical symbols, runes, Unicode characters, and keywords.

- The variable's initial character should be an alphabet ([A to Z], [a to z]). As the initial character, digits are not permitted.

- Variables have a case sensitivity. Variable age and AGE, for example, are addressed differently.

- Except for the underscore (_) and the dollar symbol ($), special characters such as #, @, &, and * are not permitted.

- The variable name should be retable and readable by the program.

Dart Variable Declaration

A variable must declare before it can use in a program. To declare a variable in Dart, use the var keyword. Because Dart is an infer type language, the Dart compiler automatically determines the type of data based on the value assigned to the variable. The syntax is shown below.

Syntax:

```
var <variable_names>  = <values>;
```

Example:

```
var name = 'Anie'
```

In the above example, the variable name has allotted some memory space. The semicolon(;) is required because it separates one program statement from another.

Type Annotations

As previously said, the Dart is an infer language, but it also has type annotation. The type of value the variable can store is suggested when it is declared. We include the data type as a prefix before the variable's name in the type annotation to ensure that the variable may hold certain data types. The syntax is shown below.

Syntax:

```
<type> <variable_names>;
```

Example:

```
int ages;
String msgs = "Welcome to Dart";
```

In the above example, we defined ages to hold the integer data. The string data was stored in the variable msgs.

Declaring the Variable as Having Multiple Values

Dart allows us to specify multiple values of the same type to variables. We can perform this in a single sentence, with commas between each value. The syntax is shown below.

Syntax:

```
<type> <var1,var2....varN>;
```

Example:

```
int a,b,c;
```

Default Value

When a variable is declared but not initialized, the Dart compiler assigns a default value (Null). Even the numeric type variables are allocated a null value at first. Consider the following scenario.

```
int counts;
assert(counts == null);
```

Final and Const

We use final and const when we don't want to update a variable in the future. It can use instead of or in addition to var. When the variable is a compile-time constant, the variable can only be set once. The following is an example of creating a final variable:

```
final name = 'Ritesh;                              //
final variable without type-annotation.
final String msg = 'How are you??';      // final
variable with type-annotation.
```

If we try to modify these values, an error will be generated.

```
name = 'Rishi';                        // Error: Final-
variable can't be changed.
```

The const keyword is used to define compile-time constants. We can assign a value to a compile-time constant such as a number, string literal, const variable, and so on.

```
const b = 2000;
```

The const keyword is also used to define a constant value that cannot modify after it is defined.

```
var g= const[];
```

It will raise an error if we try to alter it.

```
f = [14];      //Error, const variable cannot be change
```

OPERATORS IN DART

An operator is a symbol that manipulates values or performs actions on their operand. The supplied equation is 5+5, where 5 and 5 are operands, and "+" is the operator.

Dart has many built-in operators for performing many sorts of tasks. Operators can be unary or binary, which means that unary operators take only one operand and binary operators take two operands. There are several kinds of operators.

Operator Types

Dart supports the following operator types:

- Assignment operators

- Arithmetic operators

- Relational operators

- Logical operators

- Bitwise operator

- Type test operators

- Conditional operators

- Casecade notation(..) operators

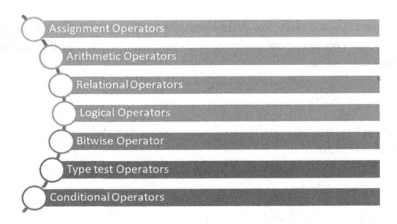

Types of operators.

Arithmetic Operators in Dart

Arithmetic operators are the most often used operators for doing addition, subtraction, multiplication, and division. If the variable has a value of 20 and variable b has a value of 10, then:

Sr.	Operator Name	Description	Example
1.	Addition (+)	It adds the left operand to the right operand.	x+y will return 20
2.	Subtraction (−)	It takes the right operand and subtracts it from the left operand.	x−y will return 30
3	Divide (/)	It takes the first operand and divides it by the second operand, returning the quotient.	x/y will return 1.0
4.	Multiplication (*)	It multiplies the first operand by the second operand.	x*y will return 100
5.	Modulus (%)	After dividing one operand into another, it returns a reminder.	x%y will return 0
6.	Division (~/)	It divides the first operand by the second operand and returns the integer quotient as a result.	x/y will return 3
7.	Unary Minus (-expr)	It changes the sign of a single operand when used with it.	−(x−y) will return −13

Example:

```
void main(){
  print("Example of Assignment operators");
  var x1 = 15;
  var x2 = 5;
  print("x1+x2 = ${x1+x2}");
  print("x1-x2 = ${x1-x2}");
  print("x1*x2 = ${x1*x2}");
  print("x1/=x2 = ${x1/x2}");
  print("x1%x2 = ${x1%x2}");
}
```

Unary Operators (Post and Pre)

In Java, the ++ and —— operators are known as increment and decrement operators, and they are also known as unary operators. Unary operators operate on a single operand, where ++ adds 1 to the operands and —— subtracts 1 from the operands.

There are two methods to employ unary operators: postfix and prefix. When ++ is used as a postfix (as in x++), it first returns the value of the operand and then increases the value of x. When — is used as a prefix (as in ++x), it raises the value of x.

Sr.	Operator Name	Description	Example
1.	++(Prefix)	It increases the operand's value.	++y
2.	++(Postfix)	It returns the operand's real value before incrimination.	y++
3.	—(Prefix)	It decreases the operand's value.	—y
4.	—(Postfix)	It returns the operand's real value before decrement.	y—

Example:

```
void main() {
    var a = 20;
    print(a++);                    //postfix value
    var b = 20;
    print(++b);                    //prefix value,
    var c = 30;
    print(--c);                    //prefix value
    var d = 15;
    print(d--);    }              //postfix value
```

Assignment Operator

Assignment operators are used to giving variables values. It can also use in conjunction with the arithmetic operators. The following is a list of assignment operators. Assume a has value of 30 and b has a value of 20.

Operators Name	Description
= (Assignment Operator)	It assigns the right operand to the right expression.
+=(Add and Assign)	It adds the value of the right operand to the left operand and assigns the result back to the left operand. For example x+=y → x = x+y → 20
−=(Subtract and Assign)	It subtracts the right operand's value from the left operand's value and assigns the result to the left operand. For example x−=y → x = x−y → 30
*=(Multiply and Assign)	It multiplies the operands and returns the result to the left operand. For example x*=y → x = x*y → 100
/=(Divide and Assign)	It divides the left operand's value by the right operand's value and assigns the result to the left operand. For example x%=y → x = x%y → 3.0
~/=(Divide and Assign)	It divides the left operand's value by the right operand's value and returns the integer remaining quotient to the left operand. For example x%=y → x = x%y → 2

(Continued)

Operators Name	Description
%=(Mod and Assign)	It divides the value of the left operand by the value of the right operand and returns the remainder to the left operand. For example x%=y → x = x%y → 0
<<=(Left shift AND assign)	The expression x<<=3 is equal to x = x<<3
>>=(Right shift AND assign)	The expression x>>=3 is equal to x = x>>3
&=(Bitwise AND assign)	The expression x&=3 is equal to x = x&3
^=(Bitwise exclusive OR and assign)	The expression x^=3 is equal to x = x^3
|=(Bitwise inclusive OR and assign)	The expression x|=3 is equal to x = x|3

Example:

```
void main(){
 print("Assignment operators");
  var x1 = 12;
  var x2 = 7;
  x1+=x2;
  print("x1+=x2 = ${x1}");
  x1-=x2;
  print("x1-=x2 = ${x1}");
  x1*=x2;
  print("x1*=x2 = ${x1}");
  x1~/=x2;
  print("x1~/=x2 = ${x1}");
  x1%=x2;
  print("x1%=x2 = ${x1}");
}
```

Relational Operator

Relational operators, often known as comparison operators, compare two expressions or operands. When two expressions are compared, the result is a Boolean true or false. Consider the following table if x has 30 and y has 10.

Sr.	Operator	Description
1.	>(greater than)	x>y will return TRUE.
2.	<(less than)	x<y will return FALSE.
3.	>=(greater than or equal to)	x>=y will return TRUE.
4.	<=(less than or equal to)	x<=y will return FALSE.
5.	==(is equal to)	x==y will return FALSE.
6.	!=(not equal to)	x!=y will return TRUE.

Example:

```
void main() {
var x = 20;
var y = 40;
print("Relational Operator");
var res = x>y;
print("x is greater than y: "+res. toString());
// We will learn the toString in next tutorial
var res0 = x<y;
print("x is less than y: "+res0. toString());
var res1 = x>=y;
print("x is greater than or equal to y: "+res1.
toString());
var res2 = x<=y;
print("x is less than and equal to y: "+res2.
toString());
var res3 = x!= y;
print("x is not equal to  y: "+res3. toString());
var res4 = x==y;
print("x is  equal to  y: "+res4. toString());
}
```

Type Test Operators

At runtime, the Type Test Operators are used to test the types of expressions. Consider the following table.

Sr.	Operator	Description
1.	As	It is used for the typecast.
2.	Is	It returns TRUE if object has a specified type.
3.	is!	It returns TRUE if object has not specified type.

Example:

```
void main()
{
  var nums = 20;
  var names = "Dart";
```

```
    print(nums is int);
    print(names is! String );
}
```

Logical Operators

Logical Operators are used to analyzing expressions and make decisions. Dart supports the logical operators are listed in the following table.

Sr.	Operator	Description
1.	&&(Logical AND)	It returns if all the expressions are true.
2.	||(Logical OR)	It returns TRUE if any of the expression is true.
3.	!(Logical NOT)	It returns a complement of expression.

Example:

```
void main(){
    bool bool_vals1 = true, bool_vals2 = false;
    print("logical operators");
    var vals1 = bool_vals1 && bool_vals2;
    print(vals1);
    var vals2 = bool_vals1 || bool_vals2;
    print(vals2);
    var vals3 = !(bool_vals1 || bool_vals2);
    print(vals3);
}
```

Bitwise Operators

The Bitwise operators perform on the value of the two operands bit by bit. The table of bitwise operators is shown below.

Sr.	Operators	Description
1.	&(Binary AND)	It returns 1 if both the bits are 1.
2.	|(Binary OR)	It returns 1 if any of the bit is 1.
3.	^(Binary XOR)	It returns 1 if both the bits are different.
4.	~(Ones Compliment)	It returns reverse of the bit. If bit is 0 then the compliment will be 1.
5.	<<(Shift left)	The value of the left operand moves left by the number of bits present in the right operand.
6.	>>(Shift right)	The value of the right operand moves left by the number of bits present in the left operand.

Example:

If $x = 7$

$y = 6$

then binary$(x) = 0111$

binary$(y) = 0011$

Hence $x \& y = 0011, x \mid y = 0111$ and $x \wedge y = 0100$

Example:

```
void main(){
  print("Example of Bitwise operators");
  var x  = 35;
  var y = 30;
  var z = 5;
  // Bitwise AND Operator
  print("x & y = ${x&y}");
  // Bitwise OR Operator
  print("x | y = ${x|y}");
  // Bitwise XOR
  print("x ^ y = ${x^y}");
  // Complement Operator
  print("~x = ${(~x)}");
  // Binary left shift Operator
  z = x <<2;
  print("z<<1= ${z}");
  // Binary right shift Operator
  z = x >>2;
  print("z>>1= ${z}");
}
```

Conditional Operators (?:)

The Conditional Operator is comparable to the if-else statement and provides similar functionality. It is the if-else statement's second form. It is also known as a "Ternary Operator." The syntaxes are shown below.

First syntax:

```
condition?  exp1 : exp2
```

If the specified condition is TRUE, it returns exp1, else it returns exp2.

Second Syntax:

```
exp1? ? expr2
```

If exp1 is not null, it returns its value; otherwise, it returns the value of exp2.

Example:

```
void main() {
    var a = null;
    var b = 30;
    var val = a?? b;
    print(val);
}
```

Cascade Notation Operators

Cascade notation Operators (..) is used to evaluate a sequence of operations on the same object. It is the same as method chaining in that it removes numerous stages and eliminates the need to store results in temporary variables.

CHAPTER SUMMARY

This chapter we discussed the basics of Flutter, including how to install the Flutter basic program and the history of Flutter, as well as its benefits and features. Furthermore, we reviewed what Dart is, including Dart's introduction, platforms, and how to install Dart. We also reviewed its features, Dart's basic syntax, comments, keywords, data types, and variables.

CHAPTER 2

Data Types and Control Flow Statements

IN THIS CHAPTER

- ➤ Constant and Number
- ➤ String and Lists
- ➤ Sets and Map and Symbol
- ➤ Symbol and Enumeration
- ➤ If, If-Else Statement
- ➤ Loops
- ➤ Boolean

We discussed Introduction to Flutter, Dart, covering history, features, advantages, and installation in the previous Chapter. We also discussed the Basic syntax of Dart, data types, keywords, and operators.

DART CONSTANTS

A Dart Constant is an immutable object, which means it cannot be updated or modified while the application is running. It cannot be reassigned once we assign a value to a constant variable.

DOI: 10.1201/9781003299363-2

Defining/Initializing a Dart Constant

Define the Dart constant in two ways.

- Using the final keyword.

- Using the const keyword.

It is helpful to maintain the value constant throughout the program. To make a continuous variable, use the terms final and const. The terms final and const are employed in conjunction with the data type. Dart will throw an exception if we try to change the constant variable.

The const keyword represents the compile-time constant, and the final variable may only be set once.

Using the Final Keyword, Define Constant

Using the final keyword, we can declare the constant. The syntax is shown below.

Syntax:

```
final const_names;
```

or

```
final data_type const_names
```

Example:

```
  void main () {
  final x = 20;
  final y = 30;
 print(x);
 print(y);
 }
```

Define Constants Using Const Keyword

The const keyword is used to declare constants. The syntax is shown below.

Syntax:

```
const const_names
```

Or

```
const data_type const_names
```

Example:
```
void main() {
    const names= "Pihu";
    print(names);
}
```

NUMBER IN DART

The Number data type is used to store the numeric value. It can be of two sorts in Dart:

- Integer
- Double

Numbers in Dart.

Dart Integer

Integer numbers are whole integers that may express without using a fractional component. For example, –20, 30, –3215, 0, and so on. An integer can be either signed or unsigned. The integer value is represented as a nondecimal number ranging from –263 to 263. In Dart, the int keyword is used to declare integer values.

```
int id = 401;
```

Dart Double

You may write a double number with a floating-point number or with a number with more decimal points. In Dart, the double keyword is used to declare a Double value.

```
double root = 1.21234;
```

or

```
double rupees  = 130000;
```

Integer value rules:

- An integer value must be a digit.

- An integer number should not contain decimal points.

- The sum of unsigned numbers is always a positive value. Numbers can be positive or negative.

- The size of the integer value depends on the platform, but it should be no more than 64 bits.

Example:

```
void main(){
  int d = 5;
  double pi = 3.147;
  double rest = 4*pi*r*r;
  print("The area of sphere = ${(rest)}");
}
```

Parse() Method in Dart

The parse() method is used to convert a numeric string to a number. Consider the following scenario:

```
void main(){
var x = num.parse("23.56");
var y = num.parse("25.63");
var z = x+y;
print("Sum is = ${z}");
}
```

Explanation: In this example, we used the parse() function to turn the numeric strings into integers, then placed them in variables. We did an add operation and printed the output to the screen when the conversion was accomplished.

Number Properties

Properties	Description
Hashcode	It returns the hash code of the number given.
isFinite	It returns true if the provided number is finite.
isInfinite	It returns true if the number is infinite.
isNan	It returns true if the number is not negative.
isNegative	It returns true if the number is negative.
Sign	Depending on the sign of the provided number, it returns −1, 0, or 1.
isEven	It returns true if the provided number is an even number.
isOdd	It returns true if the provided number is odd.

Number Methods

Method	Description
abs()	It gives the absolute value of a given number.
ceil()	It gives the ceiling value of a given number.
floor()	It gives the floor value of a given number.
compareTo()	It compares the value with other numbers.
remainder()	It gives the truncated remainder after dividing the two numbers.
round()	It returns a round of the number.
toDouble()	It gives a double equivalent representation of the number.
toInt()	Returns integer equivalent representation of the number.
toString()	Returns String equivalent representation of the number.
truncate()	Returns integer after discarding fraction digits.

STRING IN DART

Dart String is a character or UTF-16 code unit sequence. It is used to keep track of the text value. We can use single or double quotes to create the string. The triple-quotes can be used to create a multiline string. Strings are immutable, which means they are not changeable after they are created.

One can use the String keyword in Dart to declare a string. The string declaration syntax is shown below.

Syntax:

```
String msg = 'Welcome to Dart';
or
String msg1 = "This is double-quoted.";
```

```
or
String msg2 = ' ' ' line1
line2
line3'''
```

Printing String

To display the string on the screen, use the print() method. The string can be structured as a message, expression, or object. Dart supports the $expression function, which wraps the value in a string. Consider the following illustration:

```
void main() {
    String strg1 = ' an example of a single-line
string';
    String strg2 = " an example of a double-quotes
multiline line string";
    String strg3 = """ a multiline line
string using the triple-quotes""";

    var x = 20;
    var y = 30;

    print(strg1);
    print(strg2);
    print(strg3);

 // We can add expression using the ${expression}.
    print("The sum is  = ${x+y}");
}
```

String Concatenation

To combine the two strings, use the + or += operator. The following is an example.

```
void main() {
    String strg1 = 'Welcome ';
    String strg2 = "to Dart";
    String strg3 = strg1+strg2;
    print(strg3);
}
```

String Interpolation

String interpolation is a method that allows you to alter a string and produce a new string by adding another value. It can evaluate a string, including placeholders, variables, and interpolated expressions. String interpolation is accomplished using the $expression. The expressions are replaced with the values that correspond to them.

Example:

```
void main() {
    String strg1 = 'Hello ';
    String strg2 = "Everyone";
    String strg3 = strg1+strg2;

  print(strg3);

    var a = 29;
    var b = 20;

    print("The result is  = ${a%b}");

    var name = "Pihu";
    var roll_nu = 109;

    print("Name is ${name}, roll number is
${roll_nu}");
}
```

Explanation: In the above code, we declared two strings variables, concatenated them, and displayed the result.

We established two variables with integer values, performed the mod operation, and displayed the result using string interpolation.

As seen in the preceding example, we may utilize string interpolation as a placeholder.

String Properties

The string attributes provided by Dart are as follow.

Property	Description
codeUnits	It returns an unmodified list of UTF-16 code units of this string.
isEmpty	If string is empty, it returns true.
Length	It returns length of the string, including whitespace.

String Methods

The Dart offers a wide variety of approaches. The following is a list of a few key strategies.

Methods and Descriptions

- **toLowerCase()**: It lowercases all characters in the specified string.

- **toUpperCase()**: It changes all of the characters in the provided string to uppercase.

- **trim()**: It removes all whitespace from the specified string.

- **compareTo()**: It compares one string with another.

- **replaceAll()**: It replaces all substrings that match the specified pattern with the provided string.

- **split()**: It divides the string at the supplied delimiter and produces a list of the substrings.

- **substring()**: It returns the substring from a start index to an end index inclusive.

- **toString()**: It returns a string representation of the given object.

- **codeUnitAt()**: It returns a 16-bits code unit at the given index.

LISTS IN DART

Dart Lists are similar to arrays in that they are an ordered collection of things. The array is the most popular and widely used collection in any other programming language. The Dart list resembles JavaScript array literals. The syntax for defining a list is shown below:

```
list1 = [13, 15, 24, 22, 35, 55]
```

The Dart list is defined by enclosing all entries in square brackets ([]) and separating them with commas (,).

Let's look at the list's graphical representation:

- **list1:** The list variable that corresponds to the list object is list1.

- **Index:** Each element has an index number that indicates its position in the list. The index number, such as list_name[index], is used to retrieve a specific entry from the list. The indexing begins at 0 and ends at length-1, where length specifies the number of elements in the list. As an example: The preceding list is four items long.

- **Elements:** The actual value or dart object stored in the supplied list is referred to by the List elements.

Lists Types
The dart list is divided into two categories:

- Fixed Length List
- Growable List

Fixed Length List
The length of the fixed-length lists is provided. At runtime, we are unable to change the size. The syntax is shown below.

Syntax: Create a list of fixed-size

```
var list_names = new List(size)
```

The syntax shown above is used to create a fixed-size list. At runtime, we cannot add or remove elements. If we try to change its size, it will raise an exception.

The following syntax is used to initialize the fixed-size list element.

Syntax: Initialize fixed-size list element

```
list_names[index] = value;
```

Example:

```
void main() {
    var list1 = new List(5);
    list1[0] = 14;
    list1[1] = 16;
    list1[2] = 11;
    list1[3] = 19;
    list1[4] = 12;
    print(list1);
}
```

Explanation: In the preceding example, we established a variable list1 that refers to a fixed-size list. The size of the list is 5, and we added the elements matching their index position, where the 0th index contains 14, the 1st index has 16, and so on.

Growable List

A Growable list is declared without specifying a size. One can change the Growable list's size at runtime. The syntax for declaring a Growable list is shown below.

Syntax: List declaration

```
// creates list with values
var list_names = [val1, val2, val3]
```

Or

```
// creates list of the size zero
var list_names = new List()
```

Syntax: Initializing list

```
list_names[index] = value;
```

First example:

```
void main() {
    var list1 = [13,14,11,19,18,15];
    print(list1);
}
```

In the following example, the empty list or list () constructor is used to create a list. The add() function is used to add elements to a list dynamically.

Second example:

```
void main() {
    var list1 = new List();
    list1.add(14);
    list1.add(12);
```

```
        list1.add(18);
        list1.add(11);
        print(list1);
}
```

List Properties

The list's properties are shown here.

Property	Description
First	It returns the case of the first element.
isEmpty	If the list is empty, it returns true.
isNotEmpty	If list has at least one element, it returns true.
Length	It returns the list's length.
Last	It returns the list's last element.
Reversed	It returns us a list in reverse order.
Single	It determines whether the list has just one element and returns it.

Inserting an Element into a List

Dart supports four methods for inserting elements into lists. These procedures are given below:

- add()

- addAll()

- insert()

- insertAll()

The Add() Method

The specified value is inserted at the end of the list using this method. It can only add one entry and then return the changed list object. Let's have a look at an example:

Syntax:

```
list_names.add(element);
```

Example:

```
void main() {
    var odd_lists = [11,34,52,17,9];
    print(odd_lists);
    odd_lists.add(19);
    print(odd_lists);
}
```

Explanation: In the above example, we have a list called odd_list that contains odd numbers. Using the add() method, we added a new element 19 to the list. The add() method attached the element to the list's end and returned the changed list.

The AddAll() Method
This method is used to insert several values into a list. Each value is separated by a comma and enclosed by a square bracket ([]). The syntax is shown below.

Syntax:

```
list_names.addAll([val1,val2,val3,?..valN]);
```

Example:

```
void main() {
    var odd_lists = [21,32,15,72,19]
     print(odd_lists);
      odd_lists.addAll([13,11,14]);
      print(odd_lists);
}
```

Explanation: In the above example, we do not need to use the add() method numerous times. The addAll() function added many values simultaneously and returned the changed list object.

The Insert() Method
The insert() function allows us to insert an element at the provided index position. One can specify the index position of the value to be added to the list. The syntax is shown below.

Syntax:

```
list_names.insert(index,value);
```

Example:

```
void main(){
    List lsts = [13,43,22,45];
    print(lsts);
    1st.insert(21,19);
    print(lsts);
}
```

Explanation: In the preceding example, we have a list of randomly generated integers. We used the insert() method with the index 2nd value 19 as a parameter. It inserted the value at the second index before returning the changed list object.

The InsertAll() Method
Insert the multiple values at the specified index position using the insert All() method. It takes an index position and a list of values as arguments. The syntax is shown below.

Syntax:

```
list_names.insertAll(index,
iterable_list_of_value)
```

Example:

```
void main(){
    List lsts = [31,43,12,25];
    print(lsts);
    1st.insertAll(0,[61,72,10,19]);
    print(lsts);
}
```

Explanation: In the preceding example, we used the insertAll() method to append the list of items at the 0th index position. It returned the list object after edit.

Updating List
Dart allows us to update the list, and we may edit it by simply accessing its element and assigning it a new value. The syntax is shown below.

Syntax:

```
list_names[index] = new_value;
```

Example:

```
void main(){
      var lists1 = [11,25,25,21,39];
      print("List before updation: ${lists1}");
      lists1[3] = 53;
      print("List after updation:${lists1}");
}
```

Explanation: In the above example, we visited the third index, assigned the new value 53, and printed the result. The preceding list has been updated to include the new value 53.

replaceRange()

The replaceRange() method in Dart is used to update list items within a defined range. It updates the element values using the specified range. The syntax is shown below.

Syntax:

```
list_names.replaceRange(int start_val, int end_
val, iterable);
```

Example:

```
void main(){
      var lists1 = [19,11,29,22,32];
      print("List before updation: ${lists1}");
      lists1.replaceRange(0,4,[4,3,2,1]) ;
      print("List after updation using
replaceAll() function : ${lists1}");
}
```

Explanation: In the above example, we used the replaceRange() method on the list, which accepts three parameters. As a third option, we gave the starting index 0th, the ending index 4th, and the list of components changed. It returned a new list containing the substituted element from the specified range.

Removing List Elements

Dart provides the following methods for removing list items:

- remove()
- removeAt()
- removeLast()
- removeRange()

The Remove() Method

It removes one element from the provided list at a time. It recognizes elements as an argument. If several occurrences of the supplied element are in the list, it removes the first occurrence. The syntax is shown below.

Syntax:

```
list_names.remove(value)
```

Let's understand the following example.

Example:

```
void main(){
     var lists1 = [11,13,22,29,31];
     print("List before remove element :
${lists1}");
     lists1.remove(22) ;
     print("List after removing element :
${lists1}");
}
```

Explanation: In the preceding example, we called the list's remove() method and gave the value 22 as an argument. It eliminated the number 20 from the provided list and returned the updated list.

The RemoveAt() Method

It returns an element removed from the provided index point. The syntax is shown below.

Syntax:

```
list_name.removeAt(int index)
```

Example:

```
void main(){
      var lists1 = [14,11,12,19,13];
      print("List before remove element :
${lists1}");
      lists1.removeAt(3) ;
      print("List after removing element :
${lists1}");
}
```

Explanation: In the above example, we gave the third index position as an input to the removeAt() method, which deleted the 19 from the list.

The RemoveLast() Method
The removeLast() method removes the last item from a list. The syntax is shown below.

Syntax:

```
list_names.removeLast()
```

Example:

```
void main(){
      var lists1 = [11,31,69,72,81];
      print("List before removing
element:${lists1}");
      lists1.removeLast();
      print("List after removed
element:${lists1}");

}
```

We invoked the removeLast() function in the above example, which deleted and returned the last element 81 from the given list.

The RemoveRange() Method
This function removes the item inside the range specified by taking two arguments: the start index and the end index. It removes all elements that lie inside the specified range. The syntax is shown below.

Syntax:

```
list_names. removeRange();
```

Example:

```
void main(){
    var lists1 = [21,43,56,67,81];
    print("List before removing
element:${lists1}");
    lists1.removeRange(1,3);
    print("List after removed
element:${lists1}");
}
```

Explanation: In the above example, we used the removeRange() function and gave as parameters start index position 1 and end index position 3. It eliminated any elements that belonged between the given positions.

Dart Iterating List Elements

One can use the forEach function to iterate over the Dart List.

Example:

```
void main(){
    var lists1 = ["Smiti","Petir","Handsi","Devan
shi","Cruv"];
    print("Iterating the List Element");
    lists1.forEach((items){
    print("${list1.indexOf(items)}: $items");
 });
}
```

SETS IN DART

The Dart Set is an unordered collection of values of the same type. It offers a lot of the same functionality as an array, except it's not ordered. Set does not support storing duplicate values. The values in the set must be unique.

It is necessary to keep separate data of the same type in a single variable. We can only have one value of the same type after we specify the set type. The set cannot maintain the order of the items.

Initializing Set

Dart has two ways for declaring/initializing an empty set. The set can be stated using curly braces ({}) followed by a type argument, or the variable type Set can be specified using curly braces ({}). The syntax for declaring a set is as follows.

Syntax:

```
var setNames = <type>{};
```

Or

```
Set<type> setnames = {};
```

The setnames specify the name of the set variable, and the type specifies the data type of the set.

Remember to note that the syntax of the set is quite similar to that of map literals. If we fail to declare the type annotation with or without the variable to which it is allocated, the Dart compiler will generate a Map object instead of a Set object.

Example:

```
void main(){
    print("Initializing Set");
    var names = <String>{"Smiti","Petir","Handsi","
Devanshi"};
    print(names);
}
```

Add Element into Set

Dart supports two methods for inserting an element into a specified set: add() and addAll(). The add() function inserts a single item into a set. When the addAll() function adds several elements to an existing set, it can only add one at a time. The syntax is shown below.

Syntax:

```
Set_names.add(<value>);
```

Or

```
Set_names.addAll(val1,val2....valN)
```

Example:

```
void main(){
    print("Insert element into Set");
    var names = {"Jatin","Ruhi","Revanshi","Ad
ami"};
    // Declaring the empty set
    var empy = <String>{};
    empy.add("Jonathan");
    print(empy);
    // Adding the multiple elements
    empy.addAll(names);
    print(empy);
}
```

Explanation: Two sets of names and empty have been declared. The set names have few elements, whereas empy is an empy set. Then, after adding the single element "Jonathan" using the add() function, we invoked the addAll() method and gave another set of names as a parameter. Add the multiple values to the empy set.

Access the Set Element

Dart has an elementAt() function that may retrieve an item by giving its index location. The set indexing begins with 0 and progresses through size −1, where size is the number of elements in the set. If we input a more extensive index number than its size, it will error. The syntax is shown below.

Syntax:

```
Set_name.elementAt(index)
```

Example:

```
void main(){
    print("Access element from the Set");
    var name = {"Jatin","Ruhi","Devanshi","Arman"};
    print(name);

    var a = name.elementAt(3);
    print(a);
}
```

Explanation: In the preceding example, we have assigned names. One can use the elementAt() function, and index position 3 was supplied as an input. We made a variable x to retain the assessed value, and then we printed the result.

Dart Finding Element in Set

Dart has a function called contains() that may be used to find an element in a set. It takes a single item as an input and returns a Boolean result. If the given element is present in the set, it returns true; otherwise, it returns false. The syntax is shown below.

Syntax:

```
set_name.contains(value);
```

Example:

```
void main()  {

   print("Example to Find Element in the given
Set");
   var names = <String>{"Peteri","Johny","Rishi","D
evanshi","Finnie"};

   if(names.contains("Rishi")){
      print("The Element is Found");
   }

   else {
      print("The Element not found");
   }
}
```

Explanation: In the preceding program, we used the contains() function and gave the value "Rishi" as an input to discover the element in the given set. We utilized the conditional statement to determine whether or not an element belonged to the provided set. When the given element in the set was present, the condition became true, and if one wrote a block statement.

Note: In the following part, we will learn about conditional statements.

Remove Set Element

One can use the remove() function to remove or delete an element from a provided set. It accepts the value as an input and removes it from the given set. The syntax is shown below.

Syntax:

```
set_names.contains(values)
```

Example:

```
void main()  {

    print("Example of Remove Element in the given
Set");
    var name = <String>{"Peteri","Johny","Rishi","
Devanshi","Finnie"};
    print("Before remove : ${name}");

    names.remove("Peteri");
    print("After remove  :  ${name}");
}
```

Explanation: We used the remove() function to delete "Peteri" from the specified set in the preceding program. It returned the set object after it had changed it.

Dart Iterating over a Set Element

The set element in Dart may be iterated using the forEach function as shown below:

```
void main()  {
    print("Example of Remove Element in the given
Set");
    var name = <String>{"Peteri","Johny","Rishi","Deva
nshi","Finnie"};

    names.forEach((values) {
        print('Values:  $values');
    });
}
```

Dart Remove All Set Element

Using the clear() methods, we may delete a whole set element. It deletes all elements from the specified set, returning an empty set. The following is the syntax.

Syntax:

```
set_names.clear();
```

Example:

```
void main()   {
    print("Example of Remove All Element to the
given Set");
    var name = <String>{"Peteri","Johny","Rishi","
Devanshi","Finnie"};

    name.clear();
    print(name);

}
```

TypeCast Set to List

Using the toList() function, convert the Set object into a List Object. The following is the syntax.

Syntax:

```
List<type> <list_names> = <set_names>. toList();
```

Dart Set Operations

Dart Set allows us to perform the following set operations. These operations are described in detail below.

- **Union:** The union is configured to merge the values of the two provided sets, a and b.

- **Intersection:** The intersection of two sets, a and b, returns all elements shared by both.

- **Subtraction:** When two sets a and b are subtracted (a-b), the member of set b that is not present in set an is not present in set a.

Let's have a look at an example:

```dart
void main()  {

    var a = <int>{10,11,12,13,14,15};
    var b = <int>{12,18,29,43};
    var c = <int>{2,5,10,11,32};
    print("Example of Set Operations");

    print("a union b is:");
    print(a.union(b));

    print("a intersection b is: ");
    print(a.intersection(b));

    print("b difference c is: ");
     print(b.difference(c));

}
```

Dart Set Properties

The Dart's few properties are as follow:

Properties	Explanations
first	It is used to retrieve the first element from a specified set.
isEmpty	If the set has no elements, it returns true.
isNotEmpty	It returns true if the set has at least one element.
Length	The length of the specified set is returned.
Last	It's used to find the last element in a given collection.
hashcode	It is used to obtain the hash code for the specified object.
Single	It is used to determine whether a set has only one element.

MAP IN DART

Dart Map is a kind of object that holds data as a key-value pair. Each value is connected with a key, which is used to access its corresponding value. Keys and values can be of any kind. Each key in Dart Map must be unique, although the same value can appear several times. The Map model is quite similar to the Python Dictionary representation. Curly brackets ({}) are used to declare the Map, and commas (,) separate each key-value pair. Use a square bracket ([]) to obtain the key's value.

Declaring Dart Map

It can be defined in two methods.

- Using Map Literal

- Using Map Constructor

Using Map Literals

The key-value pairs are wrapped between the curly braces "{}" and separated by commas when declaring a Map using Map literal. The syntax is shown below.

Syntax:

```
var map_names = {key1:value1, key2:value2
[.......,key_n: value_n]}
```

First example:

```
void main() {
    var students = {'name':'Jay','age':'24'};
    print(students);
}
```

Second example:

```
void main() {
    var students = {'name':' Roy', 'age':24};
    student['courses'] = 'M.tech';
    print(students);
}
```

Explanation: In the preceding example, we declared a Map on a student's name. Using a square bracket, we added the value at runtime and passed the new key as a course associated with its value.

Using Map Constructor

There are two ways to declare the Dart Map using the map constructor. First, create a map with the Map () constructor and initiate the Map. The syntax is shown below.

Syntax:

```
var map_names = new map()
```

After that, initialize values.

```
map_names[key] = value
```

Example: The Map constructor

```
void main() {
    var students = new Map();
    student['names'] = 'Ria';
    student['ages'] = 24;
    student['courses'] = 'M.tech';
    student['Branchs'] = 'Computer-Science';
    print(students);
}
```

Map Properties

The Map class in the Dart:core:package defines the following properties.

Properties	Explanation
Keys	It is used to get all the keys as an iterable object.
Values	It is used to get all the values as an iterable object.
Length	It returns the length of the Map object.
isEmpty	If the Map object contains no value, it returns true.
isNotEmpty	If the Map object contains at least one value, it returns true.

Example:

```
void main() {
    var students = new Map();
    student['name'] = 'Roy';
    student['age'] = 24;
    student['course'] = 'M.tech';
    student['Branch'] = 'Computer-Science';
    print(student);

    // Get all the Keys
    print("The keys are : ${students.keys}");

    // Get all the values
    print("The values are : ${students.values}");
```

```
    // Length of the Map
    print("The length is : ${students.length}");

  //isEmpty function
  print(students.isEmpty);

  //isNotEmpty function
  print(students.isNotEmpty);
  }
```

Map Methods

The most systematic approaches are listed below.

- **addAll():** It is a function that adds several key-value pairs of others. The syntax is shown below.

  Syntax:

  ```
  Map.addAll(Map<Key, Value> other)
  ```

  Parameter:

  - **other:** It refers to a key-value pair. It yields a void type.

  Example:

  ```
  void main() {
      Map students = {'name':'Roy','age': 24};
      print('Map :${students}');

      students.addAll({'dept':'Civil','email':
  'roy@xyz.com'});
      print('Map after adding the key-values
  :${students}');
  }
  ```

- **remove ():** It removes all pairings from the Map. The syntax is shown below.

  Syntax:

  ```
  Map.clear()
  ```

Example:

```
void main() {
    Map students = {'name':'Roy','age': 24};
    print('Map :${students}');

    students.clear();
    print('Map after removing all the key-values
:${students}');

}
```

- **Remove ():** If the key and its associated value exist in the provided Map, remove() removes them. The syntax is shown below.

Syntax:

```
Map.remove(Object-key)
```

Parameter:

- **Keys:** It removes the specified entries. It returns the value that corresponds to the specified key.

Example:

```
void main() {
    Map students = {'name':'Roy','age': 24};
    print('Map :${students}');

    students.remove('age');
    print('Map after removing the given key
:${students}');
}
```

- **forEach():** It is used to loop through the Map's entries. The syntax is shown below.

Syntax:

```
Map.forEach(void f(K key, V value));
</pre></div>
<p><strong>Parameter:</strong></p>
<ul class="points">
<li><strong>f(K key, V value) -</strong> It
denotes key-value pair of the map.</li>
</ul>
```

```
<p>Let's understand following example.</p>
<p><strong>Examples</strong></p>
<div class="codeblock"><textarea name="code"
class="java">
void main() {
    Map students = {'name':'Roy','age': 24};
    print('Map :${students}');
    students.forEach((k,v) => print('${k}:
${v}'));

}
```

SYMBOL IN DART

A symbol object is used to specify a Dart programming language operator or identifier. Symbols are not required for Dart programming in general, although they are helpful for APIs. It generally refers to identifiers by name because identifier names can differ, but identifier symbols cannot.

Dart symbols are dynamic string names used to obtain metadata from a library. It primarily collects the relationship between human-readable strings that have been improved for usage by computers.

Reflection is a technique used to metadata at runtimes, like several methods used in a class, the number of constructors in a class, or the number of arguments in a function.

All reflection-related classes may be found in the Dart:mirrors library. Use it with both command-line and web-based apps.

Syntax:

In Dart, the hash(#) symbol is followed by the name to define the Symbol. The syntax is shown below.

Syntax:

```
Symbol objt = new Symbol("names")
```

In this case, one might use a valid identifier such as a function, valid class, public member name, or library name instead of the name value.

```
#bar
#radix
```

Example:

```
library foo_lib;
//the library name can be a symbol

class Foo {
   // the class name can be a symbol
   mt1() {
      // the method name can be a symbol
      print("Inside mt1");
   }
   mt2() {
      print("Inside mt2");
   }
   mt3() {
      print("Inside mt3");
   }
}
```

We declared a class Foo in the library foo in the preceding code. The methods mt1, mt2, and mt3 are included in the class. The above file is saved as foo. Dart.

Now we'll make a new file called FooSymbol. Dart and run the code below.

FooSystem.dart

```
import 'dart:core';
import 'dart:mirrors';
import 'Foo.dart';

main() {
   Symbol libr = new Symbol("foo_lib");
   //the library name stored as Symbol

   Symbol clsToSearchs = new Symbol("Foo");
   // the class name stored as Symbol

   if(checkIf_classAvailableInlibrary(libr,
clsToSearchs))
   //the searches Foo class in foo_lib library
      print("class-found");
}
```

```
bool checkIf_classAvailableInlibrary(Symbol
libraryName, Symbol className) {
   MirrorSystem mirrorSystems = currentMirrorSystem();
   LibraryMirror libMirrors = mirrorSystems.
findLibrary(libraryName);

   if (libMirror != null) {
      print("Found-Library");
      print("checkng....class details..");
      print("The No of classes found is :
${libMirrors.declarations.length}");
      libMirrors.declarations.forEach((s, d) =>
print(s));

      if (libMirrors.declarations.
containsKey(className)) return true;
      return false;
   }
}
</pre></div>
<p>Above code will show the following output.</p>
<p><strong>Output:</strong></p>
<div class="codeblock"><pre>
Found Library
checkng....class details..
No of classes found is: 1
Symbol("Foo") // Displays the class name
class found...
</pre></div>
<p><strong>Example: Print number of instance methods
of class</strong></p>
<p>In the example, The Dart provides predefine class
<strong>ClassMirror</strong> which helps us to display
number of instance methods of class.</p>
<p><strong>Example</strong></p>
<div class="codeblock"><textarea name="code"
class="java">
import 'dart:core';
import 'dart:mirrors';
import 'Foo.dart';
```

```
main() {
    Symbol libs = new Symbol("foo_lib");
    Symbol clsToSearch = new Symbol("Foo");
    reflect_InstanceMethods(libs, clsToSearch);
}
void reflect_InstanceMethods(Symbol libraryName,
Symbol className) {
    MirrorSystem mirrorSystems = currentMirrorSystem();
    LibraryMirror libMirrors = mirrorSystems.
findLibrary(libraryName);

    if (libMirrors != null) {
        print("Found-Library");
        print("checkng….class details..");
        print("No of classes found is : ${libMirrors.
declarations.length}");
        libMirrors.declarations.forEach((s, d) =>
print(s));

        if (libMirrors.declarations.
containsKey(className)) print("found class");
        ClassMirror classMirror = libMirrors.
declarations[className];

        print("No of instance methods found is
${classMirror.instanceMembers.length}");
        classMirror.instanceMembers.forEach((s, v) =>
print(s));
    }
}
```

Dart Convert Symbol to String

We can convert a Dart symbol to a string by utilizing the Dart:mirror package's built-in class MirrorClass. Let's have a look at an example.

```
import 'dart:mirrors';
void main(){
    Symbol libs = new Symbol("foo_lib");
    String name_of_libs = MirrorSystem.getName(libs);

    print(libs);
    print(name_of_libs);
}
```

RUNES IN DART

Dart String, as previously said, is a series of characters, letters, digits, and unique characters. Dart Runes are a series of UTF-16 Unicode characters, whereas the UTF-32 Unicode code points. The special symbol is printed using a UTF-32 string. For example, the theta (Θ) symbol is represented by the Unicode equivalent\u0398; '\u' refers to Unicode, and the values are hexadecimal. If the hex digits exceed four digits, they should be enclosed in curly brackets ({}). Let's look at an example to help us understand:

```
void main() {
  var heart_runes = '\u2665';
  var theta_runes = '\u{1f600}';
  print(heart_runes);
  print(theta_runes);
}
```

Dart offers the Dart: core library, which includes the Dart Runes. The String code unit can be accessed using one of the three ways listed below.

- Using String.codeUnitAt() Method

- Using String.codeUnits property

- Using String.runes property

String.codeUnitAt() Method

Using the codeUnitAt() function, we can go to the character's code unit in the provided string. It takes the index position as a parameter and returns the 16-bit UTF-16 code unit at the string's given index point. The syntax is as follows.

Syntax:

```
void main() {
  String strg = 'DartTpoint';
  print("Welcome to DartTpoint");
  print(strg.codeUnitAt(0));
}
```

Explanation: The variable str in the above code stores the string value "DartTpoint." We used the codeuUnitAt() method and gave the index position as a parameter. It returned the 0th index character's code unit.

String.codeUnits Property

The codeUnits property delivers a list of UTF-16 code units for a specified text. The syntax is shown below.

Syntax:

```
String.codeUnits;
```

Take a look at the following example:

```
void main() {
  String str = 'DartTpoint';
  print("Welcome to DartTpoint");
  print(str.codeUnits);
}
```

Explanation: The codeUnits function produced a list of the code units corresponding to the provided character.

String.runes Property

The runes property is used to iterate through the UTF-16 code unit with the provided string. The syntax is shown below.

Syntax:

```
String.runes
```

Consider the following scenario:

```
void main(){
   "DartTpoint".runes.forEach((int rune) {
      var characters=new String.fromCharCode(rune);
      print(characters);
   });
}
```

ENUMERATION IN DART

An enumeration is a collection of values known as elements, members, etc. This is critical since we performed the procedure with limited variable values. For example, consider the days of the month, which can only be one of the seven: Mon, Tue, Wed, Thur, Fri, Sat, and Sun.

Enumeration Initialization

The enumeration is defined using the enum keyword and a comma-separated list of valid identifiers. Curly braces enclose this list. The syntax is shown below.

Syntax:

```
enum <enum_name> {
const1,
const2,
....., constN
}
```

The enum name represents the enum type name and the list of identifiers included within the curly bracket.

Each identifier in the enumeration list is assigned an index point. The first enumeration has an index of 0; the second has an index of 1, and so on.

Example:

```
enum EnumofYear {
Jan,
Feb,
March,
April,
May,
June,
July,
Aug,
Sept,
Oct,
Nov,
Dec,
}
```

Let's have a look at programming examples:

First example:

```
enum EnumofYears {
Jan,
Feb,
March,
April,
May,
June,
July,
Aug,
Sept,
Oct,
Nov,
Dec,
}
void main() {
    print("DartTpoint - Dart Enumeration" );
    print(EnumofYears.values);
    EnumofWeek.values.forEach((vi) => print('value:
$vi, index: ${vi.index}'));
}
```

Second example:

```
enum Process_Status {
    none,
    running,
    stopped,
    paused
}
void main() {
    print(Process_Status.values);
    Process_Status.values.forEach((vi) =>
print('value: $vi, index: ${vi.index}'));
    print('running: ${Process_Status.running},
${Process_Status.running.index}');
    print('running index: ${Process_Status.
values[1]}');
}
```

CONTROL FLOW STATEMENT IN DART

Control statements, also known as the flow of control statements, direct the course of a Dart program. These statements are highly significant in any programming language since they determine whether they will perform subsequent statements. In general, the code statement is executed in sequential order. Based on the given condition, we may need to run or skip a collection of statements, jump to another statement, or repeat the execution of the statements.

The control statement in Dart enables the smooth flow of the program. A Dart program can be changed, redirected, or repeated based on the application logic by employing control flow statements.

Flow Statement Categories

Control flow statements in Dart may be classified into three types:

- Decision-making statements
- Looping statements
- Jump statements

Categories in flow statement in Dart.

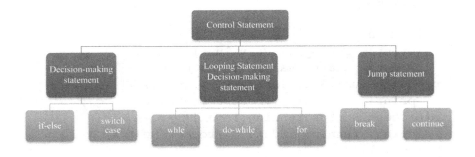

Control statement in Dart.

Dart Decision-Making Statements

We may use the decision-making statements at runtime to choose which statement to execute based on the test expression. Selection statements are another name for decision-making statements. Dart programs can have a single or several test expressions (or conditions) that evaluate the Boolean values TRUE and FALSE. These expression/condition results help determine which block of the statement(s) will be executed if the provided condition is TRUE or FALSE.

Dart supports the following decision-making statements:

- If Statement
- If-else Statements
- If else if Statement
- Switch Case Statement
- Dart Looping Statements

Dart looping statements are used to execute a block of code numerous times until it matches the specified condition. These are also known as iteration statements.

Dart supports the looping statements listed below.

- Dart for Loop
- Dart for....in Loop
- Dart while Loop
- Dart do-while Loop
- Dart Jump Statements

The jump statements are used to jump from one statement to another or to shift execution from one statement to another from the present statement.

Dart supports the following sorts of jump statements:

- Dart Break Statement
- Dart Continue Statement

The jump, as mentioned above, statements act differently.

IF STATEMENTS

When the supplied condition returns true, the If statement lets us run a code block. We have a case in Dart programming where we want to run a block of code when it meets the specified criteria. The condition analyses the Boolean values TRUE or FALSE and decides based on these Boolean values.

Flowchart:

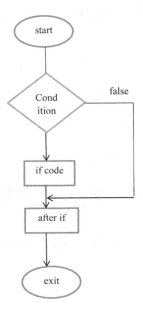

Statement of if.

The syntax of the if statement is given here.

Syntax:

```
If (condition) {
      //statement(s)
}
```

The supplied condition is if statement will evaluate TRUE or FALSE; if true, the statement inside the if the body is performed; if false, the sentence outside the if block is run.

Let's have a look at few examples.

First example:

```
void main () {
  // define variable which hold numeric value
  var a = 39;

  // if statement check given condition
  if (a<40){
    print("Number is smaller than 45")
  };
}
```

Explanation: We declared an integer variable n in the preceding program. In the if statement, we defined the condition. Is the supplied number less than 45 or more than 45? The if statement checked if the condition was true, then performed the if body and reported the result.

Second example:

```
void main () {
  // define variable which holds a numeric value
  var age = 19;

  // if statement check given condition
  if (age>20){
    print("You are eligible for the voting");
  };
  print("You are not eligible for the voting");
}
```

We can see in the preceding program that if evaluated, the condition to false, hence the execution bypassed the if body and performed the outer statement of the if block.

IF-ELSE STATEMENT

When the specified condition is true, the if-block in Dart is performed. The else-block is run if the provided condition is false. The else block is linked to the if-block.

Flowchart:

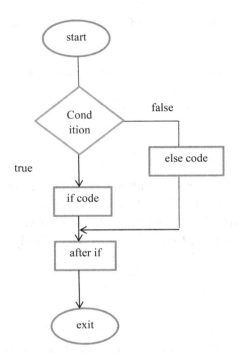

Statement of if-else.

Syntax:

```
if(condition) {
      // statement1(s);
} else {
    // statement2(s);
}
```

The if-else statement is used here for either TRUE or FALSE results. If the supplied condition is true, then if the body is executed; if the given condition is false, then the else body is executed.

First example:

```
void main() {
      var a = 30;
```

```
    var b = 40;
  print("if-else statement");

  if(a > b){
       print("a is greater than y");
} else {
       print("b is greater than x");

};
}
```

Explanation: In the preceding code, we have two variables that hold integer values. When the given condition assesses it as false, the else-block is printed.

Second example: Create a program to determine whether a given integer is even or odd.

```
void main() {
     var num = 22;

  print("if-else statement");

  if(num%4 == 0){
       print("Given number is even");
} else {
       print("Given number is odd");
};
}
```

Explanation: In the preceding example, we had an integer variable num value of 22. We used the if-else statement to determine if a given number is even or odd. The above condition assessed true since the modulus 22 is equal to 0, and the given number is printed on the screen as even.

IF ELSE-IF STATEMENT

The if else-if statement in Dart allows us to verify a series of test expressions and execute various statements. It is utilized when we have to choose amongst more than two options.

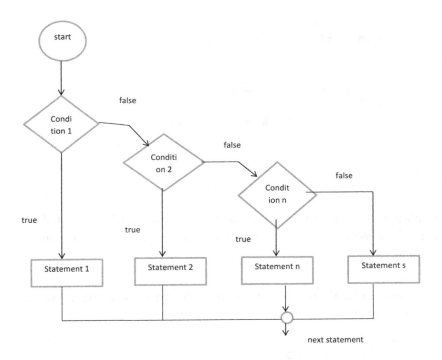

Statement of if-else-if.

Syntax:

```
if (condition1) {
    // statement
}
else if(condition2) {
    // statement
}
else if (conditionN) {
    // statement
}
.
.
else {
    // statement
}
```

This construction style is also known as the else-if ladder in this area. From top to bottom, the condition is assessed. When it finds the true condition, it executes the statement associated with that condition. When all supplied conditions are false, the else block is performed.

Example:

```
void main() {
var marks = 64;
if(marks > 95)
{
        print("Excellent");
}
  else if(marks>70)
{
        print("Very Good");
}
else if(marks>60)
{
        print("Good");
}
else
  {
        print("Average");
}
}
```

Explanation: The above application outputs the outcome depending on the test scores. To print the result, we used if else if. The integer value 64 has been assigned to the marks variable. We checked the program's many conditions.

Because the first condition is false, the marks will examine and check the second condition.

It compared to the second condition, found it to be true, and reported the result on the screen.

This operation repeats until all expressions are evaluated; control is transferred to the otherwise if ladder and default statement is displayed.

We should experiment with the setting as mentioned earlier and see what happens.

Nested If-Else Statement

A nested if-else statement in Dart implies one if-else statement within another. It is useful when we need to make a sequence of decisions.

Syntax:

```
if(condition1){
            // code-1
        if(condition2){
                    // code-2
        }
}
```

Flowchart:

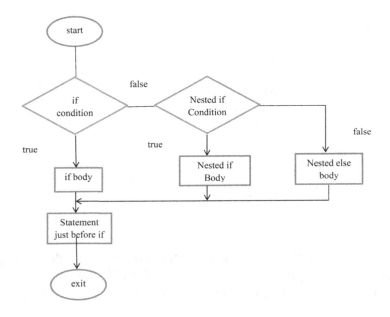

Statement of nested-if.

Example:

```
void main() {
    var x = 30;
    var y = 40;
    var z = 50;

    if (x>y){
        if(x>z){
                print("x is greater");
        }
```

```
        else{
            print("z is greater");
                }
    }
else if (y>z){
    print("y is greater");
}
else {
    print("z is greater");
}
}
```

In the preceding program, we declared three variables of 30, 40, and 50: x, y, and z. In the outer if-else condition, we specified that a must be more significant than b. The inner block will be performed; otherwise, the outer block will be executed.

Another condition in the inner block tests is if a variable is more significant than variable c. If the condition is true, the inner block will be performed.

Our software returned false in the first condition and then skipped the inner block check for the second condition. If the condition is met, the output is printed.

SWITCH CASE STATEMENT

To eliminate the lengthy chain of the if-else statement, the Dart Switch case statement is utilized. It is a shortened version of a nested if-else statement. The variable's value is compared to the various cases, and if a match is found, a block of statements associated with that case is executed.

Each instance is compared to the provided value until a match is found. When a match is detected, the block of code to be run is identified.

Syntax:

```
switch( expression )
{
    case value1:{
            //statement
            Block1;
    }
            break;
```

```
    case value2:{
          //statement
          Block2;
      }
              break;
    case valueN:{
              //statement
          BlockN;
                  }
                    break;
    default:     {
          //statement;
          }
  }
```

Example: The expression can be either an integer expression or a character expression in this case. The case labels are represented by the values 1, 2, n, and they are used to identify each case specifically. Each label must be followed by a colon (:).

The labels must be distinct since the same name label will cause difficulty while running the application.

The case label is connected with a block. A block is just a collection of several assertions for a specific situation.

Once the switch expression has been evaluated, the expression value is compared to all cases declared within the switch case. Assume the expression's value is 2, and then compare it to each case until it finds the label 2 in the program.

One must use the break statement after each case. Suppose we do not include the break statement. In that case, the specified case is identified; the program continues to execute all of the cases until the program's conclusion is reached. To declare the break statement, utilize the break keyword.

When the value of the expression does not match any of the cases, the default case is run. It is not required to write in the program.

First example:

```
void main() {
      int a = 6;
      switch (a) {
          case 1:
              print("Value is 2");
              break;
```

```
            case 2:
                print("Value is 4");
                break;
            case 3:
                print("Value is 6");
                break;
            case 4:
                print("Value is 8");
                break;
            default:
                print("Out of range");
                break;
        }
    }
```

In the above program, we set the variable n to 6. We built the switch case using the phrase, which compares each case with the variable n. Because the value is 6, case-label 3 will be executed. If case-label 3 is located successfully, the result is printed on the screen.

Second example:

```
void main()
  {
  // declaring a interger variable
  int Roll_nums =  90013;
  // Evalaute the test-expression to find the match
    switch (Roll_nums) {
    case 90008:
      print("My name is Tia");
      break;
    case 90011:
      print("My name is Peten");
      break;
    case 09008:
      print("My name is Devanshia");
      break;
  // the default block
    default:
      print("Roll number is not found");
  }
  }
```

Explanation: We assigned the number 90013 to the variable Roll num in the preceding program. The switch test expression validated all instances indicated within the switch statement. When the test expression did not match the cases, it produced the default case statement.

Benefits of the Switch Case

The switch case, as previously described, is a simplified form of if nested if-else expression. The problem with nested if-else is that it adds complexity to the program as the number of pathways increases. The switch case decreases the program's complexity. It improves the program's readability.

LOOPS IN DART

Dart Loop is used to run a block of code repeatedly for a defined number of times or until the stated condition is met. Loops are fundamental components of any programming language. It is used to iterate across Dart iterables like list, Map, and so on and execute actions many times. A loop may be divided into the loop body and control statements. The Loop's primary goal is to run the function several times. Dart supports the following loop types.

- Dart for Loop

- Dart for in Loop

- Dart while Loop

- Dart do-while Loop

For Loop in Dart

Dart for Loop is utilized when we are familiar with the number of times a piece of code has been executed. It is analogous to Loop in C, C++, and Java. To begin the loop execution, an initial variable is required. It runs a section of code until it matches the criteria supplied. When the Loop is run, the iterator's value changes after each iteration and the test expression is evaluated. This method is repeated until the specified test expression returns true. The for Loop is ended when the test expression is false. The syntax is shown below.

Syntax:

```
for(Initialization; condition; incri/decri)
{
// loop body
}
```

- The initialization function is used as a starting value in a loop and is only executed once.

- A condition or test expression returns True or False results. The for loop will continue to execute until the condition is met.

- The Loop is terminated when the condition evaluates to false.

- The incr/decr function is used to increase or reduce a variable.

Example:

```
void main()
{
    int nums = 3;
    for(nums; nums<=10; nums++)
  {
        print(nums);      //to print the number
    }
}
```

Nested for Loop

The term "nested for loop" refers to "the for loop within another for a loop." A loop within another loop is defined as an inner loop, and a loop outside another loop is defined as an outer loop. The Inner Loop will complete its cycle during each iteration of the outer loop. Let's take a look at few examples of a nested for loop:

First example:

```
void main()
{
int a, b;
int table_no = 3;
int max_no = 11;
for (a = 1; a <= table_no; a++)
{ // outer loop
   for (b = 0; b <= max_no; b++)
{ // inner loop
     print("${a} * ${b} = ${a*b}");
   //print("\n"); /* blank line between tables */
}}

}
```

Second example: Understand inner loop cycle

```
void main(){
for(int a = 1; a <=5; a++) {

    print("The Outer loop iteration : ${a}" );

            for (int b = 1; b <= a; ++b) {
                print("a = ${a} b = ${b}");
            }


        }
    }
```

For in Loop

The for in Loop differs somewhat from the for Loop. It just uses a dart object or expression as an iterator and iterates through the elements one at a time. The element's value is tied to var, which is valid and accessible to the loop body. The Loop will run until there are no more elements in the iterator. The syntax is shown below.

Syntax:

```
for (var in an expression)
{
//statement
}
```

Example:

```
void main()
{
    var list = [12,23,31,43,55];
    for(var c in list)              //for..in loop to
print list element
    {
        print(c);          //to print number
    }
}
```

While Loop

When the number of executions of a code is unknown, the while loop is employed. It will run as long as the requirement is met. It first verifies the supplied condition and then executes the while loop's lines. The while loop is most commonly used to generate an endless loop. The syntax is shown below.

Syntax:

```
while(condition) {
    //body of loop
}
```

Example:

```
void main()
{
    var c = 2;
            var maxnum = 10;
            while (c<maxnum) {            // it will
print until expression return false
                    print(c);
                    c = c+1;
// increase the value 1 after each iteration
    }
}
```

Infinite While Loop

When the while loop operates indefinitely, it is referred to as an infinite while loop. Let's look at an infinite loop example.

```
void main()
{
    int a = 1;

    while (a <= 5)
    {
        print( a);
        --a;
    }
}
```

Logical Operator While Loop

In a while loop, we may need to check numerous criteria. We may use logical operators such as (||, &&, and !). Let's have a look at the following ideas.

- while (n15 && n2>10) – This code will be executed if both criteria are met.

- while (n15 || n2>10) – This code is executed if one of the conditions is met.

- while (!n1 = 10) – This function will be executed if n1 is not equal to 10.

Example:

```
void main() {
int a1=1;
int a2=1;
    // We are checking multiple condition by using
logical operators.
    while (a1 <= 4 && a2 <= 3)
    {
     print("a1 : ${a1}, a2: ${a2}");
     a1++;
     a2++;
    }
}
```

Explanation: In the preceding code, we gave 1 to two variables, a1 and a2. In the while loop, we verified various circumstances where n1 is less than or equal to 4 and n2 is less than or equal to 3.

It tested both values and reported the result on the first iteration. When the sum of a1 and a2 equals to 4, this occurs at one place. Because a1 met condition one but a2 did not satisfy condition two, the Loop is halted, and the result is printed on the screen.

Do-While Loop

The do-while Loop is identical to the while loop, except it runs the loop statement before checking the specified condition. The syntax is shown below.

Syntax:

```
do {
    // body
} while(condition);
```

Example:

```
void main()
{
  var c = 2;
  var maxnum = 10;
do
    {
        print("Value is: ${c}");
        c = c+1;
        }while(c<maxnum);
}
```

Selection of the Loop

Choosing a loop is a challenging problem for the coder. It is difficult to determine which Loop is best suited to a particular activity. The Loop may be selected using the following points:

- Analyze the problem to determine if a pre-test or post-test Loop is required. A pre-test loop tests the condition before entering the Loop. The condition is tested after entering the Loop in the post-test Loop.

- We may use the while or for Loop if we need a pre-test loop.

- If we need a post-test loop, use the do-while loop.

BOOLEAN IN DART

The Dart Boolean data type determines if a statement is true or false. True and false are the Boolean type's two values, both compile-time constants. In Dart, the numeric values 1 and 0 do not describe whether something is true or false. The term bool is used to express a Boolean value. The syntax for defining the Boolean variable is as follows.

Syntax:

```
bool var_names = true;
```

OR

```
bool var_names = false;
```

Example:

```
void main()
{
bool check;
check = 24>10;
print("statement is = ${check}");
}
```

Explanation: We declared the bool variable check, which will use to validate the given expression. We printed the result of the expression 24>12 since it returned true.

CHAPTER SUMMARY

In this chapter, we discussed data types and control flow statements, where we also covered Constants, Strings, Lists, Sets, Maps, Symbols, Runes, and Enumeration. Moreover, we also discussed if, if-else statements, switch statements, and loops.

CHAPTER 3

Dart Functions and Object-Oriented Programming

In the previous chapter, we discussed data types and control flow statements. In this chapter, we cover data function and object-oriented where we also discuss the main function and recursion. Moreover, we discuss constructor, inheritance, methods, overriding, and interfaces.

FUNCTION IN DART

A Dart function is a collection of programs that work together to complete a specified purpose. It is used to divide big amounts of code into smaller modules that may be reused as needed. Functions make the software

DOI: 10.1201/9781003299363-3

more readable and debug. It improves the modular approach and code reusability.

Assume we develop basic calculator software in which we must conduct operations several times when the user inputs data. For each calculator operator, we may write a distinct function. We don't have to create code for adding, subtracting, multiplying, and dividing over and again by using functions. We can call the functions several times to use them multiple times.

The method allows you to run a code numerous times with varied values. A function can be called as a parameter at any time and returns some value to the place where it was called.

Function Benefits

The Dart function has a few advantages, which are listed below.

- It improves the modular method of problem-solving.

- It improves the program's reusability.

- We can link the programs together.

- It improves the code.

- It facilitates debugging.

- It simplifies development and reduces complexity.

Function Defining

A function can define by specifying the function name and the relevant parameter and return type. A function comprises a collection of statements known as the function body. The syntax is shown below.

Syntax:

```
return_type func_name (parameter_list):
{
    //statement
    return value;
}
```

Let's look at the defining function's general syntax:

- **return_type:** It can be any data type such as void, integer, float, and so on. The function's returned value must match with the return type.

- **func_name:** This should be a meaningful and valid identifier.

- **parameter_list:** It represents the list of arguments required when calling a function.

- **return value:** After completing its execution, a function returns a value.

Let's have a look at an example:

```
int mul(int x, int y)
{
    int z;
    z = x+y;
    print("The sum is:${z}");
}
```

Calling a Function

After creating a function, we may call or invoke it within the main() function body. A function is called simply by its name, with or without an argument list, if any. The syntax is shown below.

Syntax:

```
fun_name();
```

or

```
variable = function_name(argument);
```

Note: The function call must be followed by a semicolon (;).

When we call a function, control is passed to the function called. The called function performs all of the stated statements and returns the result to the calling function. The control returns to the main() function.

Example:

```
mul(20,30);
```

Passing Arguments to the Function

When a function is called, it may contain information based on the function prototype, referred to as a parameter (argument). The number of arguments given and the data type during the function call must match the number of parameters declared during the function definition. Otherwise, an error will throw. Passing parameters is also optional, which implies it is not required to do so during the function definition. There are two kinds of parameters.

- **Actual parameter:** A parameter passed during the definition of a function is referred to as the actual parameter.

- **Formal parameter:** A parameter given during a function call is referred to as a formal parameter.

Return a Value from the Function

As a result of being called, a function always returns some value. To return a value, use the return keyword. The return statement is not required. There can only be one return statement in a function. The syntax is shown below.

Syntax:

```
int sum(int a, int b)
{
......
......
return result;
}
var x = sum(30,20)
```

Syntax:

```
return <expression/values>
```

Example:

```
return results;
```

Function Examples

Let's discuss functions by creating a program that adds two integers using functions.

Dart Function with an Argument and a Return Value
We'll write a sum() method to add two numbers in the following example:

```
void main() {
  print("An Example of add two number using
function");
  // Creation of a Function
  int sum(int x, int y){
            // the function Body
            int results;
            results = x+y;
            return results;
}
// We are calling a function and storing result in
variable c
var z = sum(40,10);
print("The sum of two numbers is: ${z}");
}
```

Explanation: We declared a function named sum() and passed two integer variables as actual parameters in the preceding example. We defined a result variable in the function body to hold the sum of two integers and return the result.

We invoked a function with the same name and passed formal arguments 40 and 10 to add two numbers. The sum() function produced a result, which we saved in the variable c and reported on the console.

Dart Function with No Parameter and Return Value
As previously said, passing parameters while defining a function is optional. We can write a function with no parameters and no return value. The syntax is shown below.

Syntax:

```
return_type func_name()
{
        //Statement;
        return value;
}
```

Let's have a look at an example:

```
void main(){
// Creation of afunction without argument
String greeting(){
    return "Welcome to DartTpoint";
}
// Calling the function inside print statement
print(greeting());
}
```

Explanation: In the preceding example, we constructed a method called greeting() that took no arguments and returned a string value to the caller function. Then, within the print statement, we ran the greeting() function and output the result to the console.

Dart Function with No Parameter and without a Return Value
We can define a function that has no parameters and no return value. The syntax is shown below.

Syntax:

```
func_name()
{
 //statement..
}
```

Or

```
void fun_name()
{
   //statement..
}
```

In the preceding general syntax:

- **void:** This indicates that the function has no return type.

- **fun_name:** This is the name of the function.

Let's have a look at an example:

```
// Creation of a function without argument
void greeting()
```

```
{
    print("Welcome to DartTpoint");
}
void main() {
  print("Example of the Dart Function");
  // the function calling
  greeting();
}
```

Explanation: In the preceding example, we defined a function called greet-
ing() outside of the main() method before writing the print statement. We
invoked the defined function within the main() function and reported the
output to the console.

Dart Function with Parameter and without a Return Value
We're creating a function to determine if a given number is even or odd.
Let's have a look at an example.

```
void main()
{
  void number(int a) {
          // Check given number is even or odd
          if (a%2 ==0) {
                  print("Given number is even");
          }
          else {
                  print("Given number is odd");
          }
}
    number(30);
}
```

ANONYMOUS FUNCTION IN DART

We learned about the Dart Function specified by a user-provided name.
Dart also allows us to declare an anonymous function or a function without a name. This is referred to as an anonymous function, lambda function, or closure. An anonymous function performs the same as a regular
function, except it lacks a name. An optional type annotation can have
zero or any number of parameters.

We may assign the anonymous function to a variable and then retrieve or access the closure's value according to our needs.

An anonymous function comprises an independent chunk of code that may be passed around as function arguments in our code. The following is the syntax.

Syntax:

```
(parameter_list) {
    statement
}
```

Example:

```
void main() {
  var lists = ["Jamin","Patric","Mathini","Tony"];
  print("The Example of anonymous function");
  list.forEach((items) {
      print('${list.indexOf(items)}: $items');
});
}
```

Explanation: We defined an anonymous function with an untype parameter item in the preceding example. The function was run for each item in the list and printed the strings with specified index value.

If the function has one statement, we may express the above code in the following manner.

```
list.forEach(
(items) => print("${list.indexOf(items)}: $items"));
```

Lexical Scope

Dart is a lexical scope language, which implies that the variable's scope is determined at compile-time, as we stated in the introduction. When code is compiled, the variable's scope is determined. If the variable is defined in different curly brackets, it operates differently. Let's have a look at an example:

```
bool topVariable = true;

void main() {
```

```
  var inside_Main = true;
 // Defining a Nested Function
void myFunction() {
   var inside_Function = true;
void nestedFunction() {
      var inside_NestedFunction = true;
      // This function is using all the variable of
the previous functions.
     assert(topVariable);
     assert(inside_Main);
     assert(inside_Function);
     assert(inside_NestedFunction);
   }
 }
}
```

Lexical Closure

A closure, also known as a lexical closure, is a function object with access to variables in its lexical scope even when the function is invoked outside its original scope. In other words, it allows access to the scope of an outside function from an inside function. Let's have a look at an example:

```
void main() {
 String initial() {
     var names = 'Will Smith'; // name is local
variable created by init

     void disp_Name() {        // displayName() is   inner
function, a closure
           print(names);          // use variable
declared in parent function
   }
   disp_Name();
 }
init();
```

Explanation: The initial() method in the above code established a local variable named name and a function called disp_Name (). The disp_Name() function is defined within the initial() method; therefore, it has no local variables.

The inner function can access the variable of the outer functions. The method disp_Name() has access to the name variable defined in the outer function, which is initial().

THE MAIN() FUNCTION

Dart's top-level function is the main() function. It is the Dart programming language's most significant and critical function. The main() function initiates the execution of the programming. In a program, the main() function can only use once.

It is in responsible of all sorts of execution, including user-defined statements, functions, and library functions. The program starts with the main() function, where we declare variables and user-defined executable statements. The main method returns void and accepts a ListString> parameter as an optional input. The main() function's general syntax is shown below.

Syntax:

```
void main() {
   // the main function body
}
```

Example:

```
void main()
{
   print("Welcome To DartTpoint");
}
```

Return Value in Dart

After evaluating the function statements to the point where it is called from, the function may return a value. The outcome of the function is transferred to the function call via the return statement. The return keyword represents the return statement. If no return statement is provided, the method returns null. The return statement is optional in the function, but there can only be one return statement.

Syntax:

```
return <expression/value>;
```

Dart Value with Return Value

Syntax:

```
return_type function_name()
{
    //statement;
    return value;
}
```

Here is a description of the preceding syntax:

- **function_name:** This is the function's name, which can be any valid identifier.

- **return type:** This specifies the function's return type. Any valid data type can use. The function's return type must match the return type of the function.

Let's have a look at an example:

```
void main() {
   int mul(int x, int y){
        int z = x*y;
        return z;
}
print("The multiplication of two numbers:
${mul(20,40)}");
}
```

WHAT IS RECURSION?

Dart Recursion is a way in which a function calls itself a subroutine. It is used to tackle challenging problems by breaking them down into smaller parts. When a function is called again or recursively, this is referred to as recursion.

Iterators can solve issues, although recursion is suggested for programmers to employ when dealing with complicated problems since it is an effective problem-solving strategy. The same complex job may evaluate in less time and code.

Recursion creates several calls to the same function; nevertheless, there should be a base case that terminates the recursion.

Recursion employs the divide and conquers strategy to accomplish a complicated mathematical computing assignment. It breaks down extensive work into smaller bits.

It is not suggested to use recursion to solve all sorts of issues. It is, nevertheless, best for a few questions like searching, sorting, Inorder/ Preorder/Postorder, Tree Traversal, and DFS of Graph algorithms. However, it must do it properly; otherwise, it will result in an eternal loop.

What Is Base Condition in Recursion?

```
void main() {
    int factorial(int nums){

  if(nums<=1) { // base case
        return 1;
  else{
        return x*fact(n-1);
 }
}
}
}
```

Recursive Function in Dart

Recursive functions are quite similar to regular functions, but the distinction is that they call themselves recursively. A recursive function iterates again and over until it returns the final result. It enables programmers to handle complicated issues with a small amount of code.

How Does Recursion Work?

Let us look at the notion of recursion using the example of factorial of a given number. In the following example, we shall compute the factorial of n numbers. The following is a multiplication series.

```
Factorial of x (x!) = x*(x - 1)*(x - 2)........1
```

Recursive Function Qualities

The recursive function's characteristics are listed here.

- A recursive function is a special type of function that calls itself.

- To end the recursive function, a valid base case is necessary.

- Because of stack overheads, it is slower than iteration.

Let's have a look at the syntax of recursion:

Explanation: The factorial() method in the above example is a recursive function since it calls itself. When we supply the integer value 5 to the factorial() function, it will recursively call itself by reducing the number.

The factorial() procedure will be run until it matches the base condition or equals one. It multiplied the number by the number's factorial. Consider the following recursive call explanation.

The recursion ends when the number is reduced to one, which is the fundamental condition of recursion.

To avoid endless calls, a recursion function must contain a base condition. Recursion has the following disadvantages:

- Recursive calls use a lot of memory, so they are inefficient.

- Debugging recursive routines is challenging.

- It might be challenging to understand the rationale behind the recursion at times.

OBJECT-ORIENTED CONCEPTS IN DART

Dart is an object-oriented programming language that supports all OOP principles such as classes, objects, inheritance, mixin, and abstract classes. As the name implies, it focuses on the object, and objects are real-life entities. The object-oriented programming technique implements polymorphism, data hiding, and other concepts. The primary purpose of object-oriented programming approach (oops) is to minimize programming complexity and do several operations simultaneously. The concepts for oops are listed below.

- Class

- Object

- Inheritance

- Polymorphism

- Interfaces

- Abstract class

The following is a basic overview of these oops notions:

Class

Dart classes are the blueprints for the linked objects. A Class is a user-defined data type that outlines its attributes and behavior. To obtain all of the class's properties, we must first construct an object. The class syntax is shown below.

Syntax:

```
class Class-Name
{
    <fields>
    <getter/setter>
    <constructor>
    <functions>
}
```

Object

An object is a real-life entity such as a table, a person, a car, etc. The object has two properties: its state and its behavior. Consider an automobile, which has a name, model name, price, and behavior such as moving, stopping, and so on. Object-oriented programming allows you to identify an object's state and behavior.

By creating an object of that class, we may access its attributes. The object in Dart may create by using the new keyword followed by the class name. The syntax is shown below.

Syntax:

```
var object-tName = new
Class-Name(<constructor_arguments>)
```

Inheritance

Dart supports inheritance, which allows us to create new classes from existing ones. The class to be extended is referred to as the parent/superclass, and the newly created class is referred to as the child/subclass. Dart offers the extended keyword for inheriting parent class attributes in child classes. The syntax is shown below.

Syntax:

```
class child_class_name extends parent_class_name
```

Polymorphism

Polymorphism is a notion in object-oriented programming in which one entity has several forms. There are two forms of polymorphism: runtime polymorphism and compile-time polymorphism. For instance, a function with the same name but a distinct behavior or class. Another example is the shape() class and all the classes that inherit from Rectangle, Triangle, and Circle.

Interfaces

The interface is specified as a class blueprint. We may define methods and variables within the interface the same way we do in the class, but the interface only allows for abstract method creation. We can only declare the function signature, not the function body. The interface can be implemented by another class. It is mostly used to hide data.

Abstract Class

An abstract class has one or more abstract methods. The abstract class may declare by using the abstract keyword followed by the class definition. The syntax is shown below.

Syntax:

```
abstract class Class-Name {
   //Body of the abstract class
}
```

DART CLASSES AND OBJECT

Dart classes are the object's blueprint, often known as object constructors. A class can have fields, functions, constructors, and so on. A wrapper binds/encapsulates data and functions that may access by constructing an object. A class is a user-defined data type that defines characteristics for all of its objects.

A class can be viewed of as a sketch (prototype) or a car. It includes information such as the model's name, year, features, price, and so on. We can construct the car based on these qualities. A car is an object in this context. Because there may be several cars, we must build multiple car objects to access their characteristics.

Defining a Class in Dart

To define a class, use the class keyword followed by the class name; all fields and methods are enclosed by a pair of curly brackets ({}). The syntax is shown below.

Syntax:

```
class Class-Name
{
    <fields>
    <getters/setters>
   <constructor>
  <functions>
}
```

The Class-Name variable represents the actual name of the class, as defined by the user. A class definition is provided in curly brackets. Fields, constructors, getters, setters, and methods can all be found in a class.

Example:

```
void main()
{
    // Class Defining
  class Students {
    var stdNames;
    var stdAges;
    var stdRoll_num;
    //the Class Function
      showStdInfo() {
          print("The Student Name is :
${stdNames}");
          print("The Student Age is : ${stdAges}");
          print("The Student Roll Number is :
${stdRoll_num}")
    }
```

In the preceding class example, we declared a class called Student. This class contains three fields: standardNames, standardAges, and standardRoll_num. showStdInfo() is a class function that prints the class's fields. To access the class's properties, we must first construct its object.

Object in Dart

Dart is an object-oriented programming language in which everything is viewed as an object. An object is a variable or instance of a class used to access the properties of the class. Objects have two characteristics: state and behavior. Assume a guy has a state (name, age, and health) and a behavior (walking, running, and sleeping). Programming objects are conceptually comparable to real-world objects in that they have state and behavior. A class is a template from which an object is created.

Classes' fields are maintained as object states, whereas methods reflect an object's action.

Creating Class Objects in Dart

Once the class has been created, we may construct an instance or object of that class to access its properties and functionalities. To define a class, use the new keyword followed by the class name. The following is the typical syntax for creating a class object.

Syntax:

```
var object-name  = new
class-name(<constructor_arguments>);
```

In this case, object name and class name represent the actual object name and class name, respectively. If the constructor of the class is parameterized, the constructor parameters must pass a value.

Example:

```
// Defining class
class Students {
   var stdNames;
   var stdAges;
   var stdRoll_num;

   // Class Function
    showStdInfo() {
        print("The Student Name is :
${stdNames}");
        print("The Student Age is : ${stdAges}");
        print("The Student Roll Number is :
${stdRoll_num}")
```

```
  }
}
void main () {
 // Creation of Object called std
  var std = new Students();
}
```

We created the object std of the type Student, but simply creating an object is not enough. We must use the newly formed object to access the properties.

Assessing Instance Variable and Function

After creating an object, we may access the class's fields and methods. The (.) operator separates the class property name from the instance name. The syntax is shown below.

Syntax:

```
objectName.prop-Name or objectName.metho-Name()
```

Example:

```
// Defining class
 class Students {
    var stdNames;
    var stdAges;
    var stdRoll_num;
    // defining class function
     showStdInfo() {
         print("The Student Name is :
${stdNames}");
         print("The Student Age is : ${stdAges}");
         print("The Student Roll Number is :
${stdRoll_num}");

                      }
}
void main () {
   // Creating object called std
   var stdt = new Student();
   stdt.stdNames = "Peterin";
   stdt.stdAges =22;
```

```
    stdt.stdRoll_num = 90011;
 // Accessing class Function
  std.showStdInfo();
 }
```

Explanation: In the preceding example, we constructed a class named Student, which included the student's name, age, and roll number, as well as the showStdInfo() function, which displayed the student's data.

Then, using the (.) operator, we created a Student class object and assigned values to each field. We used the showStdInfo() method, which produced the details to the screen.

The Advantages of Objects

There are several advantages to adopting object-oriented programming. The following are a few advantages.

- **Modularity:** An object's source code can be kept separate and hidden from the source code of other objects.

- **Data: concealment:** When using oops programming, the specifics of the internal functionality of code are concealed from outsiders. Users, for example, simply interact with the application and are unfamiliar with the core implementation.

- **Reusability:** We don't have to write same code over and over again. In our software, we may utilize the class object numerous times.

- **Easy pluggability and debugging:** If any item causes an issue in our application, we may change it and plug the new object in as its replacement. The oops code may be simple to debug.

WHAT EXACTLY IS CONSTRUCTOR?

A constructor is a sort of function that is constructed with the same name as its class. When an object is created, the constructor is used to initialize it. When we create a class object, the constructor is immediately invoked. It is quite similar to class function; however, it does not have an explicit return type. The most generic type of constructor is the generative constructor, which is used to generate a new instance of a class.

Declaring within the class is an option. Every class has its constructor, but if we don't define it or forget to specify it, the Dart compiler will build a default constructor by sending the default value to the member variable. When we define our constructor, the default constructor is disregarded.

Example:

As shown below, assume we have a class name Student and want to create an object from it.

```
Student stdt = new Students()
```

It called the Student class's default constructor.

Creating Constructor

As previously stated, a constructor has the same name as its class and does not return any value. If we have the class Student, the constructor's name should also be Student.

Syntax:

```
class Class-Name {
     Class-Name() {
}
}
```

When creating a constructor, we must keep the following two rules in mind:

- The constructor and class names should be the same.

- There is no explicit return type for the constructor.

Example:

```
void main() {
     // Creating object
     Student stdt = new Students("Jonephs",29);
}
class Students{
     // Declaring a construstor
     Students(String strt, int ages){
          print("The name is: ${strt}");
          print("The age is: ${ages}");
          }
}
```

Explanation: In the preceding example, we defined a function Object() constructor method called Student(), which is also the name of the class. In the constructor, we supplied two parameters. When we created an object of the Student class and passed a value, it immediately ran the function Object() constructor and reported the result.

Types of Constructors

Dart has three types of constructors, which are listed here.

- Default Constructor or no-arg Constructor

- Parameter Constructor

- Named Constructor

Default Constructor or No-Argument Constructor

A Constructor with no argument is known as a default Constructor or a no-arg Constructor. If we don't define it in the class, the Dart compiler will generate it (with no arguments). If we build a Constructor with or without arguments, the Dart compiler ignores the default Constructor. The syntax is shown below.

Syntax:

```
class Class-Name {
    Class-Name() {
    // constructor body
    }
}
```

Example:

```
void main() {
    // Call constructor automatically when we
creates an object
    Student stdt = new Students();
}
class Students{
    // Declaring construstor
    Students(){
        print("Example of default constructor");
        }
}
```

Parameterized Constructor

We may also pass arguments to a constructor, known as a parameterized constructor. It is used to set up instance variables. We may require a constructor that accepts a single or several arguments. The parameterized constructors are mainly used to set the values of instance variables. The syntax is shown below.

Syntax:

```
class Class-Name {
   Class-Name(parameter_list)
   // constructor body
}
```

Example:

```
void main() {
      // Creating an object
      Student stdt = new Students("Jonesph",28);
}
class Students{
      // Declaring a parameterized constructor
      Student(String strt, int ages){
          print("The name is: ${strt}");
          print("The age is: ${ages}");
          }
}
```

Explanation: We specified a parameterized constructor with two parameters named names and ages in the preceding example. We created a Student class object and gave the proper value to the constructor. As an output to the screen, it printed the names and ages.

Named Constructors

Multiple constructors in a single class are declared using named constructors. The syntax is shown below.

Syntax:

```
Class-Name.constructor_name(param_list)
```

Example:

```
void main() {
      // Creating an object
      Students stdt1 = new Students();   // object
for Default constructor
      Students stdt2 = new Students.
namedConst("Computer-Science");   // object for
parameterized constructor
}
class Students{
      // Declaring construstor
      Students(){
            print("Example of the named
constructor");
            }
      // Second constructor
      Students.namedConst(String branchs){
            print("Branch is: ${branchs}");
            }
}
```

THIS KEYWORD IN DART

The term "this" is used to refer to the current class object. It represents the current instance of the class, method, or constructor. It can also be used to invoke the methods or constructors of the current class. It removes the uncertainty between class attributes because the parameter names are the same. If we declare the class attributes with the same name as the parameter name, the program will become ambiguous; however, this keyword may resolve the ambiguity by prefixing the class attributes. It may be used as a parameter in class methods and constructors.

Let's have a look at few examples of how this keyword works:

First example: Without using this keyword

```
class Mobiles {
      String modelnames;
      int man_years;
```

```
        // Creating a constructor
     Mobiles(modelnames, man_years){
              modelnames = modelnames;
              man_years = 2021;
              print("Mobile's model name:
${modelnames}, and the manufacture year is:
${man_years}");
     }
          }
void main(){
Mobiles mob = new Mobiles("iPhone 13 ",2021);
          }
```

Explanation: In the preceding program, we defined a class named Mobile, which contains two attributes: modelnames and man_years. Then we created a constructor and gave the same parameters as the names of the class attributes.

The constructor arguments with the same name are used to assign the class variables (attributes) on the left side of the constructor body. When we make an instance of a class, the constructor is automatically run, and the result is reported.

If several arguments have the same name, the Dart compiler may become confused. As a result, the compiler will generate ambiguity. That is why we use the term "this" to refer to the current class object.

Second example: Using this keyword

```
class Mobiles {
    String modelnames;
    int man_years;
     // Creating constructor
    Mobiles(modelnames, man_years){
              this.modelnames = modelnames;
              this.man_years = 2021;
              print("Mobile's model name:
${modelnames}, and the manufacture year is:
${man_years}");
    }
          }
void main(){
Mobiles mob = new Mobiles("IPhone 13",2021);
          }
```

Explanation: The preceding example is identical to the previous program, with the exception of this keyword.

this.man_years = 2021;

this.modelnames = modelnames

We utilized this keyword to distinguish an instance or class variable from a local variable.

Remember:

- This keyword is used to point to the current class object.

- It may use to refer to the variables in the current class.

- Using this term, we may instantiate or call the current class constructor.

- This keyword can be passed as an argument to the constructor call.

- This keyword can pass as a parameter in the method call.

- It resolves any ambiguity or name conflict in our instance's or object's constructor or function.

- It may use to get the current instance of the class.

Local Variables

Local variables are defined in methods, constructors, or blocks. It is formed when we create a method or constructor whose scope is limited to those objects. A local variable cannot use outside of the method, constructor, or block.

Class Variable

A class-variable, also known as a static member variable, is a variable that is declared using the static keyword. It is declared in the class but not within a constructor, function, or block. All instances share a single copy of the class variable, or all instances of that class share class variables.

Instance Variable

The instance variable, often known as the non-static variable, is used to declare variables without using the static keyword. An object specifies the instance variables. These variables may access by using the class instance.

The Difference between Class Variable and Instance Variable

The following are the distinctions between class variables and instance variables.

Sr.	Class Variable	Instance Variable
1.	The static keyword is used to specify class variables in a class, but not in methods and constructors.	In a class, the instance variable is declared without the need of a static keyword.
2.	The class variable is accessible by using the class name. **Syntax:** ClassName.variableName	The instance variable may access by using the class's instance. **Syntax:** ObjectRefernce.variableName
3.	All instances of that class share the variables of a class. All instances of the class share the static variable.	All class instances do not share the instance variables. Each specific object will keep its copy of the instance variables.
4.	These are formed when the program is started and destroyed when it is ended.	When an object of a certain class is formed using the new() keyword, instance variables are created and destroyed when the object is destroyed.

STATIC KEYWORD IN DART

The class variable and function are declared using the static keyword. It handles the memory for the global data variable in general. Instead of an individual instance, static variables and methods are members of the class. Because the static variable or methods are the same for each class instance, declaring the data member as static allows us to access it without creating an object. We may access the static method or variable without using the class object by inserting the class name before the static variable or function. We can call the class method from other classes by using the class name.

Static Variable in Dart

Dart static keyword refers to a variable specified within a class using the static keyword. Instead of a particular instance, these are class members. Static variables are regarded the same for all class instances, which imply that all instances of the class share a single copy of the static variable. It allocates memory just once, at class loading, and then uses it throughout the program.

Points to remember:

- The static variable is also known as a class variable.

- All class instances share a single copy of a static variable.

- It is accessible via the class name. We don't need to make an object of the class to which they belong.

- The static variables can easily access in the static methods.

Static Variable Declaring

The static keyword is used to declare a static variable in Dart. The static keyword, followed by the variable name, is used to declare it. The syntax is shown below.

Syntax:

```
static [datatype] [variablename];
```

Accessing the Static Variable

Instead of creating an object, we may use the class name to access the static variable. The syntax is shown below.

Syntax:

```
ClassName.staticVariableName;
```

Static Method

The concept of the static method is similar to that of the static variable. Instead of a class instance, static methods are class members. Static methods can only use static variables and call the class's static methods. We do not need to construct an instance of the class to access it. We may do so when we wish to use a static method in another class.

Remember the following:

- Instead of its object, the static methods are the member class.

- Class methods are another name for static methods.

- The class name can use to access static methods.

- A particular copy of the static method is distributed across all class instances.

Static Methods Declaration

The static method may declare by using the static keyword followed by the method name and the return type. The syntax is shown below.

Syntax:

```
static return_type method_name() {
 //statement
}
```

Static Method Calling

Instead of creating an object, static methods can be invoked simply specifying the class name to which they belong.

Syntax:

```
class-Name.staticMethod();
```

Example:

```
class Students {
   static String stdBranchs;  // Declaring static
variable
   String stdNames;
   int roll_nums;
   showStdInfo() {
     print("The Student's name is: ${empNames}");
     print("The Student's salary is:
${roll_nums}");
     print("The Student's branch name is:
${stdBranchs}");
      }
}
void main() {
  Students std1 = new Students();  // Creating
instances of the student class
  Students std2 = new Students();
  // Assigning value of the static variable using
class name
  Students.stdBranchs = "Computer-Science";
  std1.stdNames = "Benin willian";
  std1.roll_nums = 90013
```

```
    std1.showStdInfo();
    std2.stdNames = "Peterin Handsi";
    std2.roll_nums = 90038
    std2.showStdInfo();
}
```

Explanation: In the above code, we declared the Student class, which has three fields, including the static variable stdBranchs, and one function showStdInfo (). We generated two instances of the class Students and set values to the variables in the class.

The class name and associated value are used to access the static variable stdBranchs. The showStdInfo() method was then invoked by objects std1 and stu2. As an output, it printed the student's information.

SUPER KEYWORD

The super keyword signifies the current child class's immediate parent class object. Its child class uses it to invoke superclass methods and superclass constructors. The primary goal of the super keyword is to eliminate misunderstandings between parents and subclasses with the same method name. It is also used to refer to the properties and methods of the superclass.

The Use of a Static Keyword

- When both the parent and child classes contain members with the same name, the super keyword can use to access data members from the parent class in the child class.

- It is used in the child class to access the parent class's constructor.

- We may access the superclass function that is overridden by the subclass by using the super keyword.

Using a Super Keyword with Variables

This occurs when the variables in the child class have the same name as the variables in the superclass. As a result, the Dart compiler may encounter ambiguity. The super keyword can then access the superclass variables in its child class. The syntax is shown below.

Syntax:

```
Super.var-Name
```

Example:

```
 // Super class Car
class Cars
{
    int speeds = 190;
}
// sub class Bike extending Car
class Bikes extends Cars
{
    int speeds = 130;
    void display()
    {
        //print varible of the base class (Bikes)
        print("Speed of car: ${super.speeds}");
    }
}
void main() {
// Creating a object of sub class
Bikes b1 = new Bikes();
b1.display();
}
```

Explanation: In the above code, we declared the superclass as Cars, which contains speeds variable, and then the subclass Bikes inherited it.

Because the speeds of the subclass are changeable, we utilized the super keyword to retrieve the parent class variable. We generated a child class b1 object and ran a show method that reported the value of the superclass variable.

When we use print(speeds) instead of print(super.speeds), the value of the subclass variable is printed.

We may copy the preceding code, put it into a dartpad or notepad, and print the value without using the super keyword. We can tell the difference between the two outcomes.

Using the Super Keyword with the Parent Class Method

The super keyword is used to access the parent class method in the child class. If the child and parent classes have the same name, we may use the super keyword to call the parent class method from the child class. The syntax is shown below.

Syntax:

```
super.method-Name;
```

Example:

```dart
// Base class Supers
class Supers
{
    void display()
    {
        print("This is super class method");
    }
}
// Childs class inherits Supers
class Childs extends Supers
{
    void display()
    {
        print("This is child class");
    }
    // Note that message() is only in the Student
class
    void messages()
    {
        // will invoke or call the current class
display() method
        display();
        // will invoke or call the parent class
display() method
        super.display();
    }
}
void main() {
  // Creating the object of sub class
Childs c1 = new Childs();
// calling display() of Students
c1.message();
    }
```

Explanation: In the preceding code, we built a function with the same name in parent and child classes. The show() function is present in both the parent and child classes, showing that method overriding has occurred.

So we built a messages() method in the child class, called the parent class function within it using the super keyword, and then generated the child class object. We used the object to invoke the messages() function, which displayed both show() method statements on the screen.

Using a Super Keyword with the Constructor

We may also use the super keyword to go to the parent class's constructor. The super keyword can invoke both parameterized and non-parameterized constructors depending on the circumstances. The syntax is shown below.

Syntax:

```
:super();
```

Example:

```
// Base class called Parents
class Parents
{
    Parents()
    {
        print("This is super class constructor");
    }
}

// Child class Super
class Childs extends Parents
{
    Childs():super()    // Calling the super class
constructor
    {
        print("This is sub class constructor");
    }
}
void main() {
  // Creating the object of sub class
Childs c1 = new Childs();
}
```

Explanation: The syntax of the Dart language is too similar to that of the C# language. We used the super keyword to invoke the parent class constructor, separated by colon (:). We should use the superclass as an initializer when delegating a superclass constructor.

INHERITANCE IN DART

Dart inheritance is described as the process of deriving another class's features and characteristics. It allows us to construct a new class from an existing one. It is the most important notion in the oops. All of the prior class's behavior and characteristics can reuse in the new class.

- **Parent class:** A class inherited by another class is referred to as a superclass or parent class. It is sometimes referred to as a basic class.

- **Child class:** A child class inherits properties from another class. It is sometimes referred to as a derived class or a subclass.

Assume we have a fleet of cars and divided them into three classes: Duster, Maruti, and Jaguar. The modelName(), milage(), and man year() methods will be the same for all three types.

Inheritance of class.

As shown in the above figure, if we construct the class Car and write the common function in each of the classes. The program will then have more duplication and data redundancy. To avoid this kind of situation, inheritance is employed.

We can eliminate data redundancy by establishing the class Car with these functions and inheriting it in the other classes. It increases code reusability. We only need to write the code once rather than several times. Let's have a look at the following figure.

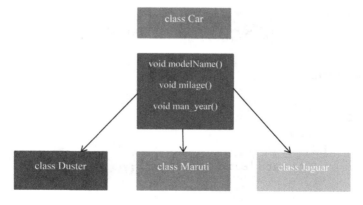

Creation of class with inheritance.

Syntax:

```
class childclass extends parentclass {
    //body of the child class
}
```

Using the extends keyword, the child class inherits functions, variables, or properties from the parent class. It cannot inherit the parent class's constructor; we shall go over this later.

Inheritance Types

There are four forms of inheritance. These are provided here.

- Single Inheritance

- Multiple Inheritance

- Multilevel Inheritance

- Hierarchical Inheritance

Single Level Inheritance

A single class or subclass inherits a class is inherited by one parent class in single inheritance. In the following example, we construct a Person class inherited from the Human class.

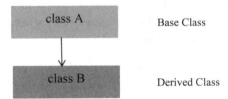

Single inheritance.

```
class Birds{
    void fly()
       {
           print("Bird can fly");
        }
  }
    // Inherits super class
```

```
class Parrots extends Birds{
        //child class function
        void speak(){
            print("Parrot can speak");
                }
}
void main() {
     // Creating object of child class
     Parrots p1=new Parrots();
     p1.speak();
     p1.fly();
}
```

Explanation: In the above code, we declare the fly() function in the parent class Birds. Then, using the extends keyword, we constructed the Parrots child class, which inherited the parent class's properties. The function speak is unique to the child class ().

The kid class now has two functions: fly() and speak(). As a result, we generated a child class object and used it to access both functions. It output the outcome to the console.

Multilevel Inheritance

A subclass is inherited by another subclass or creates a chain of inheritance in multiple inheritance. Let's have a look at an example:

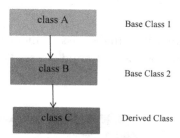

Multiple inheritance.

```
class Birds{
     void fly()
        {
            print("Bird can fly");
          }
    }
     // Inherits super class
```

```
class Parrots extends Birds{
        void speak(){
            print("Parrot can speak");
                }
}
// Inherits Parrots base class
class Eagles extends Parrots {
        void vision(){
            print("Eagle has a sharp vision");
                }
}
void main() {
    // Creating object of the child class
    Eagles e1=new Eagles();
    e1.speak();
    e1.fly();
    e1.vision();
}
```

Explanation: In the preceding example, we built a new class called Eagles and inherited it from the Parrots class. The parrot is now the parent class of Eagles, and Eagles has inherited all of the functions of both parent classes. We generated a child class object and accessed all of its attributes. It displayed the output on the screen.

Hierarchical Inheritance

Two or more classes inherit a single class in hierarchical inherence. The Persons class is inherited by the two-child classes Peterin and Jamesph in the following example:

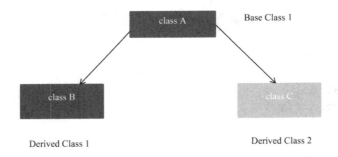

Hierarichal inheritance.

```dart
// Parent Class
class Persons {
  void dispName(String names) {
    print(names);
  }
  void dispAge(int ages) {
    print(ages);
  }
}
class Peterin extends Persons {
  void dispBranch(String nationality) {
    print(nationality);
  }
}
//Derived class created from another derived
class.
class Jamesph extends Persons {
        void result(String results){
            print(results);
}
}
void main() {
    // Creating Object of James class
    Jamesph j1 = new James();
    j1.dispName("Jamesph");
    j1.dispAge(25);
    j1.results("Passed");
  // Creating Object of Peter class
    Peter p1 = new Peterin();
    p1.dispName("Peterin");
    p1.dispAge(21);
    p1.dispBranch("Computer-Science");
}
```

SUPER CONSTRUCTOR IN DART

The child class can inherit all properties (methods, variables) and parent
behavior except parent class constructor. The superclass constructor can
be invoked in sub class by using the super() constructor. We can access
both non-parameterized and parameterized constructor of superclass.

Accessing the constructor of superclass is slightly different in the Dart. The syntax is given below.

Syntax:

```
Sub_ClassConstructor():super() {
}
```

Implicit Super

When we instantiate a class, the constructor is immediately invoked, as we all know. When we create an object of a subclass, the subclass's constructor is invoked, which automatically executes the parent class's default (non-parameterized) constructor. To invoke the superclass constructor, we may utilize the super() constructor in our subclass. Let's have a look at an example:

```
// Parent class
class Super_class {
        Super_class(){
            print("Superclass constructor");
             }
}
class Sub_class extends Super_class
{
        Sub_class(){
            print("Subclass constructor");
         }
          display(){
            print("Welcome to DartTpoint");
}
}
void main(){
        print("Dart Implicit the Superclass
constructor call");
        // We create an object of sub class which
will invoke the subclass constructor.
        // as well as the parent class constructor.
        Sub_class s1 = new Sub_class();
        // Calling sub class method
        s1.display();
}
```

Explicit Super

If the superclass constructor has parameters, we must explicitly execute the superclass constructor in the subclass by calling super() constructor with argument in. Let's have a look at an example:

```
// Parent class
class Super_class {
        Super_class(String msgs){
            print("Superclass constructor");
             print(msgs);
             }
}
class Sub_class extends Super_class
{
        Sub_class():super("We are calling the
superclass constructor explicitly "){
                print("This is a subclass
constructor");

            }
            display(){
                print("Welcome to javatpoint");
}
}
void main(){
        print("Dart Implicit the Superclass
constructor example");
        // We create an object of the sub class
which will invoke subclass constructor.
        // as well as the parent class constructor.
        Sub_class s1 = new Sub_class();
        // Calling the sub class method
        s1.display();
}
```

METHODS IN DART

A Dart method is a set of statements that include certain class object properties. It allows us to conduct various operations, and we can call it by name when we need to in the program. Methods break a huge job into little bits and carry out the program's specific operation. This strategy boosts code reusability and improves the program's modular approach. The methods can be constructed using arguments supplied as information to perform the specified task, after which it can return a value or return nothing. Methods in a class that define either instance methods or class methods.

Instance Methods

A method that may be accessed by utilizing a class instance is referred to as an instance method. The instance methods can have no or many parameters. This keyword may access via the instance method through the instance variable.

Creating Instance Methods

An instance method has a name and a valid return type. It might have a set of parameters. The syntax is shown below.

Syntax:

```
return_type method_name(<list of argument(s)>)
{
//statement
}
```

Calling the Instance Method

Instance methods may be accessible via the class object; thus, we must construct one to utilize it. The syntax is shown below.

Syntax:

```
Class_Name objName = new ClassName()
obj_Name.methodName()
```

Class Methods

The static keyword is used to declare the class method. It is accessible by utilizing the class name rather than the class object. These methods are shared by all instances of that specific class. The Static methods can only access static variables.

Creating Class Methods

The static keyword is used to declare a static method, followed by the method name and return type. The syntax is shown below.

Syntax:

```
static return_type method_name(){
    //statement
}
```

Calling the Class Method

The class method can be called by using the class name rather than the class object. The syntax is shown below.

Syntax:

```
Class_Name.classMethod()
```

METHOD OVERRIDING IN DART

In Dart, method overriding happens when a child class attempts to override the parent class's method. When a child class extends a parent class, it gains full access to the parent class's methods and thereby overrides the parent class's methods. It is accomplished by redefining the same method that exists in the parent class.

This approach is useful when conducting various tasks for each child class, because we can easily redefine the content by overriding it.

Important notes:

- A method may only overridden in the child class, not in the parent class.

- The methods described in the child and parent classes should be identical, from name to parameter list, with the exception of the content included within the method, which can and cannot be the same.

- The child class cannot override a final or static method within the parent class.

- Because constructors from the parent class cannot be inherited, they cannot be overridden by the child class.

Example:

```
// Program to illustrate the
// method overriding
class SuperClass {
  // Creating a method
  void show() {
    print("This is class SuperClass");
  }
}

class SubClass extends SuperClass {

  // Overriding show method
  void show() {
    print("This is class SubClass child of
SuperClass");
  }
}

void main() {
  // Creating objects
  //of both the classes
  SuperClass s1 = new SuperClass ();
  SubClass s2 = new SubClass ();

  // Calling the same function
  // from both classes
  // object to the show method overriding
  s1.show();
  s2.show();
}
```

What Exactly Is Polymorphism?

Polymorphism is derived from the Greek terms poly, which means many, and morph, which implies transforming into diverse forms or shapes. Polymorphism indicates that the same entity may utilize in several ways. In terms of programming, the same method can use in many classes. This method makes programming more intuitive and approachable.

For instance, we have the Shape class to define the shape of an object. The shape might be a circle, rectangle, square, straight line, or something else. So, while the aim is the same, the approach is not.

Mechanism overriding is a method for achieving polymorphism. When a subclass object uses the same function, we might want it to respond differently. This is accomplished by defining the same method in the subclass. The method has the same name, parameters, and return type as the previous one. When the method is invoked, the method defined in the subclass is performed instead of the method defined in the superclass.

Example of Method Overriding

We define two classes: one is a subclass named Human, and the other is a superclass called Boy. The Boy subclass inherits the Human superclass. The identical function void showInfo() is defined in both types but with distinct implementations. The void showInfo has its definition in the subclass ().

First example:

```dart
class Humans{
    //Overridden-method
     void run()
     {
        print("The Human is running");
     }
}
class Men extends Humans{
    //Overriding-method
     void run(){
        print("The Boy is running");
     }
}
void main(){
        Men m1 = new Men();
        //This will call  child class version of
run()
        m1.run();
}
```

Explanation: In the preceding example, we defined the identical method in the subclass and superclass. The goal of method overriding is to provide a custom implementation of a subclass method. When we built the Boy subclass object, it performed the subclass method, and printed Man is running instead of Human is running.

When we create an object of a parent class, the parent class method is always invoked.

Let's look at another example in which we build two Classes called Colleges and Students, both of which have a common function called void students details (). Let's have a look at the following code.

Second example:

```
class Colleges{
 // Declaring-variables
         String names;
         int rollnum;

// Overriden-Method
void stu_details(names,rollnum){
        this.names = names;
        this.rollnum = rollnum;
}

void display(){
        print("Student name:${names}");
        print("Student rollno: ${rollnum}");
        print("Result is passed");
    }
}
class Students extends Colleges{
// Overriding-Method
void stu_details(names,rollnum){
        this.names = names;
        this.rollnum = rollnum;
}
void show(){
        print("Student name:${names}");
        print("Student rollno: ${rollnum}");
        print("The result is failed");
}
}
void main(){
//Creating object of subclass
Students  st1 = new Students();
st1.stu_details("Josephin",121);
st1.show();
```

```
// Creating the object of superclass
Colleges cg1 = new Colleges();
cg1.stu_details("Jasonin",112);
cg1.display();
}
```

Explanation: In the above example, two classes are created: Colleges as a parent class and Students as a child class. Both classes define the function stu details with identical parameters and return types.

The Students subclass now inherits the Colleges superclass, and the stu details() function is overridden in the subclass.

We built a Students object and used appropriate inputs to call stu details(). It ran the subclass method and then reported the outcome.

Similarly, we generated an object of the Colleges superclass object, executed its methods, and printed the various outcomes.

Method Overriding Using the Super Keyword

We can call the parent class method without generating an object of it. It can attain this by using the super keyword in the subclass. The super keyword can use in the subclass to access the parent class data member. Let's have a look at an example:

```
class Humans{
   //Overridden-method
    void run()
    {
       print("The Human is running");
    }
}
class Man extends Humans{
   //Overriding method
    void run(){
       // Accessing Parent class run() method in child
class
       super.run();
       print("The Boy is running");
    }
}
void main(){
    Man m1 = new Man();
```

```
        //This will call child class version of eat()
        m1.run();
}
```

Explanation: We used the super keyword to access the Humans class method in the child class in the preceding example. We don't need to instantiate the parent class anymore. We merely constructed the subclass object called the run() methods of the child and parent classes.

The Benefit of Method Overriding

The key advantage of method overriding is that the subclass can implement the same method as required without making any modifications to the superclass function. This technique is useful when we want to subclass a method such that it behaves differently but yet has the same name.

Rules of Method Overriding in Dart

The following are a few method overriding rules. These considerations should be considered while declaring the same method in a subclass.

- The overriding method (child class method) must declare in the same way as the overridden method (the superclass method). The parent class method's return type, list of parameters, and sequence must all be the same.

- The overriding method must define in the subclass rather than in the parent class.

- Because the static and final methods are accessible in their class, they cannot be inherited in the subclass.

- A subclass cannot inherit a superclass's constructor.

- If a method cannot be inherited, it cannot be overridden.

GETTERS AND SETTERS IN DART

Getters and setters are special class methods that allow us to read and write to the properties of an object. The getter method is used to read or get the value of a variable, whereas the setter method is used to set or initialize the appropriate class fields. By default, every class has a getter and a setter function. However, we may override the default methods by explicitly specifying getter and setter methods.

Defining a Getter

The getters method may define by using the get keyword with no parameters and an appropriate return type.

Syntax:

```
return-type get field-name{
}
```

Defining a Setter

Using the set keyword, we may specify the setter method with one argument and no return type.

Syntax:

```
set field-name {
}
```

Example:

```
class Students {
        String stdNames;
        String branchs;
        int stdAges;
 // getter method
        String get std_names
            {
            return stdNames;
            }
        void set std_names(String names)
              {
            this.stdNames = names;
              }
        void set std_ages(int ages) {
            if(age> = 25){
                print("The Student age should
be greater than 25")
                }else{
                    this.stdAges = ages;
                        }
            }
        }
```

```
        int get std_ages{
            return stdAges;

}
        void set std_branchs(String branch_names) {
            this.branchs = branch_names;
}
    int get std_branchs{
        return branchs;
}
}
void main(){
Students std1 = new Students();
std1.std_names = 'Johnini';
std1.std_age = 22;
std1.std_branch = 'Computer-Science';
print("The Student name is: ${std_names}");
print("The Student age is: ${std_ages}");
print("The Student branch is: ${std_branchs}");
}
```

ABSTRACT CLASSES IN DART

Dart classes with one or more abstract methods are known as abstract classes. Abstraction is a type of data encapsulation in which the real internal workings of the function are hidden from consumers. They only interface with external functions. Using the abstract keyword, we can declare the abstract class. There is a chance that an abstract class will or will not contain abstract methods.

Abstract methods are those that are defined but not implemented. With implementation, the concrete methods or normal methods are stated. An abstract class can have both methods, but a normal class cannot have abstract methods.

We can't make an instance of an abstract class; hence, it can't be instantiated. The subclass may only expand it, and the subclass must be given access to the abstract methods available in the current class. Then an abstract subclass must declare.

Rules for the Abstract Classes

The abstract rules are outlined below.

- An abstract class may or may not have an abstract method (method without implementation).

- If the class contains at least one abstract method, it must be marked abstract.

- The abstract class object cannot create, but it may be expanded.

- The abstract class is declared with the abstract keyword.

- A conventional or concrete (method with a body) method can likewise include an abstract class.

- The parent class's abstract methods must all be implemented in the subclass.

Declaring the Abstract Class

To declare the abstract class, use the abstract keyword followed by the class name. An abstract class is typically a base for subclasses to enhance and implement abstract methods.

Syntax:

```
abstract class Class-Name {
  // Body of the abstract class
}
```

Abstract Class Usage

Assume we have a class Person with the function displayInfo() and two subclasses, Boy and Girl. Because each person's information differs from the other, there is no value to implementing displayInfo() in the parent class. Because each subclass is required to override the parent class function with its implementation; as a result, we may force the subclass to implement that method, which is one advantage of making the method abstract. The provided implementation is not required in the parent class.

Example:

```
abstract class Persons {
//declaration of abstract method

 void displayInfo();  //abstract-method
 }
```

```
class Boys extends Persons
{
// Overriding method
void displayInfo() {
    print("My name is Rohna");
        }
}
class Girls extends Persons
{
// Overriding-method
void displayInfo() {
    print("My name is Gorcia");
        }
}
void main() {
Boy b1 = new Boys();  // Creating Object of Boy
class
Girl g1 = new Girls();  // Creating Object of Girl
class
b1.displayInfo();
g1.displayInfo();
}
```

Explanation: As we can see in the above code, we implemented the abstract method in two subclasses based on its requirements, and then we invoked the displayInfo() function using the objects of both classes' objects.

DART INTERFACES

An interface establishes the syntax that all entities must follow. Dart has no specific syntax for defining interfaces. An interface is defined as a class in which an object may access any set of methods. The Class declaration has the ability to interface with itself.

The term implement must be written followed by the class name to utilize the interface. The implementing class must offer a thorough specification of all the interface's functionalities. We may say that every function with the body in the interface that we wish to achieve must be defined by a class.

Declaring an Interface

Dart does not offer syntax for explicitly declaring interfaces. A class declaration is implicitly an interface that contains the whole instance member of the class and any interfaces it implements.

Implementing an Interface

Another class must implement the interface using the implements keyword to use interface methods. A class that implements an interface must completely implement all the interface's functions. The syntax of the implementing interface is as follows.

Syntax:

```
class Class-Name implements Interface-Name
```

In the following example, we declare a class called Employees. The Engineers class implicitly implements the interface definition for the Employees class.

```
class Employees
{
    void display() {
        print("Working as an engineer");
                }
}
// Defining the interface by implanting another class
class Engineers implements Employees
{
        void display() {
                print("Engineer in this company");
}
}
void main()
{
Engineers eng1 = new Engineers();
eng1.display();
}
```

Explanation: In the preceding example, we defined the Engineers class as an interface that implements the Engineers class. Then, in both classes, we defined the identical function display(). This method is overridden in the class Engineers; therefore, we generated an Engineers object in a main() function that called the display() function. It displayed the output on the screen.

Implementing Multiple Inheritance

As we previously explained, Dart does not enable multiple inheritance, but we may use several interfaces. We may argue that multiple inheritance is possible in Dart by utilizing multiple interfaces. The syntax is shown below.

Syntax:

```
class Class-Name implements interface1,
interface2,…interface n
```

Example:

```
class Students
{
    String names;
    int ages;
    void displayNames() {
        print("I am ${names}");
                            }
    void displayAges() {
            print("My age is ${ages}");
                            }
}
class Faculty
{
    String dep_names;
    int salary;
    void displayDepartment() {
        print("I am a professor of
${dep_names}");
                        }
    void displaySalary() {
            print("Salary is ${salary}");
                        }
}
// Defining the interface by implementing another
class
class Colleges implements Students, Faculty
{
    // Overriding the Students class members
    String names;
    int ages;
    void displayNames() {
        print("I am ${names}");
                        }
```

```
void displayAges() {
        print("My age is ${ages}");
                                }
//Overriding each data member of Faculty class
   String dep_names;
   int salary;

   void displayDepartment() {
        print("I am a proffesor of
${dep_names}");
                        }
   void displaySalary() {
        print("Salary is ${salary}");
}
}
void main()
{
College cg1 = new Colleges();
cg1.names = "Josph";
cg1.age = 22;
cg1.dep_name = "Computer Science";
cg1.salary = 52000;
cg1.displayNames();
cg1.displayAges();
cg1.displayDepartments();
cg1.displaySalary();
}
```

Explanation: Different interfaces were implemented in class colleges in the above example. Each data member of the Student and Faculty classes has precedence in the Colleges class. We created a Colleges class object and called the overriding functions. It printed the outcome.

Rules for Implementing Interfaces

- Every method and instance variable of an interface must be overridden by a class that implements it.

- Dart does not provide syntax for explicitly declaring the interface. The interface might be considered in the class declaration.

- An interface class must offer a complete implementation of all interface methods.

- We can implement one or more interfaces at the same time.

- We may accomplish multiple inheritance by using the interface.

CHAPTER SUMMARY

In this chapter, we discussed Dart functions and object-oriented programming. We also discussed anonymous and main functions as well as recursion. Moreover, we learned about constructors, interfaces, inheritances, and methods.

CHAPTER 4

Dart Advanced

IN THIS CHAPTER

➤ Exceptions

➤ Collections

➤ Packages

➤ Generators

➤ Unity Testing

In the previous chapter, we discussed data functions, recursion, and object-oriented, where we also covered inheritance, interfaces, constructor, and overriding. In this chapter, we will discuss exceptions, packages, libraries, and html DOM.

DART EXCEPTIONS

Exceptions in Dart are runtime errors. It is triggered when the program is executed. When the program runs internally, and the Dart compiler finds something inappropriate, the program does not communicate the problem at build time. The application is then terminated unexpectedly after reporting a runtime error. Exceptions are the name given to this sort of problem. For instance, a given integer is divided by zero, attempting to access entries from an empty list.

DOI: 10.1201/9781003299363-4

Dart supports the built-in exceptions listed in the following table.

Sr. No.	Exceptions	Description
1.	DefferedLoadException	When a delayed library fails to load, this exception is raised.
2.	FromatException	The exception is the one that is thrown.
3.	IntegerDivisionByZeroException	When a number is split by zero, this error is thrown.
4.	IOEException	It is the most basic type of input-output exception.
5.	IsolateSpawnException	When an isolated cannot be generated, this exception is issued.
6.	Timeout	This exception is raised when a scheduling timeout occurs while waiting for an async result.

The exception's primary goal is to manage the runtime issue and keep the program from ending unexpectedly. In Dart, every exception is a subtype of the predefined class Exception. To handle exceptions, Dart supports the following techniques.

The Try/On/Catch Blocks

The try block is used to include code that may throw an exception. When we need to declare exceptions, we utilize the on the block. When the handler requires the exception object, the catch block is used.

If the try block encounters a problem, it throws the error to the catch block, which contains the code to handle the error. The try block must be followed by exactly one other block, either on/catch or finally.

The syntax for exceptional handling is as follows:

Syntax:

```
try {
// the code that might throw an exception
}
on Exception1 {
// Specify exception
}
Catch Exception2 {
// the code for handling exception
}
```

It is important to remember following points:

- We can handle numerous exceptions by utilizing several catch blocks.

- The on and catch blocks are mutually inclusive, which means we may connect both – the on and catch blocks – with the try block.

The variable x is divided by the variable y in the following example. The code is thrown when it tries to divide by zero. The code to handle the exception is included in the block. Let's look at the following code.

Example: Making use of the on block

```dart
void main() {
    int a = 17;
    int b = 0;
    int res;
    try {
        res = a ~/ b;
    }
    on IntegerDivisionByZeroException {
        print('Cannot divide by zero');
    }
}
```

Explanation: In the previous code, we defined three variables in the main () function: x, y, and res. We wrote the suspect code in a try block and divided x by 0 to see whether an exception was thrown. When the try block discovered the issue, control was moved to the on block, containing the code to handle the error. The program's execution was not stopped as a result of this.

Let's look at an example that makes use of the catch block.

Example: Making use of the catch block

```dart
void main() {
    int a = 17;
    int b = 0;
    int rest;
    try {
        rest = a ~/ b;
    }
```

```
// It returns built-in exception related to the
occurring exception
   catch(E) {
      print(E);
   }
}
```

Example 3: On...catch block

```
void main() {
   int a = 17;
   int b = 0;
   int rest;
   try {
      rest = a ~/ b;
   }
   on IntegerDivisionByZeroException catch(E) {
      print(E);
   }
}
```

Finally Block

Whether or whether an exception occurs, the finally block is always executed. After the try/on/catch, it executes unconditionally.

The syntax for the finally block is shown below.

Syntax:

```
try {
   // the code that may be throw an exception
}
on Exception1 {
   //the exception handling code or specifying the
exception
}
catch Exception2 {
   // the code for exception handling
}
finally {
   // the code that should always execute; whether
exception or not.
}
```

Example:

```
finally { void main() {
    int a = 17;
    int b = 0;
    int rest;
    try {
        rest = a ~/ b;
    }
    on IntegerDivisionByZeroException {
        print('Cannot divide by zero');
    }

        print('The Finally block always executed');
    }
}
```

Throwing an Exception

We have the option of raising an exception explicitly or forcefully. The expressly raised exception should handle to keep the application from crashing. The syntax is shown below.

Syntax:

```
throw new Exception-name()
```

Example:

```
main() {
    try {
        check_marks(-20);
    }
    catch(e) {
        print('Marks cannot be negative');
    }
}
void check_marks(int marks) {
    if(marks<0) {
        throw new FormatException();  // Raising
explanation externally
    }
}
```

Custom Exceptions

As previously stated, each exception in Dart is a subtype of the built-in class Exception. Dart allows us to build new exceptions by extending the current exception class. The syntax is shown below.

Syntax: Defining Exception

```
class Custom_exception_Name implements Exception {
    // can contain the constructors, variables and
methods
}
```

Example:

```
class AmntException implements Exception {
    String expMsg() => 'Entered the Amount should
be greater than zero';
}
void main() {
    try {
        withdraw_amnt(-1);
    }
    catch(E) {
        print(E.expMsg());
    }
    finally {
        print('Ending requested operation.....');
    }
}
void withdraw_amt(int amnt) {
    if (amnt <= 0) {
        throw new AmntException();
    }
}
```

Explanation: In the preceding example, we defined a custom exception called AmntException. If the entered amount is outside of the acceptable range, the code throws an exception, and the function call is wrapped in a try...catch block.

TYPEDEF IN DART

In Dart, the typedef function is used to create an alias for a function type, which we can then use as a type annotation when creating variables and return types for that function type. As a type annotation in variable declaration or function return type, an alias of function type can be used. When we assigned the function type to a variable, we stored the type information in a typedef.

Declaring a Typedef

A typedef keyword is used to create an alias for a function identical to the actual function. A function prototype with a set of arguments can likewise be created. The syntax is shown below.

Syntax:

```
typedef function-name(parameters)
```

Example: Let's make an alias for MultiOperation(int a1, int a2) with two integer arguments.

```
typedef MultiOperation(int a1, int a2);    //
function signature
```

Assigning the Typedef Variable

Any function with the same parameters can be assigned to the typedef variable. The syntax is shown below.

Syntax:

```
type_def var_name = function-name;
```

Let's look at an example of defining two functions with the same signature as the MultiOperation.

Example:

```
Sum(int a1, int a2) {
      print("Sum of the two number:${a1+a2}");
}
```

```
Sub(int a1, int a2 ) {
        print("Subtraction of the two
number:${a1-a2}");
  }
```

Calling Function with Typedef

Using the typdef variable, we may execute the function by passing the same parameter. The syntax is shown below.

Syntax:

```
var-name(parameter);
```

Example:

```
MultiOperation mop;
mop = Sum;
mop(30,20);
mop = Sub;
mop(20,10);
```

The mop variable is a typedef variable that can refer to any method that accepts two integer parameters. Using typedefs, the function reference can alter at runtime.

Complete the Program by Using Typedef

```
typedef MultiOperation(int num1, int num2);   //
typedef function signature
Sum(int a1, int a2) {
        print("Sum of two number:${a1+a2}");
}
Sub(int a1, int a2 ) {
        print("Subtraction of two number:${a1-a2}");
}
void main() {
MultiOperation mop = Sum;
print("DartTpoint - Dart typedef Example");
mop(30,20);
mop = Sub;
mop(20,10);
}
```

Explanation: We established an alias for the MultiOperation() method in the preceding code using the typedef keyword. We added two new functions, Sum() and Sub(), with the same signature as the typedef function.

Then we added the typedef variable mop, referencing both the Sum() and Sub() methods. We then called the function, handing it the necessary parameter, and printed the result.

Typedef as Parameter

As a parameter, we may use the typedef method. In the following example, we add a NumericOperation(int a1, int a2, MultiOperation mop) function to the same program, using the two integer variables and typedef ManyOperation mop as its parameter.

Example:

```
typedef MultiOperation(int num1, int num2);  //
typedef function signature
Sum(int a1, int a2) {
     print("Sum of the two number:${a1+a2}");
}
Sub(int a1, int a2 ) {
     print("Subtraction of the two
number:${a1-a2}");
}
NumericOperation(int a1, int a2, MultiOperation
mop){
     print("Inside Operation");
     mp(a1,a2);
        }
void main() {
print("DartTpoint - Dart typedef Example");
NumericOperation(30, 20, Sum);
NumericOperation(30, 20, Sub);
}
```

We didn't need to establish a typedef variable to refer to each method in the above code; we just invoked the NumericOperation() function, passing the required value and the typedef variable mop. It carried out the specified actions and printed the result.

Debugging in Dart

Debugging is the process of finding and removing current and potential problems in a Dart program that may generate ambiguity and uncertainty during program execution. Debugging is required to find and fix errors for the program to execute smoothly or without interruption.

When we use the Dart IDE, debugging becomes much more accessible. We will assume that we have installed the most common and appropriate IDE WebStorme on our system. The WebStorm Editor allows us to debug in stages.

What Exactly Are Breakpoints?

Breakpoints are program checkpoints used to break the program at a specific moment to test its behavior. We may insert breakpoints into the software to test for flaws in that particular place.

How Do I Create Breakpoints in WebStorm?

In WebStorm, we can create breakpoints by simply clicking on a line number in the left bar. When we run the program in debugging mode after adding the breakpoints, we'll see the Debugger window, where we can see how the breakpoints operate. We can also experiment with other variables and observe how they affect the window.

METADATA IN DART

Dart Metadata is used to provide more information to the Dart program. It often begins with @ symbol, followed by a reference to a compile-time constant or a call to a constant constructor.

Creating the Metadata Annotation

Dart allows us to create our metadata annotations.

Let's have a look at an example.

Here's an example of a @student annotation with two arguments:

```
library students;
Class Students {
    final String studentNames;
    final String rollnum;
    const Students(this.studentNames, this.code);
}
```

In the following example, we use the @student annotation:

```
import 'student.dart' ;
@Students('studentNames', 'rollnum')
void greetHii() {
    print("Hii Welcome to Dartpoint");
}
```

Metadata in Dart is often defined before a library name, class, typedef, field, type parameter, factory, function, constructor, parameter, or variable declaration and before an import or export directive. In runtime, we may access the metadata by utilizing reflection.

Let's have a look at an example:

```
class Humans{
   @Overridden method
    void run()
   {
       print("Humans are running");
   }
}
class Men extends Humans{
   @Overriding method
    void run(){
       print("The Boys are running");
   }
}
void main(){
       Men m1 = new Men();
       //This will call child class version of run()
        m1.run();
}
```

COLLECTION IN DART

Unlike the other programming languages, Dart does not offer arrays for data storage. We may use the Dart collection for the array data structure. Using the dart::core library, we may activate the collection's additional classes in our Dart script.

Dart collection may be divided into the following categories:

Dart Collection	Description
List	A list is a collection of an ordered collection of collections. The list class in the dart::core library allows us to construct and edit lists. It offers the following kinds of list:
	• Fixed Length List – We cannot adjust the length of the list during runtime.
	• Growable List – We can adjust the list's length at runtime.
Set	A set is a collection of items that each object can define at the same time. To access the dart::core library's facilities, use the Set class.
Maps	The maps are a collection of key-value data pairs. Each value is associated with a particular key. In the dart, the key and value can be of any type. A map is a living collection. We may claim that the map can change at runtime. To deal with it, the dart::core library provides the Map class.
Queue	A queue is a collection of locations stored in the first-in-first-out (FIFO) order. It can adjust on both ends. We may add the element from one end and delete it from the other.

Collections Iteration

The iterator class in the dart::core library allows for simple collection traversing. Every collection has an iterator property, as we all know. This property produces an iterator containing a list of the collection's items.

Example:

```
import 'dart:collection';
void main() {
    Queues ques = new Queues();
    ques.addAll([20,30,40]);
    Iterator c= ques.iterator;
    while(c.moveNext()) {
        print(c.current);
    }
}
```

Explanation: The moveNext() method in the preceding code returns a Boolean value indicating the following entry. The current property returns the object to which the iterator is presently pointing.

HashMap <K, V Class>

The HashMap class is based on the Map implementation. As previously discussed, the key must be unique and have consistent Object == (equal to operator) and Object.hashCode implementations. Null can also be used as a key. The elements of the Map can be arranged in any sequence. Only when the map is changed does the iteration order change. When we iterate the map, its values are iterated in the same order as their associated keys.

DART GENERICS

Dart Generics are identical to Dart collections, used to hold homogeneous data. Dart is an optionally typed language, as described in the features section.

Dart Collections are heterogeneous by default. To put it another way, a single Dart collection may store the values of many data types. On the other hand, A Dart collection can store homogeneous items or values of the same kind.

Dart Generics allows us to impose a constraint on the data type of the collection's values. These collections are known as type-safe collections.

Dart programming has a unique feature called type safety, which ensures that a memory block may only hold data of a specified data type.

Generics are a means for all Dart collections to allow type-safety implementation. The angular bracket pair is used to declare the type-safe collection. The data-types of the collection are included within the angular bracket. The syntax is shown below.

Syntax:

```
Collection-name <data_type> identifier = new
Collection-name<data_type>
```

We can type-safe implement numerous Dart objects like List, Queue, Map, and Set. It is also supported by all implementations of the collection types defined above.

Example: The Generics List

```
void main() {
    List <String> logStrs = new List <String>();
    logStrs.add("Check");
```

```
logStrs.add("Info");
logStrs.add("Error");
//iterating across list
for (String c in logStrs) {
    print(c);
}
}
```

Explanation: We generated a type-safe list and added a string entry using the add() method.

If we try to insert a value other than the one specified, we will get a compilation error. Let's have a look at an example:

```
void main() {
  List <String> logStrs = new List <String>();
  logStrs.add(511);    // Add integer value
  logStrs.add("Info");
  logStrs.add("Error");
  //iterating across list
  for (String c in logTypes) {
      print(c);
  }
}
```

Example: The Generic Set

```
void main() {
    Set <int>numberSets = new  Set<int>();
    numberSets.add(29);
    numberSets.add(32);
    numberSets.add(41);
    numberSets.add(54);
    numberSets.add(60);

    // numberSets.add("");
    // compilation error;
    print("The Default implementation
:${numberSets.runtimeType}");

    for(var c in numberSets) {
        print(c);
    }
}
```

Example: The Generics Queue

```
import 'dart:collection';
void main() {
    Queue<int> queues = new Queue<int>();
    print("The Default implementation ${queues.
runtimeType}");
    queues.addLast(100);
    queues.addLast(205);
    queues.addLast(315);
    queues.addLast(470);
    // Remove first element of queue
    queues.removeFirst();
    for(int c in queue){
        print(c);
    }
}
```

Generic Map

As we all know, declaring a map necessitates using a key and a value. The syntax is shown below.

Syntax:

```
Map <Key-type, value-type>
```

Example:

```
void main() {
    Map <String, String>m1={'name':'Josen','Rollno'
:'Std1201'};
    print('Map :${m1}');
}
```

PACKAGES IN DART

Dart packages are collections of well-organized, self-contained, and reusable code units. Third-party libraries or packages may need the use of applications. Along with the generated program and sample data, the package often comprises a collection of classes, functions, or units of code for specialized purposes. Dart has many default packages that are loaded automatically when the dart console is launched. However, if we require packages other than the default packages, we must install and load them manually to utilize them. When a package is loaded, it is available for usage throughout the Dart environment.

Package Manager in Dart

Every language has support for dealing with external packages such as Nuget for.NET, Gradle or Maven for Java, npm for Node.js, and so on. Dart features built-in package management known as a pub. It is mainly used to organize and manage third-party libraries, tools, and dependencies and install items in the repository. Every Dart application includes a pubspec.yaml file that contains the file's information. The package's metadata includes the creator, version, application name, and description. Yet Another Markup Language is the full version of yaml. The pubspec.yaml file is used to get the many libraries required by the application while programming. The pubspec.yaml file should look like this.

```
name: 'vector_victor'
version: 0.0.1
description: An absolute bare-bones web app.
...
dependencies: browser: '>=0.10.0 <0.11.0'
```

The Dart IDE includes built-in support for utilizing the pub, including building, downloading, updating, and publishing packages. Alternatively, we may use the pub command line. The following is a collection of some of the most significant pub commands.

Sr. No.	Description
pub get	It is used to obtain all application-dependent packages.
pub upgrade	It is used to update all application dependencies up to date.
pub build	It is used to develop our web application, and it will generate a build folder including all necessary scripts.
pub help	It is utilized to obtain help with all pub commands or get stuck while programming.

The following steps define the package's installation in the project:

- **Step 1:** Enter the package name in the dependencies section of the pubspec.yaml file for the project. Then execute the following command to locate the package installed in the project.

```
pub get
```

This command will download the package to the application directory's packages folder.

Example:

```
name: TestApp
version: 0.0.1
description: A simple dart application
dependencies:
xml:
```

The xml has been added to the project dependencies. By importing the Dart XML package, we can now utilize it in the project. It is possible to import it as follows:

```
import 'package:xml/xml.dart' as xml;
```

Read XML String

We can read an XML string and authenticate it; Dart XML has a parse() function for reading string input. The syntax is shown below:

Syntax:

```
xml. parse(String input):
```

Take a look at the following example:

Example: Parsing XML String Input

```
import 'package:xml/xml.dart' as xml;
void main(){
    print("xml");
    var bookstoreXml = '''<?xml version = "1.0"?>
<bookstore>
    <book>
        <title lang = "English">Who will cry when
we die </title>
        <price>153.00</price>
    </book>

    <book>
        <title lang = "English">The Drake </title>
```

```
        <price>80.00</price>
    </book>
    <price>300.00</price>
</bookstore>''';

var document = xml.parse(bookstoreXml);
print(document.toString());
}
```

LIBRARIES IN DART

The library in Dart is a collection of routines or sets of programming instructions. Dart has several built-in libraries that are useful for storing routines (functions, classes, etc.) and are often used. A Dart library comprises constants, functions, properties, exceptions, typedefs, and a collection of classes.

Importing a Library

We must first import it into the current program to use the library. The import keyword is provided by Dart and is used to make the library available in the existing file. Multiple libraries can use in a single file.

Dart built-in library URIs, for example, are used as a dart scheme to refer to a library. Other libraries can define their URIs utilizing a file system path or the package: scheme. Dart's package manager pub offers libraries and employs the package scheme.

The followings are descriptions of several widely used libraries.

Sr. No.	Library	Description
1.	dart:io	This library provides server applications with File, HTTP, socket, and other I/O functionality. This library is not intended for use in browser-based applications. We don't need to import it because it is imported by default explicitly.
2.	Dart:core	This library contains collection, built-in types, and other essential dart application functionality. It is automatically imported.
3.	Dart: math	This library includes a variety of mathematical functions, constants, and a random number generator.
4.	Dart: convert	It is used in encoders and decoders to convert various data formats such as JSON and UTF.
5.	Dart: typed_data	It represents lists that efficiently hold fixed-sized data (for example – unsigned 8-byte integer).

Importing and Using a Library as an Example

```
import 'dart:math';    // Importing the built-in library
void main() {
    print("The Square root of 25 is: ${sqrt(25)}");
}
```

Explanation: We imported the built-in library 'dart:math' in the preceding code. It has several built-in mathematical functions; in this case, we utilized the sqrt() function with a number. It accepts an integer as an input and determines its square root. We gave an integer number of 25 to the sqrt() method, and it returned a value of 5.

Library Encapsulation

Dart allows us to encapsulate or restrict access to the dart library's content. It is possible to use the _ (underscore) followed by the identification. The _ (underscore) character makes the library's content fully private. The syntax is shown below.

Syntax:

```
_identifier
```

Example:

```
library Greetings;
// We define function using the _underscore as a
prefix.
void _sayHi(msg) {
    print("We access this method in
another:${msg}");
}
```

The above file is saved as greetings.dart, let's import the library now.

```
import 'greetings.dart' as w;
void main() {
    w._sayHi("Hello DartTpoint");
}
```

Creating Custom Libraries (User-Defined Library)

We may also utilize our code as a library that can be imported as needed. A custom library is a name given to this sort of library. The processes for creating a custom library are outlined below.

Step 1: Library Declaration
The library statement is used to build a library expressly. The syntax is shown below.

Syntax:

```
library library_name
// go here  library contents
```

Step 2: Library Connecting
There are two ways to connect a library:

1. Within the same directory

   ```
   import 'library_name'
   ```

2. From a different directory

   ```
   import 'dir/library_name'
   ```

Custom Library as an Example

```
library calculator_simple;
import 'dart:math';
//the library content
int add(int numb1,int numb2){
   print("inside add method of the calculator_simple
Library ") ;
   return numb1+numb2;
}
int multiplication(int numb1,int numb2){
   print("inside multiplication method of the
calculator_simple Library ") ;
   return numb1*numb2;
}
int subtraction(int numb1,int numb2){
   print("inside subtraction  method of the
calculator_simple Library ") ;
   return numb1-numb2;
}
int modulus(int numb1,int numb2){
   print("inside modulus  method of the calculator_
simple Library ") ;
   return numb1%numb2;
}
```

Now we import the aforementioned custom file into the current file, 'library.dart.'

```dart
import 'calculator.dart';
void main() {
    var nu1 = 40;
    var nu2 = 30;
    var sum = add(nu1,nu2);
    var mod = modulus(nu1,nu2);
    var mul = multiplication(nu1,nu2);
    var div = divide(nu1,nu2);
    var sub = subtraction(nu1,nu2);
    print("$nu1 + $nu2 = $sum");
    print("$nu1 %  $nu2= $mod");
    print("$nu1 + $nu2 = $mul");
    print("$nu1 - $nu2 = $sub");
}
```

Name Alias of Library

Dart enables us to import numerous libraries into the current working file; however, if we use the same function name across libraries, it will cause a conflict when accessing these functions. The Dart compiler may be confused when defining a certain function in a separate library. Dart includes the as keyword for defining the prefix to avoid this issue. The syntax is shown below.

Syntax:

```dart
import 'library_uri' as prefix
```

Example:

```dart
To begin, let us define a library: greeting. dart
library greetings;
void sayHi(msg){
    print("Learn Dart with ${msg}");
}
```

Next, let us define the new library: hellogreetings.dart

```dart
library hellogreetings;
void sayHi(msg){
```

```
    print("${msg} provides tutorials on all technical
topic");
}
```

Now, we import the above libraries with the 'as' prefix.

```
import 'greetings.dart';
import 'hellogreetings.dart' as gret;

// using as prefix avoids function name clashes
void main(){
    sayHi("DartTpoint");
    gret.sayHi("DartTpoint");    // To eliminate the
name confliction
}
```

GENERATORS IN DART

Dart Generator is a one-of-a-kind function that generates a series of values. Generators return values on demand, which implies that the value is created when we attempt to iterate through iterators. Dart includes support for two types of generator functions.

- Synchronous Generators

- Asynchronous Generators

Synchronous Generator

It returns an iterable object that synchronously carries value. The yield keyword is used in combination with the synchronous generator function body being marked as sync* to generator values.

Let's have a look at an example of a synchronous generator:

```
main()   {
    print("the Dart Synchronous Generator Example.");
    oddNumber(20).forEach(print);
}
    // syn* functions returns an iterable
    Iterable<int> oddNumber(int numb) sync* {
    int x = numb;
    while(x >= 0) {
        if(x%2 == 1) {
            // 'yield' statement
```

```
                yield x;
                }
x--;
}
}
```

Explanation: We defined an oddNumber(20) function in the preceding program and used a foreach loop with no body. The foreach loop will iterate through the function. As a synchronous generator function, we now created the oddNumber(20) function.

We created a new variable k in the function body, assigning the input n. Then, to iterate the function, we used a while loop, and the loop body is iterated until the value of x is less than or equal to 0.

To obtain the odd numbers from the generators, we used the modulus operation on x. We used the yield statement, which stops the function and returns the value one at a time. It will return the value of each generator function run. When the while loop's condition turns false, the loop is ended, and the odd numbers are printed.

Asynchronous Generators

It returns a stream object that transmits data asynchronously. The yield keyword is used in combination with the async* to generator values indication of the asynchronous generator function body.

Example:

```
main()   {
    print("The Dart Asynchronous Generator
Example.");
    asyncNaturalsTo(20).forEach(print);
}
    // async* functions returns an stream object
   Stream<int> asyncNaturalsTo(int numb) async* {
   int x = 0;
   while(x < numb) {
            // 'yield' statement
            yield x++;
                }
x--;
}
```

Explanation: The values in the preceding code were created asynchronously. In each function body execution, the asyncNaturalsTo(int numb) method returns a stream object. In this case, the yield keyword acted similarly to the previous example: it stopped the function's execution, returned the value, and restarted its execution for the next iteration. It will keep happening till the function body is finished.

The Yield Keyword

The yield returns a single value to the sequence but does not entirely terminate the generator function's operation. It returns a value for each generator function operation.

The Sync* Keyword

The sync* keyword is used to declare the synchronize generator function. It returns the value when attempting to iterate over it rather than when it was created. Let's have a look at the following example:

```
void main() {
  print('creating-iterator');
  Iterable<int> numbers = getNumbers(5);   // Here we
are creating iterator
  print('Iteration starts');
  for (int x in numbers) {
    print('$x');            // Iterate over the
iterator
  }
  print('end of the main function');
}
Iterable<int> getNumbers(int nm) sync* {                //
define generator synchronously
  print('generator started');
  for (int x = 0; x < nm; x++) {
    yield x;
  }
  print('generator function ended');
}
```

Explanation: When we iterate through the iterator, the above generator function generates the value.

The Async* Keyword

The async* keyword is used to declare asynchronous generators. It gives the stream object. Let's have a look at an example:

```
void main() {
  print('creating-iterator');
  Stream<int> numbers = getNumbers(5);
  print('starting to listen');
  numbers.listen((int m) {
    print('$m');
  });
  print('end of main function');
}
Stream<int> getNumbers(int number) async* {   //
declaring the asynchronous generator function
  print('waiting inside generator a 3 seconds :)');
  await new Future.delayed(new Duration(seconds: 4));
//sleep 3s
  print('started generating values...');
  for (int x = 0; x < number; x++) {
    await new Future.delayed(new Duration(seconds:
2)); //sleep 1s
    yield x;
  }
  print('ended generating values');
}
```

DART CALLABLE CLASSES

Dart allows us to invoke class instances like functions. To create a callable class, we must include a call() function. Let's have a look at few examples:

Example:

```
class Students {
  String call(String names, int ages) {
             return('The Student name is $names
  and Age is $ages');

             }
}
```

```
void main() {
   Students stu1 = new Students();
   var msgs = stu1('Shreya',19);        // Class
instance called like a function.
   print('Dart Callable class');
   print(msgs);
}
```

Explanation: In the above code, we defined a call() function in the Student class that accepts two parameters. Return a message with the string name and integer age. Then we built an object of class Student and called it as if it were a function.

```
var msgs = stu1('Shreya',19);
```

Example: The Multiple callable class

```
class Students {
   String call(String names, int ages) {
              return('The Student name is $names
and Age is $ages');
              }
}

class Employees {
   int call(int empid, int ages) {
              return('Employee id is ${empid} and
Age is ${ages}');
              }
}
void main() {
   Student stu1 = new Students();
   Employees emp1 = new Employees();
   var msgs = stu1('peterin',19);  // Class
instance called like a function.
   var msgs2 = emp1(102,33);    // Class instance
called like a function.
   print('Dart Callable class');
   print(msgs);
   print(msgs2);
}
```

Explanation: We defined two callable functions in Students and Employees classes in the preceding code. The call() method of the Employees class takes two parameters: String empid and int ages. Instances of both types were referred to as callable functions.

```
var msgs = stul('peterin',19);
var msgs2 = empl(102,33);
```

DART ISOLATES

Dart supports asynchronous programming, which allows us to run our application without being blocked. To accomplish concurrency, asynchronous programming is employed. Dart isolation is a thread variant. However, there is a significant difference between the standard implementations of "Thread" and "Isolates." When compared to Thread, the isolate performs differently. The isolates are self-contained workers that do not share memory and instead communicate by sending messages through channels. Because isolation completes its operation by passing messages, it requires a method to serialize a message.

Message passing is used to communicate between the isolates as a client and server. It enables the software to make use of multicore microprocessors right away.

Dart has the dart:isolate package, which we may use to implement the isolate in our application. It provides a way for taking single-threaded Dart code and enables applications to make better use of the available hardware.

Create and Start an Isolate

To construct an isolation, use the spawn() function in Dart. It must be stated with a single argument as an "entry point." This field displays a port that is used to isolate a notification message.

First example:

```
import 'dart:isolate';
void sayhi(var msgs){
    print('execution..the message is :${msgs}');
}
void main(){
    Isolate.spawn(sayhi,'Hello!!');
    Isolate.spawn(sayhi,'Whats up!!');
    Isolate.spawn(sayhi,'Welcome!!');
    print('execution from the main1');
```

```
print('execution from the main2');
print('execution from the main3');
}
```

Explanation: In the preceding example, the isolate class's spawn method performed a function sayhi in parallel with the other code. It requires two arguments.

The function to be spawned and the string to be provided to the spawned function.

We have two functions, sayhi() and main(), which may not be executed in the same sequence each time. If we run the same program repeatedly, the outcome will be different, as seen in the second output.

Second example:

```
void start() async {
        ReceivePort   receiverPorts =
ReceiverPort();   // Port for the isolate to
receive message.
        isolate = await Isolate.spawn(runTimer,
receiverPort.sendPort);
        receivePorts.listen((data){
                stdout.write('Receiving: '+ data +
', ');
      });
}
void runTimer(SendPort, sendPort) {
int counts = 0;
Timer.periodic(new Duration(seconds: 2), (Timer t)
{
      counts++;
      String msgs = 'notification ' + counts.
toString();
      stdout.write('Sending: ' + msgs + ' -');
      sendPort.send(msgs);
});
}
```

Explanation: In the preceding code, we defined an asynchronous function start() that generates a port and spawns an isolation. We marked the start method as async to wait for the response from the isolate spawning and keep a reference to the new isolate. It is critical if we are to eliminate the running isolated. We gave two parameters to the spawn() method: the first parameter runTimer, which is a callback function that will use to execute runTimer(), and the second parameter sendPort, which is also a callback function that will use to send a message back to the caller. The start() function begins the receiverPort listening for messages from isolation. When it receives the message, it will print it to the console.

Stop an Isolate

The kill() function in the dart: isolates package terminates a running isolate.

Example:

```
void stop() {
        If (isolate != null) {
        stdout.writeln('Stopping-Isolate');
        isolate.kill(priority: Isolate.
immediate);
        isolate = null;
        }
}
```

Explanation: We defined a stop() function that destroys the currently running isolation and sets its reference to null in the preceding example. We set the priority of the isolate to immediate, which means that the isolate will be terminated as soon as possible.

Complete Program

```
import 'dart:io';
import 'dart:async';
import 'dart:isolate';
Isolate isolate1;
// Start isolate
void start() async {
        ReceivePort  receiverPort1 = ReceivePort();
// Port for isolate to receive message.
        isolate1 = await Isolate.spawn(runTimer,
receiverPort1.sendPort);
        receivePort1.listen((data){
            stdout.write('Receiving: '+ data + ', ');
    });
}
```

```
void runTimer(SendPort, sendPort) {
int count = 0;
Timer.periodic(new Duration(seconds: 2), (Timer t) {
    count++;
    String msgs = 'notification ' + count.toString();
    stdout.write('Sending: ' + msgs + ' -');
    sendPort.send(msgs);
});
}

// Stopping the isolate using the stop() function.
void stop() {
    if (isolate != null) {
        stdout.writeln('Stopping Isolate');
        isolate.kill(priority:Isolate.immediate);
        isolate = null;
    }
}
void main() async {
    stdout.writeln('Starting Isolate');
    await start();
    std.writeln('Hit enter to quit');
    await stdin.first;
    stop();
    stdout.writeln('Byebye');
    exit(0);
}
```

ASYNC IN DART

Dart Async is a programming construct that is linked to asynchronous programming. The asynchronous operation is carried out in a thread. It guarantees that the key duties are carried out until they are completed. The asynchronous action is carried out independently of the main program thread. In Dart, one operation cannot interrupt another; this implies that only one operation may run at a moment when no other component of the program can stop it. Let's have a look at an example:

```
import 'dart:io';
void main() {
    print("Enter favorite car :");
    // prompt for the user input
```

```
    String cars = stdin.readLineSync();
    // this is a synchronous method that reads user
input
    print("The car is  ${cars}");
    print("End of the main");
}
```

Explanation: We utilized the synchronous readLineSync() function in the preceding code. It implies that until the readLineSync() function completes its execution, the execution of any instructions that follow will be halted.

The stdin.readLineSync () function does nothing until it receives user input. It waits for human input before proceeding with the execution.

Difference between Synchronous and Asynchronous

Let's look at the distinction between synchronous and asynchronous.

In computer science, the term "synchronous" refers to a program that waits for an event before continuing to run. This technique has a disadvantage in that if a code section takes a long time to run, subsequent blocks through an unrelated block will prevent from executing.

This is the primary issue with the synchronous technique. A program section may need to run before the present section, but the synchronous technique does not allow for this.

This is not appropriate for webservers, as each request must be independent of the others. It indicates that the webserver does not wait for the current request to be completed before responding to requests from subsequent users.

Before performing the previous requests, the webserver should accept the request from the other user.

This method is known as asynchronous programming. Asynchronous programming is characterized by a lack of waiting or a non-blocking programming approach. Dart: async is used to make it easier to build an asynchronous programming block in a Dart script.

For example, we might create a file containing a few names and store it as names.txt, then construct a program to read this file without delaying the rest of the code.

1. Peterin

2. Johny

3. Taimur

4. Rohnson

Example:

```
import "dart:async";
import "dart:io";

void main(){
    File files1 = new File("C:\Users\DEVANSH
SHARMA\Desktop\contact.txt");
    Future<String> fs = files1.readAsString();
    // returns a future object, it is an async
method
    fs.then((data)=>print(data));
    // once file is read, call back method is
invoked
    print("End of the main");
}
```

Dart Future

The Dart Future is defined as receiving a result at some point in the future. The Future object is used to make asynchronous programming more accessible. Future objects are used to represent values returned by an expression whose execution will be completed later (in future). We can utilize async and await or the Future API to interact with the future.

Dart Async and Await

Asynchronous programming may be implemented without utilizing the Future API using the async and await keywords. To run a function asynchronously, we must include the async keyword after the function name. The syntax is as follows:

Syntax:

```
func_name() async {
    //function-body
}
```

When an async function is called, the Future object returns immediately, indicating that the async function will execute later. The function call returned the Future object after the async function's body was run. The function call will finish with the outcome of the function call.

Dart Await Keyword

The await keyword can also be used to run a function asynchronously. It pauses the current function till the result is available. When the result is returned, it continues to the next line of code. Only async functions can utilize the await keyword. The syntax is shown below.

Syntax:

```
await e;
```

Here, e is an asynchronous expression intended to evaluate a Future in this case. The await statement evaluates e before suspending the current function until the result is ready.

Example:

```
void hi() async {
        print("Hi DartTpoint");
}
void main() async {
        await hi();              // Using the await
keyword
        print("Task Completed");
}
```

Explanation: We used the async keyword to make the main() function asynchronous since we run the hi() method asynchronously. Then, we used the await modifier to call hi(), which executed asynchronously.

What Exactly Is Concurrency?

Dart concurrency allows us to execute many programs or sections of a program simultaneously. It carries out many commands at the same time. Dart provides Isolates as a tool for doing parallel tasks. Concurrency enhances the program's effectiveness and throughput by utilizing the unused capabilities of critical operating system and machine hardware.

How Does One Achieve Concurrency?

We can accomplish concurrency in Dart by utilizing Isolates. Dart isolates were covered in a prior session. Dart isolation is a thread variation. However, there is a significant difference between the standard implementations of "Thread" and "Isolates." When compared to Thread, the isolate performs differently. The isolates are self-contained workers that do not share memory and instead communicate by sending messages through channels. Because isolation completes its operation by passing messages, it requires a method to serialize a message.

Message passing is used to communicate between the isolates as a client and server. It enables the software to make use of multicore microprocessors right away.

Dart has the dart:isolate package, which we may use to implement the isolate in our program. It provides a way for taking single-threaded Dart code and enables programs to make better use of the available hardware.

Example:

```
import 'dart:isolate';
void sayhi(var msg){
    print('execution from sayhi and the message is
:${msg}');
}
void main(){
    Isolate.spawn(sayhi,'Hello');
    Isolate.spawn(sayhi,'How are you?');
    Isolate.spawn(sayhi,'Welcome');
    print('execution from the main1');
    print('execution from the main2');
    print('execution from the main3');
}
```

What Is Unit Testing?

Unit testing is a stage in the software development process in which specific units or components of an application are tested. Unit testing of each component is required to improve application speed. A unit is the smallest testable portion of a program that can be logically separated inside a system. Individual programs, subroutines, functions, methods, and classes can all be represented as Units in various programming languages. The module may include a large number of separate components. Methods belonging to a base class/superclass, or an abstract class, can be expressed as smaller units in object-oriented programming. The following figure depicts the sort of testing.

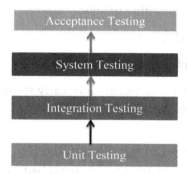

Unit testing.

Unit Testing Task

The unit testing task is provided below.

- Unit Test Plan
  - Prepare
  - Review
  - Rework
  - Baseline
- Unit Test Cases/Scripts
  - Prepare
  - Review
  - Rework
  - Baseline
- Unit Test
  - Perform

Advantages of Unit Testing

A few benefits of unit testing are listed below:

- We can simply maintain code.

- It increases the reusability of code.

- It speeds up development.

- The code is simple to debug.

- Because any error is detected at an early stage, it detects the cost of testing and resolving defects.

Dart Unit Testing

We required to include an external library called "test" in Dart to support a consistent manner of authoring and executing individual unit tests. The following steps can use to do unit testing.

- **Step 1:** Installing the "test" package
  To include unit testing into our project, we must first install a third-party package called "test" in our present working project. Let's open our project's pubspec.yaml file and type the following statements:

  ```
  dependencies:
  test:
  ```

  Right-click the pubspec.yaml file and select Pub: get dependencies. This will include the installation of the "test" package in our project.

  We may also use the following command to install it.

  ```
  pub get
  ```

- **Step 2:** Importing the "test" package
  Add the following line to include the "test" package in our project.

  ```
  import "package:test/test.dart";
  ```

- **Step 3:** Writing the Test Cases
  The Test cases add the top-level test() method. The expect() method is used in the test() function to create the test assertion. The actualValue and MatchValue inputs are passed to the expert() method.

Syntax:

```
test("Test Description", () {
    expert(actualValue, matchingValue)
});
```

Group of Test Cases

Using the group() function, we can build a group of numerous test cases. It aids in the grouping of test instances depending on certain characteristics. Each group's description appears at the start of the test's description.

Syntax:

```
group("Test_Group_Name", () {
    test("test_case_name_1", () {
        expect(actual, equals(exptected));
    });
    test("test_case_name_2", () {
        expect(actual, equals(expected));
    });
})
```

Example: Passing Test

Here's an example of defining an add() function for unit testing. It takes two integer arguments and returns an integer reflecting the total. Understand the following example to test the add() function:

- **Step 1:** We import the test package.

- **Step 2:** We define the test using the test() method, and it makes an assertion with the expert() function.

```
import 'package:test/test.dart';
// Importing test package
int add(int a,int b)
// this function to be tested {
    return a+b;
}
void main() {
    // Defining test function
    test("test to check the add method", (){
```

```
        // Arrange
        var expected = 40;
        // Act
        var actual = add(20,30);
        // Asset
        expect(actual,expected);
    });
}
```

Example: A failed test

We define the sub() method, which contains a logical error. Consider the following example.

```
import 'package:test/test.dart';
int add(int a,int b){
    return a+b;
}
int sub(int a,int b){
    return a-b-1;
}
void main(){
    test('test to check sub',(){
        var expected = 20;
        // Arrange
        var actual = sub(40,30);
        // Act
        expect(actual,expected);
        // Assert
    });
    test("test to check add method",(){
        var expected = 40;
        // Arrange
        var actual = add(20,10);
        // Act
        expect(actual,expected);
        // Asset
    });
}
```

In the above example, the add() method passed the unit test, but the sub() function failed owing to a logical mistake.

Grouping Test Cases

Multiple test cases can write in the form of a group. These methods are grouped together using group(). It aids in the creation of considerably cleaner code.

We'll write a test case for the split() and trim() functions in the next example. We collected these functions and named it String.

Let's have a look at an example:

```dart
import "package:test/test.dart";
void main() {
    group("String", () {
      // First test case
        test("testing on split() method of string
class", () {
          var string = "Hii,Helloo,Heyy";
          expect(string.split(","), equals(["Hii",
"Helloo", "Heyy"]));
      });
      // Second test case
        test("testing on trim() method of string class",
() {
          var string = "  Helloo ";
          expect(string.trim(), equals("Helloo"));
      });
    });
}
```

DART HTML DOM

Every webpage may be thought of as an entity that resides within a browser window. We may access the webpage using the web browser, which must link to the Internet. Document object model is abbreviated as DOM. A Document object represents the HTML document that is shown in that window. The DOM comprises numerous attributes that relate to other objects and allow us to edit the document's content.

The DOM is the technique through which a document's content is accessible. The Objects are arranged in a hierarchical order. A hierarchical structure is used to organize objects in a web content.

- **Window:** It is the initial item in the hierarchy. It is the highest level of the object hierarchy.

- **Document:** When an HTML document loads into a window, it becomes a window object. The page's contents are included in the document.

- **Elements:** This term refers to the website's content. For instance, a title, a text field, and so on.

- **Nodes:** Nodes are frequent elements, but they can also be attributes, comments, text, or other DOM kinds.

The hierarchy of the most significant DOM objects is shown in the following figure.

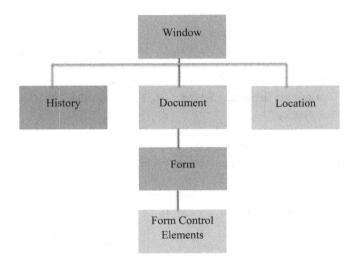

Objects of DOM.

Using the dart:html library, we can control objects and elements in the DOM. The dart:html library cannot be used in a console application. In order to deal with the HTML library in the web application, we must import the dart:html package.

```
import 'dart.html';
```

Finding the DOM Elements

A document may include several attributes, and we may sometimes need to search for a certain attribute. The querySelector method in the dart:html library is used to search for elements in the DOM.

```
Element querySelector(String selector);
```

The querySelector() method returns the first element that matches the selector's provided group.

Syntax:

```
var elements1 = document.querySelector('.
className');
var elements2 = document.querySelector('#id');
```

Let's have a look at an example:

```
<!DOCTYPE html>
<html>
    <head>
        <meta charset = "utf-8">
        <meta http-equiv = "X-UA-Compatible" content =
"IE = edge">
        <meta name = "viewport" content = "width =
device-width, initial-scale = 1.5">
        <meta name = "scaffolded-by" content = "https://
github.com/google/stagehand">
        <title>DemoWebApp</title>
        <link rel = "stylesheet" href = "styles.css">
        <script defer src = "main.dart" type =
"application/dart"></script>
        <script defer src = "packages/browser/dart.
js"></script>
    </head>
    <body>
        <h1>
            <div id = "output"></div>
        </h1>
    </body>
</html>
```

Main.dart

```
import 'dart:html';
void main() {
   querySelector('#output').text = 'Our Dart web dom
app is running';
}
```

Event Handling

The onClick event for DOM Elements is provided by the dart:html library. The syntax demonstrates how an element may handle a series of click events.

```
querySelector('#Id').onClick.
listen(eventHanlderFunction);
```

OnClick, the querySelector() method returns the element from the specified DOM. Listen() will accept an eventHandler method, which will be called when a click event occurs. The syntax of eventHandler is as follows:

```
void eventHanlderFunction (MouseEvent event){ }
```

TestEvent.html

```
<!DOCTYPE html>
<html>
    <head>
        <meta charset = "utf-8">
        <meta http-equiv = "X-UA-Compatible" content =
"IE = edge">
        <meta name = "viewport" content = "width =
device-width, initial-scale = 1.5">
        <meta name = "scaffolded-by" content ="https://
github.com/google/stagehand">
        <title>DemoWebApp</title>
        <link rel = "stylesheet" href = "styles.css">
        <script defer src = "TestEvent.dart"
type="application/dart"></script>
        <script defer src = "packages/browser/dart.
js"></script>
    </head>
    <body>
        <div id = "output"></div>
        <h1>
            <div>
                Enter you name : <input type = "text" id =
"txtName">
```

```
            <input type = "button" id = "btnWish"
value="Wishs">
         </div>
      </h1>
      <h2 id = "display"></h2>
```

TestEvent.dart

```
import 'dart:html';
void main() {
   querySelector('#btnWish').onClick.
listen(wishHandler);
}
void wishHandler(MouseEvent event){
   String name = (querySelector('#txtName')  as
InputElement).value;
   querySelector('#display').text = 'Hello'+ name;
}
```

CHAPTER SUMMARY

In this chapter, we discussed exceptions in Dart, typedef, collections, packages, and libraries. Moreover, we also discussed callable classes, async, unit testing, and html DOM.

CHAPTER 5

Basics of Flutter

IN THIS CHAPTER

➤ Flutter Widgets

➤ Layouts and Gestures

➤ State Management

➤ Details of Flutter Widgets

In the previous chapter, we covered advanced topics in Dart such as collection, typedef, libraries, generators, and unit testing. In this chapter, we will discuss flutter widgets, layouts, gestures. Moreover, we will also discuss state management, Flutter IDE, and all flutter widgets in detail.

FIRST APPLICATION IN FLUTTER

We will learn how to construct a simple application in Android Studio to grasp the fundamentals of the Flutter application. To build a Flutter application, follow these steps:

- **Step 1:** Launch the Android Studio application.

- **Step 2:** Begin working on the Flutter project. To start a project, select File->New->New Flutter Project. The following screen might help us comprehend things better.

- **Step 3:** In the following step, select the Flutter Application. Select Flutter Application and then click Next.

DOI: 10.1201/9781003299363-5

- **Step 4:** After that, customize the application information and click the Next button.

    - **Project Name:** Fill in the blanks with the name of application.

    - **Path to the Flutter SDK:** <path to flutter sdk>

    - **Path to Project Folder:** <path to project folder>

    - **Descriptions:** <A new Flutter hello everyone application>.

- **Step 5:** In the next wizard, enter the company domain name and click the Finish button.

    After pressing the Finish button, it will take some time to construct a project. We will have a fully functional Flutter application with limited functionality when the project is finished.

- **Step 6:** Let's look at the structure and purpose of the Flutter project application. The many folders and components of the Flutter application structure are:

    - **.idea:** This folder is at the top of the project structure and contains the Android Studio setup. It makes no difference because we are not going to utilize Android Studio; thus, the contents of this folder may be ignored.

    - **.android:** This folder contains a whole Android project needed for building the Flutter application for Android. When the Flutter code is turned into native code, it is injected into this Android project, resulting in a native Android app. When we use the Android emulator, this Android project is used to develop the Android app, which is then published to the Android Virtual Device.

    - **.ios:** This folder contains a complete Mac project and is used for building the Flutter app for iOS. It is identical to the android folder used when designing an Android app. When the Flutter code is turned into native code, it is injected into this iOS project, yielding a native iOS application. Building a Flutter application for iOS is only feasible while using macOS.

    - **.lib:** This is an important folder that stands for the library. It is a folder where we will do 99 percent of the project work.

The Dart files that comprise the code for our Flutter application can be found in the lib folder. This folder contains the file main.dart by default, which is the Flutter application's entrance file.

- **.test:** This folder includes Dart code developed for the Flutter application to run automated tests when the app is built.

In the Flutter application, we may also have specific default files. In 99.99 percent of circumstances, we do not manually touch these files. These are the files:

- **.gitignore:** This is a text file that contains a list of files, file extensions, and directories that notify Git which files in a project should be ignored. Git is a version-control file used to monitor source code changes during software development.

- **.metadata:** It is a file created automatically by the flutter tools and is used to monitor the attributes of the Flutter project. This file handles internal activities, so we never have to modify the content manually.

- **.packages:** It is a file created by the Flutter SDK that contains a list of dependencies for our Flutter project.

- **Flutter demoapp.iml:** It is always titled after the Flutter project name and contains different project settings. This file handles internal operations controlled by the Flutter SDK, so you never have to modify the content yourself.

- **pubspec.yaml:** This is the project's configuration file, which will be used often while working with the Flutter project. It enables you to control how your application functions. This file contains the following:

    - General project parameters include the project's name, description, and version.

    - Dependencies in the project.

    - Assets for the project (e.g., images).

- **pubspec.lock:** It is a file created automatically depending on the. yaml file. It has a more detailed setup of all requirements.

- **README.md:** This is an auto-generated file that contains project information. If we wish to share information with the developers, we may update this file.

- **Step 7:** Open the main.dart file and replace the following code with it.

```
import 'package:flutter/material.dart';
void main() => runApp(App());
class App extends StatelessWidget {
  // This widget is root of our application.
  @override
  Widget build(BuildContext context) {
    return MaterialApp(
      title: 'Hello Everyone Flutter Application',
      theme: ThemeData(
        // This is theme of your application.
        primarySwatch: Colors.blue,
      ),
      home: HomePage(title: 'Homepage'),
    );
  }
}
class MyHomePage extends StatelessWidget {
  MyHomePage({Key key, this.title}) : super(key:
key);
  // This widget is home page of our application.
  final String title;
  @override
  Widget build(BuildContext context) {
    return Scaffold(
      appBar: AppBar(
        title: Text(this.title),
      ),
      body: Center(
        child: Text('Hello Everyone'),
      ),
    );
  }
}
```

FLUTTER ARCHITECTURE

This section goes through the architecture of the Flutter framework. The Flutter architecture is made up of four primary components.

- Flutter Engine
- Foundation Library
- Widgets
- Design Specific Widgets

Flutter Engine

The Flutter Engine is a portable runtime for high-quality mobile apps mostly built on the C++ programming language. It includes animation and graphics, file and network I/O, plugin architecture, accessibility support, and a dart runtime for writing, constructing, and executing Flutter applications. Google's open-source graphics package, Skia, is used to produce low-level visuals.

Foundation Library

The Foundation Library provides all of the packages necessary for the basic building blocks of constructing a Flutter application. These libraries are written in the Dart programming language.

Widgets

Everything in Flutter is a widget, the framework's primary notion. In Flutter, a widget is a user interface (UI) component that impacts and controls the app's display and interface. It is an immutable description of a portion of the UI that contains graphics, text, shapes, and animations made with widgets. The widgets are similar to React components.

Specific Widgets Design

The Flutter framework has two widgets that adhere to different design languages. Material Design for Android applications and Cupertino Style for iOS applications are the two options.

Gestures

It is a widget in Flutter that offers interactivity (how to listen for and respond to gestures) by utilizing GestureDetector. GestureDector is an invisible widget that interacts with its child widget via tapping, dragging, and scaling. Combining with the GestureDetector widget can also add more interactive elements into the current widgets.

State Management

The StatefulWidget widget in Flutter is used to keep the widget's state. When its internal state changes, it is always re-rendered. The re-rendering is optimized by measuring the distance between the old and new widget UIs and rendering the necessary modifications.

Layers

Layers are a key notion in the Flutter framework, classified into several categories based on complexity and organized in a top-down manner. The highest layer is the application's UI, unique to the Android and iOS platforms. All of the Flutter native widgets are located on the second-highest layer. The rendering layer comes next, responsible for rendering everything in the Flutter app. The layers then fall to Gestures, the foundation library, the engine, and the core platform-specific code.

FLUTTER WIDGETS

This part looks at the notion of a widget, how to make one, and the many types accessible in the Flutter framework. We already know that everything in Flutter is a widget.

Flutter is simple to grasp if you are familiar with React or Vue.js.

Every time we write code in Flutter, it will be within a widget. The main goal is to create an app consisting of widgets. It specifies how your app's view should appear in its current setup and state. When we modify the code, the widget rebuilds its description by calculating the difference between the previous and current widgets to identify the minimal modifications for rendering in the app's UI.

To construct the app, widgets are nested with one another. It signifies that your app's root is a widget, and everything underneath it is also a widget. A widget, for example, can show things, define design, manage interaction, and so on.

The widget tree is depicted graphically in the following figure.

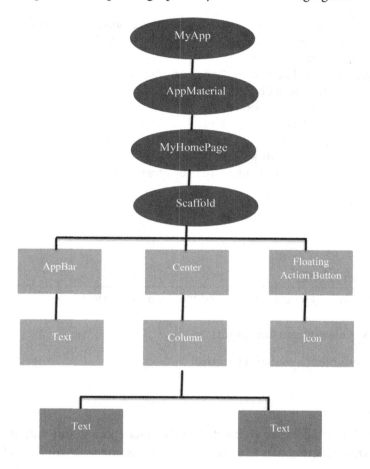

Tree of widget.

We can make the Flutter widget as follows:

```
Class ImageWidget extends StatelessWidget {
        // Class-Stuff
}
```

Example: Hello Everyone

```
import 'package:flutter/material.dart';
class HomePage extends StatelessWidget {
```

```
  HomePage({Key key, this.title}) : super(key:
key);
  // This widget is home page of your application.
  final String title;
  @override
  Widget build(BuildContext context) {
    return Scaffold(
      appBar: AppBar(
        title: Text(this.title),
      ),
      body: Center(
        child: Text('Hello Everyone'),
      ),
    );
  }
}
```

WIDGET TYPES

The Flutter widget may be divided into two categories:

- Visible (Output and Input)
- Invisible (Layout and Control)

Visible Widget

The visible widgets are connected to the data entered and output by the user. This widget comes in a variety of forms, some of which are as follow:

Text

A Text widget contains text that will show on the screen. We may align the text widget by using the textAlign property, and the style property allows us to customize the text by changing the font, font weight, font style, letter spacing, color, and many other things. We may utilize it in the following code snippets.

```
new text (
'Hello, Dartpoint!',
textAlign: TextAlign.center,
style: new TextStyle(fontWeight: FontWeight.bold),
)
```

Button

This widget allows us to perform a specific action with a single click. Flutter does not support the Button widget natively; instead, it employs buttons like the FlatButton and the RaisedButton. We may utilize it in the following code snippets.

```
// Example of FlatButton
new FlatButton(
  child: Text("Clickhere"),
  onPressed: () {
    // Do something here
  },
),
// Example of RaisedButton
new RaisedButton(
  child: Text("Clickhere"),
  elevation: 4.0,
  onPressed: () {
    // Do something here
  },
),
```

The onPressed property in the above example lets us to conduct an action when you click the button, and the elevation property is used to adjust how much it stands out.

Image

This widget contains an image that may be retrieved from various sources, including the asset folder or straight from the URL. It has many constructors for loading images, which are listed below:

- **image:** It is a generic image loader that ImageProvider uses.

- **asset:** It loads images from your project's asset folder.

- **file:** It reads pictures from the system's folder.

- **memory:** It loads the image from memory.

- **network:** It retrieves photos from the network.

To include a picture in the project, first establish an assets folder to store your images, and then add the following line to the pubspec.yaml file:

```
assets:
  - assets/
```

Now, in the dart file, add the following line:

```
Image.asset('assets/comp.png')
```

In the hello everyone example, the complete source code for inserting an image is displayed below:

```
class HomePage extends StatelessWidget {
  HomePage({Key key, this.title}) : super(key: key);
  // This widget is the home page of our application.
  final String title;
  @override
  Widget build(BuildContext context) {
    return Scaffold(
      appBar: AppBar(
        title: Text(this.title),
      ),
      body: Center(
        child: Image.asset('assets/comp.png'),
      ),
    );
  }
}
```

Icon

This widget serves as a container for the Icon in Flutter. The following code describes it in further detail.

```
new Icon(
  Icons.add,
  size: 35.0,
)
```

Invisible Widget

The invisible widgets are associated with widget layout and control. It allows us to change how the widgets behave and appear on the screen. Among the most critical sorts of these widgets are as follow:

Column

A column widget is a widget that arranges all of its children's widgets vertically. It uses the mainAxisAlignment and crossAxisAlignment attributes to establish space between widgets. The major axis in these attributes is the vertical axis, while the cross axis is the horizontal axis.

Example: The following code builds two widget items vertically.

```
new Column (
  mainAxisAlignment: MainAxisAlignment.center,
  childrens: <Widget>[
    new Text (
      "Veg-Element",
    ),
    new Text (
      "Nonveg-Element"
    ),
  ],
),
```

Row

Row widget is similar to the column widget in that it builds a widget horizontally rather than vertically. In this case, the horizontal axis is the primary axis, while the vertical axis is the cross axis.

Example: The following code lines create two widget items horizontally.

```
new Row (
  mainAxisAlignment: MainAxisAlignment.
spaceEvenly,
  childrens: <Widget>[
    new Text (
      "Veg-Element",
    ),
```

```
      new Text(
        "Nonveg-Element"
      ),
    ],
  ),
```

Center

This widget is used to center the child widget that is contained within it. The center widget is present in all of the preceding examples.

Example:

```
Center(
  child: new clumn(
    mainAxisAlignment: MainAxisAlignment.
spaceEvenly,
    childrens: <Widget>[
      new Text(
        "Veg-Element",
      ),
      new Text(
        "Nonveg-Element"
      ),
    ],
  ),
),
```

Padding

This widget covers other widgets to provide padding in specific directions. Padding can also provide in all directions. We can see this in the example below, which shows a text widget with a padding of 5.0 in all directions.

```
Padding(
  padding: const EdgeInsets.all(5.0),
  child: new Text(
    "Element 1",
  ),
),
```

Scaffold

This widget offers a framework for adding standard material design features such as AppBar, Floating Action Buttons, Drawers, and so on.

Stack

This is a necessary widget mainly used to overlap a widget such as a button on a background gradient.

State Management Widget

There are primarily two sorts of widgets in Flutter:

- StatefulWidget

- StatelessWidget

StatefulWidget

A StatefulWidget keeps information of its current state. It primarily consists of two classes: the state object and the widget. It is dynamic because the inside data might change over the widget's lifespan. This widget lacks a build() function. It provides a method called createState() that returns a class that extends the Flutters State Class. Checkbox, Radio, Slider, InkWell, Form, and TextField are instances of StatefulWidget.

Example:

```
class Cars extends StatefulWidget {
  const Cars({ Key key, this.title }) : super(key:
key);
  @override
  _CarState createState() => _CarState();
}
class _CarState extends State<Cars> {
  @override
  Widget build(BuildContext context) {
    return Container(
      color: const Color(0xFEEFE),
          childs: Container(
          childs: Container( //childs:
Container() )
        )
    );
  }
}
```

StatelessWidget

The StatelessWidget has no state information. Throughout its existence, it stays static. Text, Row, Column, Container, and so on are instances of StatelessWidget.

Example:

```
class MyStatelessCarsWidget extends
StatelessWidget {
  const MyStatelessCarsWidget ({ Key key }) :
super(key: key);
  @override
  Widget build(BuildContext context) {
    return Container(color: const
Color(0x0xFEEFE));
  }
}
```

FLUTTER LAYOUTS

The widget is the layout mechanism's central notion. We know that Flutter treats everything as if it were a widget. So your app's picture, icon, content, and even its layout are all widgets. Some of the items we don't see on our app's UI, such as rows, columns, and grids that arrange, constrain, and align the visible widgets, are also widgets in this case.

Flutter allows us to design more sophisticated widgets by assembling numerous widgets. For example, consider the following image, which has three symbols, each with a label beneath them.

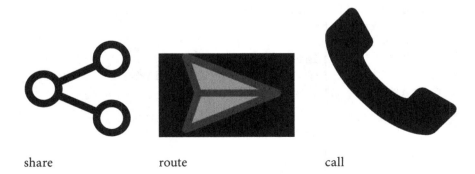

share　　　　　　　route　　　　　　　call

The visual layout of the above image may be seen in the following figure that depicts a row of three columns, each with an icon and label.

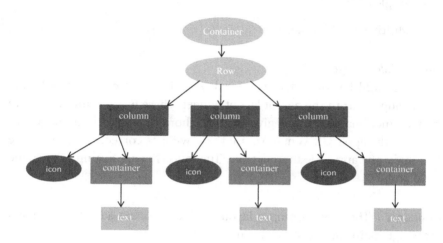

Layout of Flutter.

The container in the above image is a widget class that configures the child widget. It is mainly used to create borders, padding, margins, background color, and various other features. The text widget is placed beneath the container for adding margins in this case. In addition, the entire row is enclosed in a container to add margin and padding around the row. Additionally, characteristics like color, text style, and so on are used to manage the remainder of the UI.

Layout a Widget

Let's look at how to make and show a simple widget. The following instructions demonstrate how to layout a widget:

- **Step 1:** First, we must choose a Layout widget.

- **Step 2:** After that, create a visible widget.

- **Step 3:** Finally, add the visible widget to the layout widget.

- **Step 4:** Finally, add the layout widget to the page where you want the widget to appear.

Sorts of Layout Widgets

There are two types of layout widgets:

- Single Child Widget

- Multiple Child Widget

Single Child Widgets

A single child layout widget is a kind of widget that can have only one child widget within the parent layout widget. These widgets may also have layout functionality. Flutter gives us a plethora of single child widgets to enhance the app's UI. When we use these widgets correctly, we save time and make the app code more legible. The following are examples of single child widgets.

Container   The most common layout widget, it offers adjustable choices for widget painting, positioning, and sizing.

```
Center(
  child: Container(
    margin: const EdgeInsets.all(14.0),
    color: Colors.yellow,
    width: 48.0,
    height: 48.0,
  ),
)
```

Padding   It is a widget that is used to organize its child widgets based on the padding specified. It includes EdgeInsets and EdgeInsets.fromLTRB for the specified side where padding is wanted.

```
const Greetings(
  child: Padding(
    padding: EdgeInsets.all(13.0),
    child: Text('Hello Dartpoint!'),
  ),
)
```

Center   With this widget, we may center the child widget within itself.

Align   It is a widget that aligns its child widget inside itself and sizes is dependent on the size of the child. It gives more control to place child widget exactly where we want it.

```
Center(
  child: Container(
    height: 120.0,
    width: 120.0,
    color: Colors.black,
    child: Align(
      alignment: Alignment.topRight,
      child: FlutterLogo(
        size: 40,
      ),
    ),
  ),
)
```

SizedBox   This widget allows us to specify the size of the child widget across all screens.

```
SizedBox(
  width: 310.0,
  height: 440.0,
  child: const Card(child: Text('Hello DarTpoint!')),
)
```

AspectRatio   This widget allows us to limit the child widget's size to a certain aspect ratio.

```
AspectRatio(
  aspectRatio: 6/3,
  child: Container(
    color: Colors.black,
  ),
),
```

Baseline   This widget moves the child widget based on the baseline of the child.

```
child: Baseline(
        baseline: 40.0,
```

```
            baselineType: TextBaseline.alphabetic,
            child: Container(
                height: 40,
                width: 30,
                color: Colors.black,
            ),
)
```

ConstrainedBox   It's a widget that lets us impose extra limits on its child widget. It implies that we may force the child widget to have a constraint without affecting its characteristics.

```
ConstrainedBox(
  constraints: new BoxConstraints(
    minHeight: 160.0,
    minWidth: 160.0,
    maxHeight: 310.0,
    maxWidth: 310.0,
  ),
  child: new DecoratedBox(
    decoration: new BoxDecoration(color: Colors.blue),
  ),
),
```

CustomSingleChildLayout   It is a widget that delegates the layout of a single child to a delegate. The delegate determines the child widget's position and the size of the parent widget.

FittedBox   It scales and arranges the child widget based on the fit parameter.

```
import 'package:flutter/material.dart';

void main() => runApp(App());

class App extends StatelessWidget {
  // It is root widget of our application.
  @override
  Widget build(BuildContext context) {
    return MaterialApp(
      title: 'Multiple Layout Widget',
```

```
      debugShowCheckedModeBanner: false,
      theme: ThemeData(
        // This is the theme of your application.
        primarySwatch: Colors.yellow,
      ),
      home: HomePage(),
    );
  }
}
class HomePage extends StatelessWidget {
  @override
  Widget build(BuildContext context) {
    return Scaffold(
        appBar: AppBar(title: Text("FittedBox
Widget")),
        body: Center(
        child: FittedBox(child: Row(
          children: <Widget>[
            Container(
              child: Image.asset('assets/comp.png'),
            ),
            Container(
              child: Text("This is widget"),
            )
          ],
        ),
        fit: BoxFit.contain,
      )
      ),
    );
  }
}
```

FractionallySizedBox   This widget allows you to size its child widgets based on the fraction of available space.

IntrinsicHeight and IntrinsicWidth   They are widgets that allow us to size its child widget to the intrinsic height and width of the child.

LimitedBox   We can restrict the size of this widget only when it is unconstrained.

Offstage   It is used to measure the size of a widget without bringing it onto the screen.

OverflowBox   A widget allows us to impose different limitations on its child widget than it receives from its parent. In other words, it permits the child widget to overflow the parent widget.

Example:

```
import 'package:flutter/material.dart';
void main() => runApp(App());
class App extends StatelessWidget {
  // It is root widget of your application.
  @override
  Widget build(BuildContext context) {
    return MaterialApp(
      title: 'Single Layout Widget',
      debugShowCheckedModeBanner: false,
      theme: ThemeData(
        // This is the theme of your application.
        primarySwatch: Colors.red,
      ),
      home: HomePage(),
    );
  }
}
class HomePage extends StatelessWidget {
  @override
  Widget build(BuildContext context) {
    return Scaffold(
      appBar: AppBar(
        title: Text("OverflowBox Widget"),
      ),
      body: Center(
      child: Container(
        height: 40.0,
        width: 40.0,
        color: Colors.white,
        child: OverflowBox(
          minHeight: 60.0,
          minWidth: 60.0,
          child: Container(
```

```
            height: 40.0,
            width: 40.0,
            color: Colors.yellow,
            ),
          ),
        ),
      ),
    );
  }
}
```

Multiple Child Widgets

Multiple child widgets are widgets that have more than one child widget, and their layout is unique. For example, a Row widget puts out its child widget horizontally, and a Column widget sets out vertically. When we combine the Row and Column widgets, we may create any level of the complicated widget.

We will learn about many forms of numerous child widgets in this section.

Row   It allows its child widgets to be positioned horizontally.

```
import 'package:flutter/material.dart';

void main() => runApp(App());
class App extends StatelessWidget {
  // It is root widget of your application.
  @override
  Widget build(BuildContext context) {
    return MaterialApp(
      title: 'Multiple Layout Widget',
      debugShowCheckedModeBanner: false,
      theme: ThemeData(
        // This is theme of our application.
        primarySwatch: Colors.blue,
      ),
      home: HomePage(),
    );
  }
}
```

```
class HomePage extends StatelessWidget {
  @override
  Widget build(BuildContext context) {
    return Center(
      child: Container(
        alignment: Alignment.left,
        color: Colors.white,
        child: Row(
          children: <Widget>[
            Expanded(
              child: Text('Peter', textAlign:
TextAlign.left),
            ),
            Expanded(
              child: Text('John', textAlign:
TextAlign.left ),
            ),
            Expanded(
              child: FittedBox(
                fit: BoxFit.contain, // otherwise logo
will be tiny
                child: const FlutterLogo(),
              ),
            ),
          ],
        ),
      ),
    );
  }
}
```

Column   It allows us to arrange its child widgets vertically.

ListView   It is the most common scrolling widget, allowing us to arrange its child widgets in the scroll direction one after the other.

GridView   Its child widgets may be arranged as a scrollable, 2D array of widgets. It comprises a repetitive pattern of cells organized horizontally and vertically.

Expanded   It allows you to make the children of a Row and Column widget take up the most space possible.

Table   A table-based widget that allows us to organize its children.

Flow   It enables us to create a flow-based widget.

Stack   This is a necessary widget mainly used to overlap many child widgets. It enables us to display numerous layers on the screen.
The following example assists us in comprehending it.

```
import 'package:flutter/material.dart';
void main() => runApp(App());
class App extends StatelessWidget {
  // It is root widget of your application.
  @override
  Widget build(BuildContext context) {
    return MaterialApp(
      title: 'Multiple Layout Widget',
      debugShowCheckedModeBanner: false,
      theme: ThemeData(
        // This is theme of our application.
        primarySwatch: Colors.blue,
      ),
      home: HomePage(),
    );
  }
}
class HomePage extends StatelessWidget {
  @override
  Widget build(BuildContext context) {
    return Center(
      child: Container(
        alignment: Alignment.center,
        color: Colors.green,
        child: Stack(
          children: <Widget>[
            // Max Size
            Container(
              color: Colors.blue,
            ),
            Container(
              color: Colors.yellow,
              height: 410.0,
              width: 310.0,
            ),
```

```
            Container(
              color: Colors.black,
              height: 230.0,
              width: 210.0,
            )
        ],
      ),
    ),
  );
  }
}
```

Building the Complex Layout

In this part, we'll look at how to build a complicated UI using both single and numerous child layout widgets. The layout framework allows us to arrange rows and columns inside rows and columns to create a complex UI layout.

Create a product list to view an example of a complex UI. To accomplish this, first, replace the code in the main.dart file with the following code snippet.

```
import 'package:flutter/material.dart';
void main() => runApp(App());
class App extends StatelessWidget {
  // It is the root widget of our application.
  @override
  Widget build(BuildContext context) {
    return MaterialApp(
      title: 'Flutter Demo Application', theme:
ThemeData(
      primarySwatch: Colors.yellow,),
      home: HomePage(title: 'Complex layout example'),
    );
  }
}
class HomePage extends StatelessWidget {
  MyHomePage({Key key, this.title}) : super(key: key);
  final String title;
  @override
  Widget build(BuildContext context) {
    return Scaffold(
      appBar: AppBar(title: Text("Product List")),
      body: ListView(
```

```
            padding: const EdgeInsets.fromLTRB(4.0,
13.0, 2.0, 11.0),
            children: <Widget>[
              ProductBox(
                  name: "iPhone11",
                  description: "iPhone is top branded
phone ever",
                  price: 50000,
                  image: "iphone11.png"
              ),
              ProductBox(
                  name: "AndroidS2",
                  description: "Android is very stylish
phone",
                  price: 12000,
                  image: "androidS2.png"
              ),
              ProductBox(
                  name: "Tablet",
                  description: "Tablet is popular device
for official meetings",
                  price: 26000,
                  image: "tablet.png"
              ),
              ProductBox(
                  name: "DellLaptop",
                  description: "Laptop is most famous
electronic device",
                  price: 38000,
                  image: "delllaptop.png"
              ),
              ProductBox(
                  name: "Desktop",
                  description: "Desktop is most popular
for regular use",
                  price: 13000,
                  image: "computer.png"
              ),
            ],
        )
    );
  }
}
```

```
class ProductBoxes extends StatelessWidget {
  ProductBoxes({Key key, this.names, this.
descriptions, this.prices, this.images}) :
        super(key: key);
  final String names;
  final String descriptions;
  final int prices;
  final String images;

  Widget build(BuildContext context) {
    return Container(
        padding: EdgeInsets.all(2),
        height: 120,
        child: Card(
            child: Row(
                mainAxisAlignment: MainAxisAlignment.
spaceEvenly,
                children: <Widget>[
                  Image.asset("assets/" + image),
                  Expanded(
                      child: Container(
                          padding: EdgeInsets.all(5),
                          child: Column(
                              mainAxisAlignment:
MainAxisAlignment.spaceEvenly,
                              children: <Widget>[
                                Text(
                                    this.names, style:
TextStyle(

                                        fontWeight:
FontWeight.bold
                                )
                                ),
                                Text(this.description),
Text(
                                    "Prices: " + this.
price.toString()
                                ),
                              ],
                          )
                      )
                  )
                ]
```

```
                )
             )
        ) ;
    }
}
```

In the above code, we construct the widget ProductBox, which holds product details like an image, name, price, and description. We utilize the following child widgets in the ProductBox widget: Container, Row, Column, Expanded, Card, Text, Image, and so on.

GESTURES IN FLUTTER

Flutter's gestures are an exciting feature that allows us to interact with the mobile app (or any touch-based device). In general, gestures are any physical motion or movement performed by a user to control a mobile device. Here are some examples of gestures:

- When the smartphone screen is locked, we unlock it by swiping our fingers over it.

- Tapping a button on our mobile screen and moving an app icon between screens on a touch-based device.

These gestures are used in everyday life to interact with our phone or another touch-based device.

Flutter separates the gesture system into two levels, which are described below:

1. Pointers

2. Gestures

Pointers

The first layer is pointers, which represent primary data regarding user interaction. It provides events that explain the location and movement of points across the displays such as touches, mice, and style. Flutter does not provide a means for canceling or stopping the dispatch of pointer events. Flutter has a Listener widget that allows us to listen to pointer events straight from the widgets layer. The pointer-events are classified into four types:

- **PointerDownEvents:** This allows the pointer to touch the screen at a particular position.

- **PointerMoveEvents:** It allows the pointer to move from one location on the screen to another.

- **PointerUpEvents:** These events enable the pointer to quit contacting the screen.

- **PointerCancelEvents:** This event is sent when pointer interaction is terminated.

Gestures

The second layer represents semantic actions like tap, drag, and scale detected from many individual pointer events. It can also send out several events related to the gesture lifecycle such as drag start, drag update, and drag end. The following are some of the most commonly used gestures.

Tap

This involves briefly contacting the screen's surface with our finger-tip and releasing it. The following occurrences occur as a result of this gesture:

- onTapDown
- onTapUp
- onTap
- onTapCancel

Double Tap   It is identical to a Tap gesture, but we must tap twice in a brief period of time. The following occurrences occur as a result of this gesture:

- onDoubleTap

Drag

It allows us to use our fingertips to touch the screen's surface and move it from one spot to another before releasing it. Flutter divides drag into two types:

1. **Horizontal Drag:** With this action, the cursor may move horizontally. It includes the following events:

   • onHorizontalDragStart

   • onHorizontalDrag

   • Update

   • onHorizontalDragEnd

2. **Vertical Drag:** This motion enables the cursor to travel vertically. It includes the following events:

   • onVerticalDragStart

   • onVerticalDragStart

   • onVerticalDragStart

Long Press

This refers to touching the screen's surface in a specific spot for an extended period of time. The following occurrences occur as a result of this gesture:

   • onLongPress

Pan

It refers to touching the screen's surface with a fingertip that can travel in any direction without releasing the fingertip. The following occurrences occur as a result of this gesture:

   • onPanStart

   • onPanUpdate

   • onPanEnd

Pinch

It refers to zooming into or out of a screen by pinching (moving one's finger and thumb or bringing them together on a touchscreen).

Gesture Detector

Using the GestureDetector widget, Flutter provides great support for all forms of motion. The GestureWidget is a non-visual widget used to detect the user's gesture. The gesture detector's basic concept is a stateless widget with parameters in its constructor for various touch events.

In some cases, there may be multiple gesture detectors at the same position on the screen, and the framework determines which gesture should be called. The GestureDetector widget determines which gestures to identify based on which callbacks are not null.

Let's see how we can utilize these gestures in our app with a simple onTap() event and how the GestureDetector handles it. This section creates a box widget, design it to our specifications, and then add the onTap() code to it.

Create a new Flutter project and replace the code in the main.dart file with the following:

```
import 'package:flutter/material.dart';
void main() => runApp(App());
class App extends StatelessWidget {
  // This widget is the root of your application.
  @override
  Widget build(BuildContext context) {
    return MaterialApp(
      title: 'Flutter Demo Application', theme:
ThemeData(
      primarySwatch: Colors.blue,),
      home: HomePage(),
    );
  }
}
class HomePage extends StatefulWidget {
  @override
  MyHomePageState createState() => new
HomePageState();
}

class HomePageState extends State<HomePage> {
  @override
  Widget build(BuildContext context) {
    return new Scaffold(
      appBar: new AppBar(
```

```
            title: new Text('Gestures-Example'),
            centerTitle: true,
         ),
         body: new Center(child: GestureDetector(
            onTap: () {
              print('Box-Clicked');
            },
            child: Container(
              height: 62.0,
              width: 110.0,
              padding: EdgeInsets.all(12.0),
              decoration: BoxDecoration(
                color: Colors.blueGrey,
                borderRadius: BorderRadius.
circular(18.0),
              ),
              child: Center(child: Text('Click-Me')),
            )
         )),
      );
   }
}
```

Example of Multiple Gesture

In this part, we'll look at how multiple gestures function in flutter apps. This sample program is made up of two containers: parent and kid. Everything is done by hand, with a "RawGestureDetector" and a custom "GestureRecognizer." The custom GestureRecognizer adds the attribute "AllowMultipleGestureRecognizer" to the gesture list and creates a "GestureRecognizerFactoryWithHandlers." Text is printed to the console when the onTap() event is called.

Replace the following code in the main.dart file in the flutter project:

```
import 'package:flutter/gestures.dart';
import 'package:flutter/material.dart';
//It is entry point for your Flutter app.
void main() {
   runApp(
     MaterialApp(
        title: 'Multiple-Gestures Demo',
        home: Scaffold(
```

```
        appBar: AppBar(
          title: Text('Multiple-Gestures Demo'),
        ),
        body: DemoApp(),
      ),
    ),
  );
}


class DemoApp extends StatelessWidget {
  @override
  Widget build(BuildContext context) {
    return RawGestureDetector(
      gestures: {
        AllowMultipleGestureRecognizer:
GestureRecognizerFactoryWithHandlers<
            AllowMultipleGestureRecognizer>(
            () => AllowMultipleGestureRecognizer(),
            (AllowMultipleGestureRecognizer instance) {
            instance.onTap = () => print('It is parent
container gesture');
          },
        )
      },
      behavior: HitTestBehavior.opaque,
      //Parent Container
      child: Container(
        color: Colors.yellow,
        child: Center(
          //Now, wraps the second container in
RawGestureDetector
          child: RawGestureDetector(
            gestures: {
              AllowMultipleGestureRecognizer:
              GestureRecognizerFactoryWithHandlers<
                AllowMultipleGestureRecognizer>(
                () =>
AllowMultipleGestureRecognizer(), //constructor
                (AllowMultipleGestureRecognizer
instance) { //initializer
                instance.onTap = () => print('It is
the nested container');
              },
```

```
                    )
                },
                //Creates the nested container within the
first.
                child: Container(
                  color: Colors.deepOrange,
                  width: 260.0,
                  height: 360.0,
                ),
              ),
            ),
          ),
        );
    }
}
class AllowMultipleGestureRecognizer extends
TapGestureRecognizer {
  @override
  void rejectGesture(int pointer) {
    acceptGesture(pointer);
  }
}
```

STATE MANAGEMENT

This section goes over state management and how we can handle it in Flutter. We already know that everything in Flutter is a widget. The widget may be divided into two types: stateless widgets and stateful widgets. There is no internal state in the Stateless widget. It implies that we can't edit or modify it once generated until it's initialized again. A Stateful widget, on the other hand, is dynamic and has a state. It implies that we can simply modify it during its lifecycle without reinitializing it.

What Exactly Is a State?

A state is an information that may be read when the widget is formed and may change or be adjusted throughout the app's existence. If we wish to alter our widget, you must first update the state object, which we can accomplish by calling the setState() function on Stateful widgets. The setState() function lets us modify the attributes of the state object that causes the UI to redraw.

State management is one of the most common and essential activities in an application's lifecycle. Flutter, according to official documentation, is declarative. This implies that Flutter's UI is created by reflecting our app's current state (see the following figure).

Application state.

To further grasp the notion of state management, consider the following example. Assume we have a list of customers or items on our app. Assume we've added a new client or product dynamically to that list. The list must then refresh to see the newly added item in the record. As a result, anytime we add a new item, we must reload the list. This sort of programming necessitates state management to handle such a circumstance and increase performance. It's because the state is updated every time we make a modification or update it.

Flutter's state management is divided into two conceptual categories, which are listed below:

- Ephemeral State

- App State

Ephemeral State
Ephemeral state is also called a UI state or local state. It is a sort of state associated with a particular widget, or we can say that it is a state contained within a single widget. We do not need to utilize state management techniques in this type of state. Text Field is a frequent example of this condition.

Example:

```
class Homepage extends StatefulWidget {
  @override
  HomepageState createState() => HomepageState();
}

class HomepageState extends State<Homepage> {
  String _name = "Peterin";
```

```
@override
Widget build(BuildContext context) {
  return RaisedButton(
      child: Text(_name),
      onPressed: () {
        setState(() {
          _name = _name == "Peterin" ? "Johny"
: "Peterin";
          });
        },
      );
  }
}
```

In the above example, the _name is an ephemeral state. Only the setState() function within the StatefulWidget's class has access to the _name in this case. The build method invokes the setState() function, modifying the state variables. When this method is called, the widget object is replaced with a new one with the updated variable value.

App State

It is not the same as the ephemeral state. It is a form of state that we wish to preserve throughout user sessions and distribute across different portions of our program. As a result, this form of state may be applied globally. It is also called an application state or shared state at times. User preferences, login information, alerts in a social networking app, the shopping cart in an e-commerce app, the read/unread status of articles in a news app, and so on are examples of this state.

The following figure clearly demonstrates the distinction between the ephemeral state and the app state.

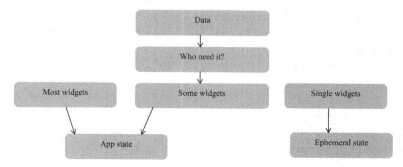

App and ephemeral state difference.

We may learn the most basic example of app state management using the provider package. The provider's state management is simple to grasp and needs little code. A third-party library is a supplier. To use this library, we must first grasp three key ideas.

- ChangeNotifier

- ChangeNotifierProvider

- Consumer

ChangeNotifier   A ChangeNotifier is a basic class that notifies its listeners when anything changes. It is simple to comprehend, implement, and optimize for a small group of listeners. It is utilized for the listener to notice a change model. We simply use the notifyListener() function to notify the listeners in this case.

Let us develop a model based on ChangeNotifier as an example. The Counter in this model has been enhanced with a ChangeNotifier, which alerts its listeners when we run notifyListeners (). It is the sole method that a ChangeNotifier model must implement. We declared two functions in this example, increment and decrement, used to raise and reduce the value. We may use the notifyListeners() function if the model changes to affect the UI of our project.

```dart
import 'package:flutter/material.dart';
class Counter with ChangeNotifier {
  int _counters;
  Counter(this._counters);
  getCounter() => _counters;
  setCounter(int counters) => _counters = counters;
  void increment() {
    _counters++;
    notifyListeners();
  }
  void decrement() {
    _counters--;
    notifyListeners();
  }
}
```

ChangeNotifierProvider   It is a widget that delivers a ChangeNotifier instance to its children. It is part of the provider package. The following code samples will help us grasp the notion of ChangeNotifierProvider.

In this section, we developed a builder that would produce a new instance of the Counter model. ChangeNotifierProvider does not rebuild Counter until it is required. When the instance is no longer required, it will also automatically invoke the dispose() function on the Counter model.

```
class App extends StatelessWidget {
  @override
  Widget build(BuildContext context) {
    return MaterialApp(
      theme: ThemeData(
        primarySwatch: Colors.blue,
      ),
      home: ChangeNotifierProvider<CounterModel>(
        builder: (_) => CounterModel(),
        child: CounterView(),
      ),
    );
  }
}
```

We can use MultiProvider if we need to offer more than one class. The MultiProvider is a list of the providers utilized inside its scope. We would have to nest our Providers if we didn't use this, with one being the child of another and another. We may deduce this from the following code.

```
void main() {
  runApp(
    MultiProvider(
      providers: [
        ChangeNotifierProvider(builder: (context) =>
Counter()),
        Provider(builder: (context) =>
SomeOtherClass()),
      ],
      child: App(),
    ),
  );
}
```

Consumer It is a provider who does not perform anything special. It invokes the provider in a new widget and passes the build implementation to the builder. The following code describes it in further detail.

```
return Consumer<Counter>(
    builder: (context, counts, child) {
        return Text("Total price is: ${counts.total}");
    },
);
```

The consumer widget in the above example requires a constructor, which is invoked whenever the ChangeNotifier changes. The context, count, and child parameters are sent to the builder function. Every construct() function takes the first parameter, context. The second parameter is the ChangeNotifier object, and the third argument is the child utilized for optimization. The consumer widget should be placed as deep in the tree as possible.

FLUTTER IDE

Interactive development environments (IDEs) are software tools that allow users to create and modify text files. Editors are commonly used in the development profession to refer to source code editors, which have particular functions for creating and modifying code.

We can build Flutter apps with any text editor that works well with our command-line tools. However, for a better experience, editor plugins (IDE) are recommended. These plugins include syntax highlighting, code completion, widget editing assistance, run and debug support, and various other capabilities. Flutter supports a variety of IDEs for app development. Some of these are covered here, but we can use a different editor.

The most popular IDEs that provide the best support for Flutter application development are:

- Android Studio

- IntelliJ Idea

- Visual Studio

- Emac

- Codemagic

Android Studio

It is a free, open-source, and rapid tool for developing apps for all types of Android devices. It offers a comprehensive development experience for Flutter applications, including code completion, navigation, syntax highlighting, refactoring, widget editing assistance, and run and debug support, among other things. The major goal of the Android Studio is to speed up development and create high-quality apps for all Android devices. It enables the developer to resolve specific code errors automatically.

To download the android studio, click here: https://developer.android.com/studio

IntelliJ Idea

JetBrains Company created and maintained IntelliJ IDEA, the most powerful and popular IDE among developers. It is released under the Apache 2.0 license. It allows you to create apps in a variety of languages. Because it supports good plugins and has a wide built-in feature set, it will quickly become a preferred IDE for many developers. When it comes to developing applications in the Dart language, it is the clear winner compared to other IDEs. It provides a complete app development experience, including smart coding aid for Dart, code completion, formatting, navigation, intents, refactoring, a built-in debugger, interaction with pub, and the Dart Analysis Server. It enables us to resolve specific code bugs automatically.

IntelliJ Idea is primarily offered in two editions:

- The Community Edition (it is free and open-source).

- Edition ULTIMATE (a paid version but a free trial for 30 days).

Click here https://www.jetbrains.com/idea/download/#section=windows to download IntelliJ Idea.

Visual Studio Code

Visual Studio Code, sometimes known as the VS Code IDE, is a well-known editor in the market for building Flutter applications. It is free and simple to use. Most developers use this IDE for Flutter application development because Microsoft supports it. It has a strong rate of growth and support. It includes a basic Dart plugin that speeds up app development (within 10 minutes or less). Syntax highlighting, Code Completion, Real-time errors/warnings/TODOs, Pub Get Packages command, Pub Upgrade

Packages command, Type Hierarchy, and more features are available. The VS code editor is compatible with macOS, Windows, and Linux.

To download the VS Code, click here https://code.visualstudio.com/download

Emacs (Dart Mode)

It is a lightweight IDE that supports the building of apps in Flutter and Dart. It's a free and open-source plugin available on GitHub. It is immediately usable in our Emacs installation for Dart coding. It is a real-time display editor with over 10000 built-in commands that is expandable, customizable, and self-documenting. Emacs is compatible with a variety of operating systems, including GNU, GNU/Linux, MacOS, Windows, FreeBSD, OpenBSD, and Solaris.

To download the Emacs, access this website: https://www.gnu.org/software/emacs/download.html

Codemagic

It is also a handy tool for quickly developing, testing, and delivering Flutter applications. Using the Flutter framework to create an app will speed up the development process. It enables Cinemagic to test and publish the app. It also aids in marketing our app without causing too many problems. It is a completely free and open-source IDE. It also allows us to submit anything we want to help enhance its documentation.

Click here https://codemagic.io/start/ to download Codemagic.

FLUTTER SCAFFOLD

In Flutter, the Scaffold widget constructs the fundamental material design visual layout framework. It is fast enough to build a general-purpose mobile app and offers practically everything we need to create effective and responsive Flutter apps. This widget can take up the entire screen of the device. In other words, it is primarily responsible for establishing a foundation for the app screen on which the child widgets may hold and render on the screen. It includes a plethora of widgets and APIs for displaying Drawer, SnackBar, BottomNavigationBar, AppBar, FloatingActionButton, and many others.

Scaffold class provides a shortcut for the setting up appearance and feel of program, allowing us to avoid manually building the individual visual elements. It saves our time from building extra code for the app's look and feel.

The Scaffold widget class's constructor and attributes are as follows:

```
const Scaffold({
  Key key,
  this.appBar,
  this.body,
  this.floatingActionButton,
  this.floatingActionButtonLocation,
  this.persistentFooterButtons,
  this.drawer,
  this.endDrawer,
  this.bottomNavigationBar,
  this.bottomSheet,
  this.floatingActionButtonAnimator,
  this.backgroundColor,
  this.resizeToAvoidBottomPadding = true,
  this.primary = true,
})
```

Let's take a closer look at each of the properties listed above:

1. **appBar:** This horizontal bar appears at the top of the Scaffold widget. It is the Scaffold widget's main component and appears at the top of the screen. The Scaffold widget is incomplete without this attribute. It makes use of the appBar widget, which has several features like elevation, title, brightness, and so on. Consider the following example:

```
Widget build(BuildContext context)
{
  return Scaffold(
    appBar: AppBar(
      title: Text('First Application'),
    ), )
}
```

The title attributes in the above code uses a Text widget to show text on the screen.

2. **body:** This widget's other primary and required property, which displays the main content in the Scaffold. It denotes the area beneath the appBar and behind the floatingActionButton and drawer. By default,

the widgets inside the body are positioned at the top-left of the available space. Look at the following code:

```
Widget build(BuildContext context) {
return Scaffold(
    appBar: AppBar(
    title: Text('First Application'),
    ),
    body: Center(
    child: Text("Welcome to DartTpoint",
        style: TextStyle( color: Colors.yellow,
fontSize: 33.0,
        ),
        ),
    ),
}
```

The text "Welcome to DartTpoint" was shown in the body property of the preceding code. Using the Middle widget, this text is positioned in the center of the page. We've also used the TextStyle widget to style the text, changing the color, font size, and so on.

3. **drawer:** This is a slider panel located on the body's side. On mobile devices, it is usually concealed, but the user may access the drawer menu by swiping left to right or right to left. It shows navigation links in the application by horizontally sliding the Drawer widget attributes from the Scaffold edge. In an appBar property, a suitable icon for the drawer is automatically set. The gesture is also programmed to open the drawer automatically. Look at the following code:

```
drawer: Drawer(
        child: ListView(
        children: const <Widget>[
        DrawerHeader(
            decoration: BoxDecoration(
            color: Colors.yellow,
            ),
            child: Text(
            'Welcome to Dartpoint',
            style: TextStyle(
                color: Colors.green,
                fontSize: 35,
            ),
            ),
```

```
            ),
            ListTile(
                title: Text('1'),
            ),
            ListTile(
                title: new Text("Mail Inboxes"),
                leading: new Icon(Icons.mail),
            ),
            Divider(
                height: 0.2,
            ),
            ListTile(
                title: new Text("Prime"),
            ),
            ListTile(
                title: new Text("Socials"),
            ),
            ListTile(
                title: new Text("Promotion"),
            ),
            ],
             ),
    ),
```

We utilize Scaffold's drawer property in the preceding code to create a drawer. We also used some additional widgets to make it more appealing. We separated the panel in the ListView widget into two sections: Header and Menu. The DrawerHeader property changes the panel header, including an icon or information depending on the application. We used ListTile once more to add the list items to the menu.

4. **floatingActionButton:** This button appears in the bottom right corner of the screen and floats above the body. It is a circular icon button that floats over the content of a screen at a designated location to encourage a key action in the program. The location of the page cannot be modified while scrolling. Scaffold is used to access the FloatingActionButton widget attributes floatingActionButton. Look at the following code:

```
Widget build(BuildContext context) {
        return Scaffold(
    appBar: AppBar(title: Text('First
Application')),
```

```
        body: Center(
            child: Text("Welcome to Dartpoint!!"),
        ),
        floatingActionButton: FloatingActionButton(
            elevation: 8.0,
            child: Icon(Icons.add),
            onPressed: (){
                print('Floating Action Button');
            }
        );
}
```

We utilized the elevation attribute in the preceding code to create the button a shadow effect. We also utilized the Icon widget to provide the button an icon using preloaded Flutter SDK icons. When the user presses button, the onPressed() property is called, and the statements "Floating Action Button" are displayed to the console.

5. **backgroundColor:** This parameter is used to provide the background color of the Scaffold widget as a whole.

```
backgroundColor: Colors.red,
```

6. **primary:** It determines whether or not the Scaffold will be shown at the top of the screen. Its default value is true, which shows that the appBar's height is increased by the screen's status bar height.

```
the primary: true/false
```

7. **persistentFooterButton:** This is a collection of buttons that appear at the bottom of the Scaffold widget. These property items are always displayed, even when we browse the Scaffold's body. It's always wrapped by a ButtonBar widget. They appear under the body but above the bottomNavigationBar.

```
persistentFooterButtons: <Widget>[
  RaisedButton(
    onPressed: () {},
    color: Colors.white,
    child: Icon(
      Icons.add,
      color: Colors.black,
    ),
  ),
```

```
RaisedButton(
  onPressed: () {},
  color: Colors.blue,
  child: Icon(
    Icons.clear,
    color: Colors.red,
  ),
),
],
```

We utilized the RaisedButton that appears at the bottom of the Scaffold in the above code. We may also use the FlatButton for the RaisedButton.

8. **bottomNavigationBar:** This property functions similarly to a menu in that it shows a navigation bar at the bottom of the Scaffold. It may be found in the majority of mobile applications. This attribute enables the developer to include several icons or words as items in the bar. It should appear beneath the body and persistentFooterButtons. Look at the following code:

```
bottomNavigationBar: BottomNavigationBar(
  currentIndex: 0,
  fixedColor: Colors.white,
  items: [
    BottomNavigationBarItem(
      title: Text("MyHome"),
      icon: Icon(Icons.home),
    ),
    BottomNavigationBarItem(
      title: Text("Search"),
      icon: Icon(Icons.search),
    ),
    BottomNavigationBarItem(
      title: Text("User-Profile"),
      icon: Icon(Icons.account_circle),
    ),
  ],
  onTap: (int itemIndex){
    setState(() {
      _currentIndex = itemIndex;
    });
  },
),
```

To display the menu bar, we utilized the BottomNavigationBar widget in the preceding code. The fixedColor parameter determines the active icon's color. The BottomNavigationBarItems widget adds items to the bar that include text and an icon as child properties. We also used the onTap(int itemIndex) function to perform an action when we tapped on the items based on their index position.

9. **endDrawer:** This property is identical to a drawer property, except it is shown on the right side of the screen by default. It may swipe from right to left or from left to right.

10. **resizeToAvoidBottomInset:** If true, the body and the Scaffold's floating widgets should adjust to avoid the onscreen keyboard. The bottom attribute specifies the height of the onscreen keyboard.

11. **floatingActionButtonLocation:** It is by default located at the bottom right corner of the screen. It is used to determine the floatingAction-Button's location. It has a wide range of predefined constants such as centerDocked, centerFloat, endDocked, endFloat, etc.

FLUTTER CONTAINER

In Flutter, the container is a parent widget that can hold several child widgets and manage them effectively through width, height, padding, background color, etc. It is a widget that combines the child widgets' common painting, positioning, and sizing. It is also a class for storing widgets and positioning them on the screen based on our requirements. In general, it is similar to a box used to store contents. It provides the user with numerous properties for customizing its child widgets, such as margin, which divides the container from other contents.

A container widget is equivalent to the HTML <div> element. If this widget does not have any child widgets, it will automatically occupy the entire screen. Otherwise, it wraps the child widget according to specified height and width. It should be noted that this widget cannot render directly in the absence of a parent widget. As its parent widget, we can use Scaffold widget, Center widget, Padding widget, Row widget, or Column widget.

Why Is a Container Widget Required in Flutter?

We may consider wrapping it in a container widget if we have a widget that requires background styling due to color, shape, or size limitations.

This widget assists us in composing, decorating, and positioning its child widgets. We wouldn't notice any change in look if we wrapped our widgets in a container without utilizing any parameters. However, by including characteristics such as color, margin, padding, and so on in a container, we may layout our widgets on the screen to suit our needs.

Container Class Constructors

The syntax of the container class constructor is as follows:

```
Container({Key key,
          AlignmentGeometry alignment,
          EdgeInsetsGeometry padding,
          Color colors,
          double width,
          double height,
          Decoration decorations,
          Decoration foregroundDecoration,
          BoxConstraints constraints,
          Widget child,
          Clip clipBehavior: Clip.none
});
```

Container Widget Properties

In depth, let us go through some of the most important container widget attributes.

1. **child:** This property is used to hold the container's child widget. Assume we have a Text widget as its child widget, as illustrated in the following example:

```
Container(
    child: Text("Hello, container widget", style:
TextStyle(fontSize: 29)),
    )
```

2. **color:** Color property is used to set background color of the text. It also changes the background color of the entire container.

```
Container(
    color: Colors.yellow,
    child: Text("Hello, container widget", style:
TextStyle(fontSize: 29)),
    )
```

3. **height and width:** This property is used to set container's height and width according to our needs. By default, container always takes the space based on its child widget.

```
Container(
    width: 210.0,
    height: 110.0,
    color: Colors.yellow,
    child: Text("Hello, container widget", style:
TextStyle(fontSize: 29)),
)
```

4. **margin:** This attribute is used to enclose the container's empty space. We can notice this by looking at the white area around the container. Assume we used the EdgeInsets.all(29) function to establish an equal margin in all four directions, as demonstrated in the following example:

```
Container(
    width: 210.0,
    height: 110.0,
    color: Colors.yellow,
    margin: EdgeInsets.all(22),
    child: Text("Hello, container widget", style:
TextStyle(fontSize: 29)),
)
```

5. **padding:** This parameter specifies the space between the container's border (in all four dimensions) and its child widget. This may be seen by looking at the gap between the container and the child widget. In this case, we used EdgeInsets.all(39) to establish the spacing between the text and all four container directions.

```
Container(
    width: 210.0,
    height: 110.0,
    color: Colors.red,
    padding: EdgeInsets.all(39),
    margin: EdgeInsets.all(22),
    child: Text("Hello, container widget", style:
TextStyle(fontSize: 29)),
)
```

6. **alignment:** This attribute specifies the child's location within the container. Flutter's elements may be aligned in a variety of ways, including center, bottom, bottom center, topLeft, centerRight, left, right, and many more. We will align its kid to the bottom right position in the next example:

```
Container(
    width: 210.0,
    height: 110.0,
    color: Colors.red,
    padding: EdgeInsets.all(39),
    margin: EdgeInsets.all(22),
    alignment: Alignment.bottomRight,
    child: Text("Hello, container widget", style:
TextStyle(fontSize: 29)),
)
```

7. **decoration:** The developer may use this attribute to add decoration to the widget. It paints or decorates the widget behind the child. We must utilize the forgroundDecoration option if we wish to decorate or paint in front of a child. The following image demonstrates the distinction between them, with the foregroundDecoration covering the kid and the decorative paint behind the child.

   Many parameters were supported by the decorating property, including color, gradient, background image, border, shadow, and so on. Its purpose is to ensure that we may use the color property in either a container or a decoration, but not both. Look at the following code, where we've added a border and shadow property to adorn the box.

```
import 'package:flutter/material.dart';
void main() => runApp(App());
/// This Widget is the main application widget.
class App extends StatelessWidget {
  @override
  Widget build(BuildContext context) {
    return MaterialApp(
      home: Scaffold(
        appBar: AppBar(
          title: Text("Container Example"),
        ),
```

```
        body: Container(
          padding: EdgeInsets.all(39),
          margin: EdgeInsets.all(22),
          decoration: BoxDecoration(
            border: Border.all(color: Colors.
black, width: 3),
            borderRadius: BorderRadius.
circular(9),
            boxShadow: [
              new BoxShadow(color: Colors.red,
offset: new Offset(5.0, 5.0),),
            ],
          ),
          child: Text("Hello, container widget
decoration box",
            style: TextStyle(fontSize: 32)),
        ),
      ),
    );
  }
}
```

8. **transform:** Developers can rotate the container using the transform attribute. It has the ability to rotate the container in any direction, hence changing the container coordinates in the parent widget. In the following example, we will rotate the container along the z-axis.

```
Container(
    width: 210.0,
    height: 110.0,
    color: Colors.yellow,
    padding: EdgeInsets.all(39),
    margin: EdgeInsets.all(22),
    alignment: Alignment.bottomRight,
    transform: Matrix4.rotationZ(0.2),
    child: Text("Hello container widget", style:
TextStyle(fontSize: 29)),
)
```

9. **constraints:** When we want to add extra limitations to the child, we utilize this property. It includes constructors like tight, loose, expand, and so forth. Let's look at how we can utilize these constructors in our app.

- **tight:** If we use the size property in this, it will give fixed value to the child.

```
Container(
    color: Colors.red,
    constraints: BoxConstraints.tight(Size size)
        : minWidth = size.width, maxWidth =
size.width,
            minHeight = size.height, maxHeight =
size.height;
    child: Text("Hello, container widget",
style: TextStyle(fontSize: 29)),
)
```

- **expand:** Here, we can choose height, width, or both values to the child.

```
Container(
    color: Colors.yellow,
    constraints: BoxConstraints.expand(height:
63.0),
    child: Text("Hello, container widget",
style: TextStyle(fontSize: 29)),
)
```

FLUTTER ROW AND COLUMN

We covered how to create a small Flutter application and apply basic style to widgets in previous sections. We will now learn how to arrange the widgets on the screen in rows and columns. Rows and columns are not the same widget; they are two distinct widgets: Row and Column. We'll combine these two widgets since they have comparable properties to help us grasp them more efficiently and swiftly.

Row and column are two fundamental Flutter widgets that allow developers to position children horizontally and vertically based on our needs. When designing the application UI in Flutter, we need these widgets.

Key points:

- The most widely used layout patterns in the Flutter application are row and column widgets.
- Both can have several child widgets.

- A row or column widget can also be a child widget.

- We can extend or constrain a particular children's widget.

- Flutter also allows developers to specify how the child widgets can use in row and column widgets.

Row Widget

This widget distributes its children horizontally on the screen. In other words, it will expect child widgets in the form of a horizontal array. If the child widgets must occupy the available horizontal area, they must be wrapped in an Expand widget.

Because it shows the widgets within the viewable view, a row widget does not look scrollable. As a result, it is regarded wrong to have more children in a row than would fit in the given area. The ListView widget is required to create a scrollable list of row widgets.

Using the properties of crossAxisAlignment and mainAxisAlignment, we can modify how a row widget aligns its children based on our preferences. The cross-axis of the row will run vertically, while the main axis will run horizontally.

The following properties may use to align the row's children widget:

- **start:** It will start the children at the beginning of the main axis.

- **end:** It will put the children at the very end of the main axis.

- **center:** It will place the children in the center of the main axis.

- **space between:** It will evenly distribute the open space between the children.

- **spaceAround:** It will uniformly distribute the free space between the children, with half of that space placed before and after the first and final children's widgets.

- **space Evenly:** It will evenly distribute the free space between the children and before and after the first and final children's widgets.

Let's look at an example where we're going to align the material such that there's an even gap around the children in a row.

```
import 'package:flutter/material.dart';
void main() { runApp(App()); }
```

```
class App extends StatelessWidget {
  @override
  Widget build(BuildContext context) {
    return MaterialApp(
      home: HomePage()
    );
  }
}

class HomePage extends StatefulWidget {
  @override
  _HomePageState createState() => _HomePageState();
}
class _HomePageState extends State<MyHomePage> {
  @override
  Widget build(BuildContext context) {
    return Scaffold(
      appBar: AppBar(
        title: Text("Row Example"),
      ),
      body: Row(
          mainAxisAlignment: MainAxisAlignment.
spaceEvenly,
          children:<Widget>[
            Container(
              margin: EdgeInsets.all(11.0),
              padding: EdgeInsets.all(7.0),
              decoration:BoxDecoration(
                  borderRadius:BorderRadius.
circular(7),
                  color:Colors.blue
              ),
              child: Text("React.js",style:
TextStyle(color:Colors.redAccent,fontSize:29),),
            ),
            Container(
              margin: EdgeInsets.all(14.0),
              padding: EdgeInsets.all(9.0),
              decoration:BoxDecoration(
                  borderRadius:BorderRadius.
circular(9),
                  color:Colors.blue
              ),
```

```
                child: Text("Flutter",style:
TextStyle(color:Colors.redAccent,fontSize:29),),
             ),
             Container(
                margin: EdgeInsets.all(11.0),
                padding: EdgeInsets.all(9.0),
                decoration:BoxDecoration(
                   borderRadius:BorderRadius.
circular(9),
                   color:Colors.blue
                ),
                child: Text("MySQL",style:
TextStyle(color:Colors.redAccent,fontSize:29),),
             )
          ]
       ),
     );
   }
}
```

Column

This widget arranges its children vertically on the screen. In other words, it expects a vertical array of child widgets. If the child widgets must occupy the available vertical space, they must be wrapped in an Expand widget.

Because it displays the widgets within the viewable view, a column widget does not look scrollable. As a result, it is considered incorrect if we have more children in a column than would fit in the given area. The ListView Widget is required to create a scrollable list of column widgets.

Using the properties of mainAxisAlignment and crossAxisAlignment, we can customize how a column widget aligns its children. The cross-axis of the column will run horizontally, while the main axis will run vertically.

Let's look at an example where we're going to align the content such that there's an even amount of space between the children in a column.

```
import 'package:flutter/material.dart';

void main() { runApp(App()); }
class App extends StatelessWidget {
  @override
  Widget build(BuildContext context) {
    return MaterialApp(
```

```
          home: HomePage()
      );
  }
}

class HomePage extends StatefulWidget {
  @override
  _HomePageState createState() => _HomePageState();
}

class _HomePageState extends State<HomePage> {
  @override
  Widget build(BuildContext context) {
    return Scaffold(
      appBar: AppBar(
        title: Text("Column Example"),
      ),
      body: Column(
        mainAxisAlignment: MainAxisAlignment.
spaceBetween,
        children:<Widget>[
          Container(
            margin: EdgeInsets.all(22.0),
            padding: EdgeInsets.all(11.0),
            decoration:BoxDecoration(
                borderRadius:BorderRadius.
circular(7),
                color:Colors.blue
            ),
            child: Text("React.js",style:
TextStyle(color:Colors.redAccent,fontSize:20),),
          ),
          Container(
            margin: EdgeInsets.all(22.0),
            padding: EdgeInsets.all(11.0),
            decoration:BoxDecoration(
                borderRadius:BorderRadius.
circular(7),
                color:Colors.blue
            ),
            child: Text("Flutter",style:
TextStyle(color:Colors.redAccent,fontSize:22),),
          ),
```

```
            Container(
                margin: EdgeInsets.all(21.0),
                padding: EdgeInsets.all(11.0),
                decoration:BoxDecoration(
                    borderRadius:BorderRadius.
circular(7),
                    color:Colors.yellow
                ),
                child: Text("MySQL",style:
TextStyle(color:Colors.redAccent,fontSize:22),),
            )
        ]
    ),
    );
}
}
```

The disadvantages of the row and column widgets:

- The row widget in Flutter does not support horizontal scrolling. So, if we put a huge number of children in a single row that cannot accommodate, we will receive the Overflow message.

- Vertical scrolling is not available in the Column widget in Flutter. So, if we enter a big number of children in a single column whose total children size is greater than the screen's height, we will get the Overflow message.

FLUTTER TEXT

A Text widget in Flutter allows us to show a string of text in our application on a single line. Depending on the layout limitations, we may split the string across numerous lines or show it entirely on the same line. If no styling is specified for the text widget, it will use the closest DefaultTextStyle class style. There is no specified style in this class. In this post, well look at using a Text widget and design it in our application.

Here's an easy example to help us understand this widget. This example displays the title of our project in the application bar and a message in the application body.

```
import 'package:flutter/material.dart';
void main() { runApp(App()); }
```

```
class App extends StatelessWidget {
  @override
  Widget build(BuildContext context) {
    return MaterialApp(
        theme: ThemeData(
          primarySwatch: Colors.yellow,
        ),
        home: TextPage()
    );
  }
}
class TextPage extends StatelessWidget {
  @override
  Widget build(BuildContext context) {
    return Scaffold(
      appBar: AppBar(
          title:Text("Widget Example")
      ),
      body: Center(
          child:Text("Welcome to Dartpoint")
      ),
    );
  }
}
```

We utilized a MaterialApp widget to access the home screen via the MyTextPage() class in the preceding code. This class includes the scaffold widget, which consists of the appBar and body widgets, where we utilized the Text widget to show the title and body, respectively. It is a simple Text widget scenario in which we must give the string that we want to display on our page.

Text Widget Constructor

The text widget constructor is used in Flutter to provide a custom look and feel for our text.

```
const Text(String data,{
    Key key,
    TextStyle style,
    StrutStyle strutStyle,
    TextAlign textAlign,
```

```
TextDirection textDirection,
TextOverflow overflow,
bool softWrap,
double textScaleFactor,
int maxLines,
String semanticsLabel,
TextWidthBasis textWidthBasis,
TextHeightBehavior textHeightBehavior
}
)
```

The Text widget utilized in our application has the following basic properties:

- **TextAlign:** This property describes how our text should be oriented horizontally. It also has control over the text's position.

- **TextDirection:** This property determines how textAlign values influence the layout of our text. Usually, we write text from left to right, but this argument allows us to modify that.

- **Overflow:** This word indicates when the text will not fit in the available space. It signifies we've provided more text than there for room.

- **TextScaleFactor:** This property is used to scale the text shown by the Text widget. If we set the text scale factor to 1.5, our text will be 50 percent larger than the chosen font size.

- **SoftWrap:** It is used to determine whether or not to display full-text widget content when there is insufficient space. If this is correct, it will display all material. Otherwise, it will not display all of the text.

- **MaxLines:** This property specifies the maximum number of lines displayed in the text widget.

- **TextWidthBasis:** It specifies how the text width is defined.

- **TextHeightBehavior:** This property regulates how the paragraph looks between the first and end lines.

- **Style:** This widget's most famous attribute allows developers to style their text. It supports style by specifying the foreground and background color, font size, font weight, letter and word spacing, location, shadows, and so on. See the following table for a better understanding.

Attributes	Descriptions
foreground	It selects the paint as the text's foreground.
Background	It selects the paint to be used as the text's background.
fontWeight	It determines the text's thickness.
fontSize	It determines the text's size.
fontFamily	It is used to determine the font's typeface. To do this, we must first download a typeface file for our project and then place it in the assets/font folder. Finally, configure the pubspec.yaml file so that it can use in the project.
fontStyle	It is used to change the font's style to bold or italic.
Color	It is used to determine the text's color.
letterSpacing	It is used to calculate the distance between the text's characters.
wordSpacing	It is used to describe the distance between two text words.
Shadows	It is employed to paint behind the text.
Decoration	This beautifies text by passing three parameters: decoration, decorationColor, and decorationStyle.

```
import 'package:flutter/material.dart';
void main() { runApp(App()); }
class App extends StatelessWidget {
  @override
  Widget build(BuildContext context) {
    return MaterialApp(
        theme: ThemeData(
          primarySwatch: Colors.red,
        ),
        home: TextPage()
    );
  }
}
class TextPage extends StatelessWidget {
  @override
  Widget build(BuildContext context) {
    return Scaffold(
      appBar: AppBar(
          title:Text("Widget Example")
      ),
      body: Center(
          child:Text(
            "Hello World, Text Widget.",
            style: TextStyle(
              fontSize: 39,
              color: Colors.purple,
```

```
                    fontWeight: FontWeight.w720,
                    fontStyle: FontStyle.italic,
                    letterSpacing: 7,
                    wordSpacing: 22,
                    backgroundColor: Colors.blue,
                    shadows: [
                        Shadow(color: Colors.yellowAccent,
offset: Offset(3,1), blurRadius:12)
                    ]
                ),
            )
        ),
    );
    }
}
```

Flutter RichText Widget

Sometimes we wish to display a line or a paragraph in numerous styles such as bold, italicized, underlined, a different color, a different font, or everything all at once. We should utilize the RichText widget in such a situation, which allows us to run numerous test styles without switching between several widgets.

RichText is a convenient widget in Flutter for showing a paragraph of text on the UI in various ways. We may have several styles within the widget by providing it with a tree of TextSpan widgets. Each TextSpan can override the default style by specifying its style.

FLUTTER TEXTFIELD

A TextField or TextBox is an input element that stores alphanumeric data such as a name, password, address, etc. It is a graphical UI control element that allows users to enter text data using programmable code. It can be a single-line text field (for information that only requires one line) or a multiple-line text field (when more than one line of information is needed).

TextField is the most often used text input widget in Flutter, allowing users to take keyboard inputs and save them in an app. The TextField widget may create forms, convey messages, create search experiences, and much more. Flutter adds underlining to the TextField by default. Using an InputDecoration as the decoration, we can add numerous properties to

TextField such as a label, icon, inline hint text, and error text. If we want to delete the decorative properties, we must set the decoration to null.

The following code is a TextFiled widget demo in Flutter.

```
TextField (
  decoration: InputDecoration(
    border: InputBorder.none,
    labelText: 'Enter-name',
    hintText: 'Enter-your-name'
  ),
);
```

The following are some of the most popular characteristics associated with the TextField widget:

- **decoration:** It is used to display the design around TextField.

- **border:** This property generates a rounded rectangular border around TextField by default.

- **labelText:** It displays the label text on the TextField selection.

- **hintText:** This property displays the hint text within a TextField.

- **icon:** It is used to add icons to the TextField directly.

We'll go through how to utilize the TextField widget in the Flutter app in the following steps:

- **Step 1:** In the IDE you used, create a Flutter project. We are going to utilize Android Studio in this case.

- **Step 2:** Navigate to the lib folder in Android Studio after opening the project. Open the main.dart file in this folder and import the material.dart package as shown below:

  ```
  import 'package:flutter/material.dart';
  ```

- **Step 3:** Next, use the void main run app method to call the main MyApp class, and then construct our main widget class, MyApp extends with StatefulWidget:

  ```
  void main() => runApp( App() );
  class App extends StatefulWidget { }
  ```

- **Step 4:** Next, in the class widget build area, add the Scaffold widget -> Column widget as shown below:

```
class App extends StatefulWidget {
  @override
  Widget build(BuildContext context) {
    return Scaffold(
        appBar: AppBar(
          title: Text('TextField Example'),
        ),
        body: Padding(
            padding: EdgeInsets.all(16),
            child: Column(
              children:   [

              ]
            )
          )
        )
      );
  }
}
```

- **Step 5:** Finally, create the TextField widget as shown in the following code:

```
child: TextField(
                  obscureText: true,
                  decoration: InputDecoration(
                    border: OutlineInputBorder(),
                    labelText: 'Password',
                    hintText: 'Enter-Password',
                  ),
                ),
```

BUTTONS IN FLUTTER

Buttons are graphical control elements that allow a user to initiate an event such as performing actions, making choices, searching for items, and so on. They may be put anywhere in our UI such as dialog, forms, cards, toolbars, and so on.

Buttons are Flutter widgets, which are included in the material design library. Flutter consists of various buttons with varying shapes, styles, and functionalities.

The following are the usual features of a button in Flutter:

- Themes may easily apply to buttons, shapes, color, animation, and behavior.

- We may also customize the icons and text that appear inside the button.

- Buttons can be made up of various child widgets to represent various properties.

Flutter Buttons and Their Varieties

The following are the many sorts of buttons accessible in Flutter:

- Flat Button

- Floating Button

- Raised Button

- Drop Down Button

- Menu Button

- Inkwell Button

- Popup

- Outline Button

- Icon Button

Flat Button

It is a text label button with little decoration and is presented without elevation. The flat button must have two properties: kid and onPressed (). It is typically seen in toolbars, dialogues, or in-line with other content. The flat button has no color by default, and its text is black. However, using the color and textColor properties, we can add color to the button and text, respectively.

Example:

```
import 'package:flutter/material.dart';
void main() {
  runApp(App());
}
class App extends StatefulWidget {
  @override
  _AppState createState() => _AppState();
}

class _AppState extends State<MyApp> {
  @override
  Widget build(BuildContext context) {
    return MaterialApp(
      home: Scaffold(
          appBar: AppBar(
            title: Text('FlatButton Example'),
          ),
          body: Center(child: Column(children:
<Widget>[
              Container(
                margin: EdgeInsets.all(28),
                child: FlatButton(
                  child: Text('SignUp', style:
TextStyle(fontSize: 21.0),),),
                  onPressed: () {},
                ),
              ),
              Container(
                margin: EdgeInsets.all(29),
                child: FlatButton(
                  child: Text('LogIn', style:
TextStyle(fontSize: 22.0),),),
                  color: Colors.blueAccent,
                  textColor: Colors.grey,
                  onPressed: () {},
                ),
              ),
            ]
          ))
        ),
      );
  }
}
```

Raised Button

It is a button with a rectangular body based on the material widget. It seems like a flat button, but it has an elevation that rises when the button is pressed. It provides depth to the UI along the Z-axis. It contains numerous attributes such as text color, shape, padding, button color, the color of a disabled button, animation duration, elevation, etc.

There are two callback functions associated with this button.

- **onPressed():** This function is called when the button is pressed.

- **onLongPress():** This function is called when the button is held in place for an extended period.

It should note that if the onPressed() and onLongPressed() callbacks are not given, this button is disabled.

Example:

```
Replace the following code in the main.dart file.
import 'package:flutter/material.dart';
void main() {
  runApp(App());
}
class App extends StatefulWidget {
  @override
  _AppState createState() => _AppState();
}

class _AppState extends State<MyApp> {
  String msg = 'RaisedButton Example';
  @override
  Widget build(BuildContext context) {
    return MaterialApp(
      home: Scaffold(
          appBar: AppBar(
            title: Text('RaisedButton Example'),
          ),
        body: Container(
          child: Center(
            child: Column(
              mainAxisAlignment:
MainAxisAlignment.center,
```

```
                    children: [
                        Text(msg, style: TextStyle(
    fontSize: 32, fontStyle: FontStyle.italic),),
                        RaisedButton(
                            child: Text("ClickHere", style:
    TextStyle(fontSize: 22),),
                            onPressed: _changeText,
                            color: Colors.blue,
                            textColor: Colors.red,
                            padding: EdgeInsets.all(7.0),
                            splashColor: Colors.white,
                        )
                    ],
                ),
              ),
            ),
          ),
        ),
      );
    }
    _changeText() {
      setState(() {
        if (msg.startsWith('F')) {
          msg = 'We have learned button example.';
        } else {
          msg = 'RaisedButton Example';
        }
      });
    }
}
```

Floating Activity Button (FAB)

FAB button is a circular icon button in our application that performs the
principal action. In today's apps, it is the most often utilized button. This
button can use to add, update, or share content. Flutter recommends utilizing no more than one FAB button per screen. A Floating Action Button
can be of two types:

- **FloatingActionButton:** This class generates a basic circular floating button that contains a child widget. To display a widget, it must
  include a child parameter.

- **FloatingActionButton.extended:** This method generates a large floating button with an icon and label. Labels and icon parameters are used instead of a child.

Example:

```
import 'package:flutter/material.dart';
void main() {
  runApp(App());
}
class App extends StatefulWidget {
  @override
  _AppState createState() => _AppState();
}
class _AppState extends State<App> {
  @override
  Widget build(BuildContext context) {
    return MaterialApp(home: Scaffold(
      appBar: AppBar(
        title: Text("Button Example"),
        backgroundColor: Colors.red,
        actions: <Widget>[
          IconButton(icon: Icon(Icons.camera_alt),
onPressed: () => {}),
          IconButton(icon: Icon(Icons.account_
circle), onPressed: () => {})
        ],
      ),
      floatingActionButton: FloatingActionButton(
        child: Icon(Icons.navigation),
        backgroundColor: Colors.yellow,
        foregroundColor: Colors.grey,
        onPressed: () => {},
      ),
      /*floatingActionButton:FloatingActionButton.
extended(
        onPressed: () {},
        icon: Icon(Icons.save),
        label: Text("Save"),
      ), */
    ),
    );
  }
}
```

The Drop-Down Button

A drop-down button is used to provide a nice overlay on the screen that allows the user to choose any item from a list of possibilities. Flutter offers a straightforward method for implementing a drop-down box or drop-down button. This button displays the presently selected item and an arrow that opens a menu allowing us to choose an item from a list of possibilities.

To implement a drop-down list, Flutter includes a DropdownButton widget. It may place anywhere in our app.

Example:

```
import 'package:flutter/material.dart';
void main() => runApp(MaterialApp(
  home: App(),
));
class App extends StatefulWidget {
  @override
  _AppState createState() => _AppState();
}

class _AppState extends State<App> {
  List<ListItem> _dropdownItems = [
    ListItem(1, "Huboftutorial"),
    ListItem(2, "Dartpoint"),
    ListItem(3, "tutorialexample"),
    ListItem(4, "Zone")
  ];
  List<DropdownMenuItem<ListItem>>
_dropdownMenuItems;
  ListItem _itemSelected;
  void initState() {
    super.initState();
    _dropdownMenuItems =
buildDropDownMenuItems(_dropdownItems);
    _itemSelected = _dropdownMenuItems[1].value;
  }
  List<DropdownMenuItem<ListItem>>
buildDropDownMenuItems(List listItems) {
    List<DropdownMenuItem<ListItem>> items =
List();
    for (ListItem listItem in listItems) {
      items.add(
```

```
          DropdownMenuItem(
            child: Text(listItem.name),
            value: listItem,
          ),
        );
      }
    return items;
  }
  @override
  Widget build(BuildContext context) {
    return Scaffold(
      appBar: AppBar(
        title: Text("Button Example"),
      ),
      body: Column(
        children: <Widget>[
          Padding(
            padding: const EdgeInsets.all(12.0),
            child: Container(
              padding: const EdgeInsets.all(6.0),
              decoration: BoxDecoration(
                  color: Colors.blueAccent,
                  border: Border.all()),
              child: DropdownButtonHideUnderline(
                child: DropdownButton(
                    value: _itemSelected,
                    items: _dropdownMenuItems,
                    onChanged: (value) {
                      setState(() {
                        _itemSelected = value;
                      });
                    }),
              ),
            ),
          ),
          Text("We selected ${_itemSelected.
name}"),
        ],
      ),
    );
  }
}
```

```
class ListItem {
  int value;
  String name;
  ListItem(this.value, this.name);
}
```

Button Icon

An IconButton is a graphic that has been printed on the Material widget. It is a useful widget that adds a material design feel to the Flutter UI. We may also change the appearance and feel of this button. Simply put, it is an icon that responds when the user touches it.

Example:

```
import 'package:flutter/material.dart';
void main() => runApp(App());
class App extends StatelessWidget {
  @override
  Widget build(BuildContext context) {
    return MaterialApp(
      home: Scaffold(
        appBar: AppBar(
          title: Text("Button Example"),
        ),
        body: Center(
          child: MyStatefulWidget(),
        ),
      ),
    );
  }
}
double _speakervolume = 0.0;
class MyStatefulWidget extends StatefulWidget {
  MyStatefulWidget({Key key}) : super(key: key);
  @override
  _MyStatefulWidgetState createState() =>
_MyStatefulWidgetState();
}
class _MyStatefulWidgetState extends
State<MyStatefulWidget> {
  Widget build(BuildContext context) {
    return Column(
```

```
        mainAxisSize: MainAxisSize.min,
        children: <Widget>[
          IconButton(
            icon: Icon(Icons.volume_up),
            iconSize: 52,
            color: Colors.blue,
            tooltip: 'Increase volume by 6',
            onPressed: () {
              setState(() {
                _speakervolume += 6;
              });
            },
          ),
          Text('SpeakerVolume: $_speakervolume')
        ],
      );
    }
  }
```

Inkwell Button

The InkWell button is a material design idea for touch response. This widget is part of the Material widget, where the ink responses are drawn. It makes the app's UI more interactive by incorporating gesture feedback. It is mainly used to create a splash ripple effect.

Example:

```
import 'package:flutter/material.dart';
void main() => runApp(App());
class App extends StatefulWidget {
  @override
  _AppState createState() => _AppState();
}
class _AppState extends State<App> {
  int _volume = 0;
  @override
  Widget build(BuildContext context) {
    return MaterialApp(
      home: Scaffold(
        appBar: AppBar(
          title: Text('Button Example'),
        ),
```

```
        body: Center(
          child: new Column(
            mainAxisAlignment: MainAxisAlignment.
center,
              children: <Widget>[
                InkWell(
                  splashColor: Colors.yellow,
                  highlightColor: Colors.green,
                  child: Icon(Icons.ring_volume,
size: 54),
                  onTap: () {
                    setState(() {
                      _volume += 3;
                    });
                  },
                ),
                Text (
                  _volume.toString(),
                  style: TextStyle(fontSize: 54)
                ),
              ],
            ),
          ),
        ),
      );
    }
  }
```

PopupMenu Button

It is a button that, when pressed, displays the menu and then calls the onSelected method to dismiss the menu. It is because one of the various possibilities has been chosen. This button has both text and an image. It will mostly use with the Settings menu to show all available choices. It contributes to a positive user experience.

Example:

```
import 'package:flutter/material.dart';
void main() { runApp(App());}
class App extends StatefulWidget {
  @override
  _AppState createState() => _AppState();
}
```

```
class _AppState extends State<App> {
  Choice _selectedOption = choices[0];
  void _select(Choice choice) {
    setState(() {
      _selectedOption = choice;
    });
  }
  @override
  Widget build(BuildContext context) {
    return MaterialApp(
      home: Scaffold(
        appBar: AppBar(
          title: const Text('Button Example'),
          actions: <Widget>[
            PopupMenuButton<Choice>(
              onSelected: _select,
              itemBuilder: (BuildContext context)
{
                return choices.skip(0).map((Choice
choice) {
                  return PopupMenuItem<Choice>(
                    value: choice,
                    child: Text(choice.name),
                  );
                }).toList();
              },
            ),
          ],
        ),
        body: Padding(
          padding: const EdgeInsets.all(12.0),
          child: ChoiceCard(choice:
_selectedOption),
        ),
      ),
    );
  }
}
class Choice {
  const Choice({this.name, this.icon});
  final String name;
  final IconData icon;
}
```

```
const List<Choice> choices = const <Choice>[
  const Choice(name: 'Wi-Fi', icon: Icons.wifi),
  const Choice(name: 'Bluetooth', icon: Icons.
bluetooth),
  const Choice(name: 'Battery', icon: Icons.
battery_alert),
  const Choice(name: 'Storage', icon: Icons.
storage),
];
class ChoiceCard extends StatelessWidget {
  const ChoiceCard({Key key, this.choice}) :
super(key: key);
  final Choice choice;
  @override
  Widget build(BuildContext context) {
    final TextStyle textStyle = Theme.of(context).
textTheme.headline;
    return Card(
      color: Colors.greenAccent,
      child: Center(
        child: Column(
          mainAxisSize: MainAxisSize.min,
          crossAxisAlignment: CrossAxisAlignment.
center,
          children: <Widget>[
            Icon(choice.icon, size: 120.0, color:
textStyle.color),
            Text(choice.name, style: textStyle),
          ],
        ),
      ),
    );
  }
}
```

Outline Button

It looks similar to the flat button, except it has a thin grey rounded rectangle border around it. The shape property defines its outline boundary.

Example:

```
import 'package:flutter/material.dart';
void main() {
  runApp(App());
}
class App extends StatefulWidget {
  @override
  _AppState createState() => _AppState();
}
class _AppState extends State<App> {
  @override
  Widget build(BuildContext context) {
    return MaterialApp(
      home: Scaffold(
        appBar: AppBar(
          title: Text('Button Example'),
        ),
        body: Center(child: Column(children:
<Widget>[
          Container(
            margin: EdgeInsets.all(28),
            child: OutlineButton(
              child: Text("Outline Button",
style: TextStyle(fontSize: 22.0),),
              highlightedBorderColor: Colors.
blue,
              shape: RoundedRectangleBorder(
                borderRadius: BorderRadius.
circular(17)),
              onPressed: () {},
            ),
          ),
          Container(
            margin: EdgeInsets.all(28),
            child: FlatButton(
              child: Text('Flat Button', style:
TextStyle(fontSize: 22.0),),
              color: Colors.blueAccent,
              textColor: Colors.grey,
              onPressed: () {},
            ),
          ),
```

```
                ]
              ))
          ),
        );
    }
}
```

FLUTTER FORMS

Forms are a necessary component of any current mobile and online apps. It is mainly used to interact with the app and collect information from users. They may execute a variety of functions, depending on the nature of your business requirements and logic such as user authentication, user addition, searching, filtering, ordering, booking, and so on. A form may have text fields, buttons, checkboxes, radio buttons, and so on.

Creating a Form

To create a form, use the Form widget provided by Flutter. The form widget serves as a container, allowing us to group and check the various form fields. When you build a form, you must include the GlobalKey. This key identifies the form and allows us to validate the form fields.

The form widget uses the child widget TextFormField to allow users to enter text into the text field. This widget displays a material design text field and validation errors as they occur.

Let's make a form. Create a Flutter project first, and then change the following code in the main.dart file. We've developed a custom class called MyCustomForm in this code snippet. We define a global key as _formKey within this class. This key contains a FormState, which may be used to obtain the form widget. We've added some custom styling to this class's create function, and we're using the TextFormField widget to give form fields like name, phone number, date of birth, or simply a regular field. We utilized InputDecoration within the TextFormField to offer the appearance and feel of your form attributes such as borders, labels, icons, hint, styles, and so on. Finally, we've included a button for submitting the form.

```
import 'package:flutter/material.dart';
void main() => runApp(App());
class App extends StatelessWidget {
    @override
```

```
  Widget build(BuildContext context) {
    final appTitle = 'Form Demo';
    return MaterialApp(
      title: appTitle,
      home: Scaffold(
        appBar: AppBar(
          title: Text(appTitle),
        ),
        body: MyCustomForm(),
      ),
    );
  }
}
// Create Form widget.
class MyCustomForm extends StatefulWidget {
  @override
  MyCustomFormState createState() {
    return MyCustomFormState();
  }
}
// Create the corresponding State class. This class
holds data related to form.
class MyCustomFormState extends State<MyCustomForm> {
  // Create global key that uniquely identifies the
Form widget
  // and allows validation of the form.
  final _formKey = GlobalKey<FormState>();
  @override
  Widget build(BuildContext context) {
    // Build Form widget using the _formKey created
above.
    return Form(
      key: _formKey,
      child: Column(
        crossAxisAlignment: CrossAxisAlignment.start,
        children: <Widget>[
          TextFormField(
            decoration: const InputDecoration(
              icon: const Icon(Icons.person),
              hintText: 'Enter name',
              labelText: 'Name',
            ),
          ),
```

```
            TextFormField(
              decoration: const InputDecoration(
                icon: const Icon(Icons.phone),
                hintText: 'Enter phone number',
                labelText: 'Phone',
              ),
            ),
            TextFormField(
              decoration: const InputDecoration(
              icon: const Icon(Icons.calendar_today),
              hintText: 'Enter date of birth',
              labelText: 'DOB',
              ),
              ),
            new Container(
                padding: const EdgeInsets.only(left:
160.0, top: 50.0),
                child: new RaisedButton(
                  child: const Text('Submit'),
                    onPressed: null,
                )),
          ],
        ),
      );
  }
}
```

Validation of a Form

Validation is a method that allows us to fix or confirm a certain standard. It guarantees that the data entered is legitimate.

Form validation is a standard practice in all digital interactions. To verify a form in Flutter, we must first create three phases.

- **Step 1:** Create a global key and use the Form widget.

- **Step 2:** Give the input field the validator property by using TextFormField.

- **Step 3:** Make a button to validate form data and display validation errors.

ICONS IN FLUTTER

An icon is a graphic image representing a program or any unique entity that has meaning for the user. It can be either selectable or non-selectable. The company's logo, for example, is not selectable. It may also include a hyperlink that leads to another page. It also serves as a symbol instead of a complete description of the real thing.

Flutter offers an Icon Widget to build icons for our apps. In Flutter, we may create icons using either built-in or custom icons. Flutter returns a list of all the icons in the Icons class. This tutorial will teach us how to utilize Flutter icons in your application.

Icon Widget Attributes

The Flutter icons widget has several properties to customize the icons. These characteristics are described here.

Property	Descriptions
Icon	It is used to give the icon's name that will display in the program. Flutter, in general, use material design icons as representations for common actions and items.
Color	It is used to determine the icon's color.
Size	It is used to specify the icon's size in pixels. Icons are typically identical in height and width.
textDirection	It is used to determine the direction in which the icon will show.

In the following example, we'll look at a basic icon widget with default settings. Create a new project in the IDE, then navigate to the lib folder and open the main.dart file. Replace the following code in the main.dart file:

```
import 'package:flutter/material.dart';
void main() => runApp(App());
class App extends StatelessWidget {
  // Widget is the root of your application.
  @override
  Widget build(BuildContext context) {
    return MaterialApp(
      theme: ThemeData(
        primarySwatch: Colors.blue,
      ),
      home: IconPage(),
    );
  }
}
```

```
class IconPage extends StatefulWidget {
  @override
  _IconPageState createState() => _IconPageState();
}

class _IconPageState extends State<IconPage> {
  @override
  Widget build(BuildContext context) {
    return Scaffold(
      appBar: AppBar(
        title: Text('Icon Tutorial'),
      ),
      body: Row(
        mainAxisAlignment: MainAxisAlignment.
spaceAround,
          children: <Widget>[
            Icon(Icons.camera_enhance),
            Icon(Icons.camera_front),
            Icon(Icons.camera_rear),
      ]),
    );
  }
}
```

IMAGES IN FLUTTER

In this part, we'll look at showing images in Flutter. When we build a Flutter app, we include code and assets (resources). A file that is packed and deployed with the available program at runtime is referred to as an asset. Static data, configuration files, icons, and images are all examples of assets. Flutter supports many image formats, including JPEG, WebP, PNG, GIF, animated WebP/GIF, BMP, and WBMP.

The basic principle of most mobile apps is to display photos. Flutter includes an Image widget that lets us show several images in our mobile application.

How to Display Images in Flutter

To display an image in Flutter, follow these steps:

- **Step 1:** First, we'll make a new folder called assets in the root of the Flutter project. If you choose, we may give it another name.

- **Step 2:** Next, manually add one image to this folder.

- **Step 3:** Make changes to the pubspec.yaml file. If the image's name is tablet.png, the pubspec.yaml file is as follows:

```
assets:
    - assets/tablets.png
    - assets/bg.png
```

If the assets folder has many images, we may include them by appending the directory name with a slash (/).

```
flutter:
  assets:
    - assets/
```

- **Step 4:** Finally, open the main.dart file and insert the following code into it.

```
import 'package:flutter/material.dart';
void main() => runApp(App());
class App extends StatelessWidget {
  @override
  Widget build(BuildContext context) {
    return MaterialApp(
      home: Scaffold(
        appBar: AppBar(
            title: Text('ImageDemo'),
        ),
        body: Center(
          child: Column(
            children: [
              Image.asset('assets/tablets.
png'),
              Text(
                'A tablet is a wireless touch
screen computer that is smaller than a notebook
but larger than smartphone.',
                style: TextStyle(fontSize:
22.0),
              )
            ],
          ),
        ),
```

```
      ),
    );
  }
}
```

- **Step 5:** Run the application. We will see something similar to the image below.

Display Images from the Internet

It is quite simple to display images from the Internet or network. To interact with photos from a URL, Flutter has a built-in function Image.network. We may also utilize extra attributes like height, width, color, fit, and more with the Image.network function. To display an image from the Internet, we may use the following syntax:

```
Image.network(
'https://picsum.photos/250?image=9',
)
```

Imag.Network provides one crucial feature that enables animated gifs. For showing gifs from the Internet, we may use the following syntax:

```
Image.network(
'https://github.com/flutter/plugins/raw/master/
packages/video_player/doc/demo_ipod.gif?raw=true',
);
```

Look at an example of how to show an image from the network:

```
import 'package:flutter/material.dart';
void main() => runApp(App());
class App extends StatelessWidget {
  @override
  Widget build(BuildContext context) {
    return MaterialApp(
      home: Scaffold(
        appBar: AppBar(
            title: Text('Image Demo'),
        ),
        body: Center(
          child: Column(
```

```
        children: <Widget>[
            Image.network(
                'https://pixabay.com/photos/
pigeons-flock-of-birds-flying-birds-5277317/',
                height: 420,
                width: 280
            ),
            Text(
                'It is an image displays from given
url.',
                style: TextStyle(fontSize: 22.0),
            )
        ],
    ),
  ),
 ),
);
 }
}
```

FLUTTER LISTS

Lists are the most common components of any web or mobile application. They are composed of many rows of objects such as text, buttons, toggles, icons, thumbnails, and many others. We may use it to show information such as menus and tabs or break up the monotony of plain text files.

This section discusses how to interact with Lists in Flutter. Flutter allows us to deal with Lists in a variety of ways, as detailed below:

- Basic Lists

- Long Lists

- Grid Lists

- Horizontal Lists

Basic Lists

Flutter comes with a ListView widget for working with Lists, which is the basic notion of displaying data in mobile apps. The ListView is an excellent standard for showing lists with only a few elements. ListView also includes the ListTitle widget, which adds extra visual structure to a list of data.

Example:

```dart
import 'package:flutter/material.dart';
void main() => runApp(App());
class App extends StatelessWidget {
  @override
  Widget build(BuildContext context) {
    final appTitle = 'Basic List Demo';
    return MaterialApp(
      title: appTitle,
      home: Scaffold(
        appBar: AppBar(
          title: Text(appTitle),
        ),
        body: ListView(
          children: <Widget>[
            ListTile(
              leading: Icon(Icons.map),
              title: Text('Map'),
            ),
            ListTile(
              leading: Icon(Icons.photo_album),
              title: Text('Album'),
            ),
            ListTile(
              leading: Icon(Icons.phone),
              title: Text('Phoneno'),
            ),
            ListTile(
              leading: Icon(Icons.contacts),
              title: Text('Contactno'),
            ),
            ListTile(
              leading: Icon(Icons.settings),
              title: Text('Settings'),
            ),
          ],
        ),
      ),
    );
  }
}
```

Working with Long Lists

When we want to display a very long list on a single screen of your app, the above way for displaying the lists is not ideal. To work with a list with a high number of elements, we must utilize the ListView.builder() constructor. The primary distinction between ListView and ListView.builder is that ListView creates all items at once, whereas ListView.builder() creates things as they are scrolled into the screen.

Example:

```dart
import 'package:flutter/material.dart';
void main() {
  runApp(MyApp(
    products: List<String>.generate(600, (x) =>
"Product List: $x"),
  ));
}
class App extends StatelessWidget {
  final List<String> products;
  App({Key key, @required this.products}) :
super(key: key);
  @override
  Widget build(BuildContext context) {
    final appTitle = 'Long-List Demo';
    return MaterialApp(
      title: appTitle,
      home: Scaffold(
        appBar: AppBar(
          title: Text(appTitle),
        ),
        body: ListView.builder(
          itemCount: products.length,
          itemBuilder: (context, index) {
            return ListTile(
              title: Text('${products[index]}'),
            );
          },
        ),
      ),
    );
  }
}
```

Creating Grid Lists

We sometimes want to display the items in a grid layout rather than the standard list that appears one after the other. A GridView widget in Flutter lets us construct a grid list. The GridView.count() constructor, which provides the number of rows and columns in a grid, is the easiest method to create a grid.

Example:

```
import 'package:flutter/material.dart';
void main() {runApp(App());}
class App extends StatelessWidget {
  @override
  Widget build(BuildContext context) {
    final appTitle = "Grid-List Demo";
    return MaterialApp(
        title: appTitle,
        home: Scaffold(appBar: AppBar(
          title: Text(appTitle),
        ),
            body: GridView.count(
                crossAxisCount: 3,
                children: List.generate(choices.
length, (index) {
                  return Center(
                    child: SelectCard(choice:
choices[index]),
                  );
                }
                )
            )
        )
    );
  }
}

class Choices {
  const Choices({this.title, this.icon});
  final String title;
  final IconData icon;
}
```

```
const List<Choices> choice = const <Choice>[
  const Choices(title: 'Home', icon: Icons.home),
  const Choices(title: 'Contact', icon: Icons.
contacts),
  const Choices(title: 'Map', icon: Icons.map),
  const Choices(title: 'Phone', icon: Icons.
phone),
  const Choices(title: 'Camera', icon: Icons.
camera_alt),
  const Choices(title: 'Setting', icon: Icons.
settings),
  const Choices(title: 'Album', icon: Icons.
photo_album),
  const Choices(title: 'WiFi', icon: Icons.wifi),
  const Choices(title: 'GPS', icon: Icons.
gps_fixed),
];
class SelectCard extends StatelessWidget {
  const SelectCard({Key key, this.choice}) :
super(key: key);
  final Choices choice;
  @override
  Widget build(BuildContext context) {
    final TextStyle textStyle = Theme.of(context).
textTheme.display1;
    return Card(
        color: Colors.lightYellowAccent,
        child: Center(child: Column(
            mainAxisSize: MainAxisSize.min,
            crossAxisAlignment:
CrossAxisAlignment.center,
            children: <Widget>[
              Expanded(child: Icon(choice.icon,
size:53.0, color: textStyle.color)),
              Text(choice.title, style:
textStyle),
            ]
        ),
        )
    );
  }
}
```

Creating a Horizontal List

Horizontal lists are also supported via the ListView widget. Sometimes we want to make a list that can scroll horizontally instead of vertically. In this situation, ListView gives the horizontal scrollDirection, taking precedence over the vertical direction.

Example:

```
import 'package:flutter/material.dart';
void main() => runApp(App());
class App extends StatelessWidget {
  @override
  Widget build(BuildContext context) {
    final title = 'Horizontal Demo List';
    return MaterialApp(
      title: title,
      home: Scaffold(
        appBar: AppBar(
          title: Text(title),
        ),
        body: Container(
          margin: EdgeInsets.symmetric(vertical:
25.0),
          height: 160.0,
          child: ListView(
            scrollDirection: Axis.horizontal,
            children: <Widget>[
              Container(
                width: 160.0,
                color: Colors.red,
                child: new Stack(
                  children: <Widget>[
                    ListTile(
                      leading: Icon(Icons.home),
                      title: Text('Home'),
                    ),
                  ],
                ),
              ),
              Container(
                width: 149.0,
```

```
                        color: Colors.yellow,
                        child: new Stack(
                          children: <Widget>[
                            ListTile(
                              leading: Icon(Icons.
camera_alt),

                              title: Text('Camera'),
                            ),
                          ],
                        ),
                      ),
                      Container(
                        width: 149.0,
                        color: Colors.yellow,
                        child: new Stack(
                          children: <Widget>[
                            ListTile(
                              leading: Icon(Icons.phone),
                              title: Text('Phoneno'),
                            ),
                          ],
                        ),
                      ),
                      Container(
                        width: 149.0,
                        color: Colors.green,
                        child: new Stack(
                          children: <Widget>[
                            ListTile(
                              leading: Icon(Icons.map),
                              title: Text('Map'),
                            ),
                          ],
                        ),
                      ),
                      Container(
                        width: 198.0,
                        color: Colors.grey,
                        child: new Stack(
                          children: <Widget>[
                            ListTile(
                              leading: Icon(Icons.settings),
```

```
                        title: Text('Setting'),
                    ),
                ],
            ),
          ),
        ],
      ),
    ),
  ),
),
);
}
}
```

FLUTTER TOAST NOTIFICATION

A Toast Notification message is another name for Flutter Toast. At the bottom of the device's screen, a message appears. It will vanish on its own when the developers' time limit has expired. A developer often used a toast notification to provide feedback on a user's action.

The ability to display a toast notification message is a must-have feature in Android applications. We can accomplish this with a few lines of code. In this part, we'll look at displaying toast messages on Android and iOS using Flutter. To provide toast notification, we must first import the fluttertoast library into Flutter.

To display toast notifications in Flutter, perform the following steps:

- Construct a Flutter Project.

- Flutter Toast Dependencies should add to the project.

- In the library, add the fluttertoast dart package.

- In Flutter, implement the code for displaying a toast message.

Property	Description
Msg	String(Required)
Toastlength	Toast.LENGTH_SHORT or Toast.LENGTH_LONG
Gravity	ToastGravity.TOP or ToastGravity.CENTER or ToastGravity.BOTTOM
timeInSecForIos	It is used only for the Ios (1 sec or more)
backgroundColor	It specifies background color.
textColor	It specifies the text color.
fontSize	It specifies font size of the notification message.

FlutterToast.cancel()

This function is used to cancel all requests to display messages to the user.

Let's have a look at how we can display toast notifications in the Flutter app using the following steps:

- **Step 1:** In the IDE, create a Flutter project. We are going to utilize Android Studio in this case.

- **Step 2:** In Android Studio, open the project and browse to the lib folder. Open the pubspec.yaml file in this folder. Add the flutter toast library to the dependencies area and then click on the get package link to import the library into our main.dart file.

```
pubspec.yaml
dependencies:
  flutter:
    sdk: Flutter
  cupertino_icons: ^0.1.2
  fluttertoast: ^3.1.0
```

It guarantees that you have left two spaces off the left side of a flutter-toast dependency when adding dependencies. The fluttertoast requirement makes it possible to display toast notifications straightforwardly. It also allows us to alter the appearance of the toast popup easily.

- **Step 3:** Open the main.dart file and add a toast notification to the widget using the following code provided.

```
Fluttertoast.showToast(
        msg: 'This is a toast notification',
        toastLength: Toast.LENGTH_SHORT,
        gravity: ToastGravity.BOTTOM,
        timeInSecForIos: 2,
        backgroundColor: Colors.blue,
        textColor: Colors.red
    );
```

Let's look at the whole code for the preceding phases. Replace the following code in the main.dart file. This code has a button, and when we push it, the toast message is shown by executing FlutterToast. showToast.

```
import 'package:flutter/material.dart';
import 'package:fluttertoast/fluttertoast.dart';
```

```dart
class ToastExample extends StatefulWidget {
  @override
  _ToastExampleState createState() {
    return _ToastExampleState();
  }
}

class _ToastExampleState extends State {
  void showToast() {
    Fluttertoast.showToast(
        msg: 'This is a toast notification',
        toastLength: Toast.LENGTH_SHORT,
        gravity: ToastGravity.BOTTOM,
        timeInSecForIos: 2,
        backgroundColor: Colors.blue,
        textColor: Colors.grey
    );
  }
  @override
  Widget build(BuildContext context) {
    return MaterialApp(
      title: 'Toast-Notification Example',
      home: Scaffold(
          appBar: AppBar(
            title: Text('Toast-Notification
Example'),
          ),
          body: Padding(
            padding: EdgeInsets.all(14.0),
            child: Center(
              child: RaisedButton(
                child: Text('click-to-show'),
                onPressed: showToast,
              ),
            ),
          )
      ),
    );
  }
}

void main() => runApp(ToastExample());
```

CHECKBOX IN FLUTTER

A checkbox is an input component that stores a Boolean value. It is a graphical UI element that lets the user to pick numerous alternatives from a list of possibilities. A user can simply provide a yes or no answer in this case. A checked/marked checkbox indicates yes, whereas an unmarked/unchecked checkbox indicates no value. Checkboxes are often represented as a square box with white space or a tick mark on the screen. The significance of the checkboxes was described by a label or caption that corresponded to each checkbox.

This section looks at how to use checkboxes in Flutter. There are two sorts of checkboxes in Flutter: a tiny form of the Checkbox called "checkbox" and the "CheckboxListTile" checkbox, which includes a header and a subtitle. The following are extensive explanations of these checkboxes:

Checkbox

Attributes	Descriptions
Value	It is utilized regardless of whether the checkbox is ticked or not.
onChanged	When the value is modified, it will be called.
Tristate	By default, it is false. It can also have a value of true, false, or null.
activeColor	It provided the color of the checkbox that was chosen.
checkColor	When they are selected, it specifies the color of the check icon.
materialTapTargetSize	It's used to set the size of the tap target.

Example:

```
Checkbox(
  value: this.showvalue,
  onChanged: (bool value) {
    setState(() {
      this.showvalue = value;
    });
  },
),
```

Let's write the entire code to see how a checkbox appears in Flutter. To begin, create a project in Android Studio, open the main.dart file, and replace the following code:

```dart
import 'package:flutter/material.dart';

void main() {
  runApp(MaterialApp( home: MyHomePage(),));
}
class HomePage extends StatefulWidget {
  @override
  _HomePageState createState() => _HomePageState();
}
class _HomePageState extends State<HomePage> {
  bool valuefirst = false;
  bool valuesecond = false;
  @override
  Widget build(BuildContext context) {
    return MaterialApp(
      home: Scaffold(
        appBar: AppBar(title: Text('Checkbox
Example'),),
        body: Container(
          child: Column(
            children: <Widget>[
              Row(
                children: <Widget>[
                  SizedBox(width: 13,),
                  Text('Checkbox without Header and
Subtitle: ',style: TextStyle(fontSize: 18.0), ),
                  Checkbox(
                    checkColor: Colors.yellowAccent,
                    activeColor: Colors.blue,
                    value: this.valuefirst,
                    onChanged: (bool value) {
                      setState(() {
                        this.valuefirst = value;
                      });
                    },
                  ),
                  Checkbox(
                    value: this.valuesecond,
```

```
                    onChanged: (bool value) {
                      setState(() {
                        this.valuesecond = value;
                      });
                    },
                  ),
                ],
              ),
            ],
          )
        ),
      ),
    );
  }
}
```

FLUTTER RADIO BUTTON

A radio button, often known as an options button, is a button that contains a Boolean value. It lets the user select only one choice from a group of possibilities. This distinguishes it from a checkbox, where we can pick more than one choice, and the unselected state is restored. The radio buttons can be arranged in groups of two or more and displayed as circular holes with white space (for unselected) or as a dot (for selected). We may additionally include a label for each related radio button that describes the option represented by the radio button. A radio button may select by clicking the mouse on the circular hole or using a keyboard shortcut.

This part explains how to utilize radio buttons in Flutter. With the aid of "Radio," "RadioListTile," or "ListTitle" Widgets, we may use radio buttons in Flutter.

The flutter radio button does not keep any state. When choosing a radio button, the onChanged callback is called, and the value is sent as a parameter. The radio option will be selected if the value and groupValue match.

- **Step 1:** In the IDE, create a Flutter project. We are going to utilize Android Studio in this case.

- **Step 2:** In Android Studio, open the project and browse to the lib folder. Open the main.dart file in this folder and build a RadioButtonWidget class (MyStatefulWidget). The Column widget will be created next, along with three RadioListTile components. We will also construct a Text widget to display the selected item. The characteristics of the ListTitle are as follows:

- **groupValue:** It specifies the presently chosen item for the radio button group.

- **title:** It is used to set the label for the radio button.

- **value:** It defines the backhand value, represented as a radio button.

- **onChanged:** This function is invoked whenever the user selects a radio button.

```
ListTile(
    title: const Text('www.google.com'),
    leading: Radio(
      value: BestTutor.dartpoint,
      groupValue: _site,
      onChanged: (BestTutorSite value) {
        setState(() {
          _site = value;
        });
      },
    ),
  ),
```

Let's look at the whole code for the preceding phases. Replace the following code in the main.dart file.

The Radio widgets are wrapped in ListTiles in this case, and the currently chosen text is provided into groupValue and kept by the example's State. The first Radio button will deselect because _site is set to BestTutorSite. dartpoint. If the second radio button is hit, setState is used to alter the example's State, changing _site to BestTutorSite.w3schools. It rebuilds the button with the new groupValue and selects the second button.

```
import 'package:flutter/material.dart';
void main() => runApp(App());
/// This Widget is the main application widget.
class App extends StatelessWidget {
  static const String _title = 'Radio-Button-Example';
  @override
```

```
Widget build(BuildContext context) {
  return MaterialApp(
    title: _title,
    home: Scaffold(
      appBar: AppBar(title: const Text(_title)),
      body: Center(
        child: MyStatefulWidget(),
      ),
    ),
  );
}
}
enum BestTutorSite { dartpoint, w3school,
tutorialpoint }
class MyStatefulWidget extends StatefulWidget {
  MyStatefulWidget({Key key}) : super(key: key);
  @override
  _MyStatefulWidgetState createState() =>
_MyStatefulWidgetState();
}
class _MyStatefulWidgetState extends
State<MyStatefulWidget> {
  BestTutorSite _site = BestTutorSite.dartpoint;
  Widget build(BuildContext context) {
    return Column(
      children: <Widget>[
        ListTile(
          title: const Text('www.dartpoint.com'),
          leading: Radio(
            value: BestTutorSite.dartpoint,
            groupValue: _site,
            onChanged: (BestTutorSite value) {
              setState(() {
                _site = value;
              });
            },
          ),
        ),
        ListTile(
          title: const Text('www.w3school.com'),
          leading: Radio(
            value: BestTutorSite.w3school,
```

```
          groupValue: _site,
          onChanged: (BestTutorSite value) {
            setState(() {
              _site = value;
            });
          },
        ),
      ),
      ListTile(
        title: const Text('www.tutorialpoint.com'),
        leading: Radio(
          value: BestTutorSite.tutorialpoint,
          groupValue: _site,
          onChanged: (BestTutorSite value) {
            setState(() {
              _site = value;
            });
          },
        ),
      ),
    ],
  );
}
}
```

PROGRESS BAR IN FLUTTER

It is a graphical control element that displays the status of a task such as downloading, uploading, installing, or transferring files. In this part, we'll look at displaying a progress bar in a flutter application.

Flutter may display a progress bar by using the two widgets listed below:

- LinearProgressIndicator

- CircularProgressIndicator

LinearProgressIndicator

The linear progress bar displays the task's progress in a horizontal line.

Flutter primarily provides two sorts of linear progress indicators:

1. **Determinate:** The Determinate progress bar shows the real amount of progress made at each assignment stage. Its value will rise monotonically from 0.0 to 1.0 to reflect the quantity of work accomplished

at the moment. To create a deterministic progress indicator, we must utilize a non-null number ranging from 0.0 to 1.0.

2. **Indeterminate:** An indeterminate progress bar does not reflect how far you are along in finishing the activity. It suggests we don't know when the work will complete. It makes progress without expressing how far it has come. Using a null value, we may create an indeterminate progress indication.

The following are the most prevalent characteristics of a linear progress indicator:

- **double value:** It is used to indicate a non-null number between 0.0 and 1.0, representing the completion of task progress.

- **Color BackgroundColor:** This property is used to specify the color of the widget's background.
  <Color> value for animation

- **Color:** As an animated value, it is used to determine the color of the progress indication.
  Example: The code demonstrates the usage of an indeterminate linear progress bar to display a download where we do not know when it will complete. A floating button is utilized to change the status from not downloading to downloading. It displays a text when there is no downloading; otherwise, it displays the progress indicator.

```
import 'package:flutter/material.dart';
void main() => runApp(App());
class App extends StatelessWidget {
  @override
  Widget build(BuildContext context) {
    return MaterialApp(
      home: LinearProgressIndicatorApp(),
    );
  }
}
class LinearProgressIndicatorApp extends
StatefulWidget {
  @override
```

```
  State<StatefulWidget> createState() {
    return LinearProgressIndicatorAppState();
  }
}
class LinearProgressIndicatorAppState extends Stat
e<LinearProgressIndicatorApp> {
  bool _loading;
  @override
  void initState() {
    super.initState();
    _loading = false;
  }

  @override
  Widget build(BuildContext context) {
    return Scaffold(
      appBar: AppBar(
        title: Text("Linear Progress Bar"),
      ),
      body: Center(
        child: Container(
          padding: EdgeInsets.all(14.0),
          child: _loading?
LinearProgressIndicator() : Text(
                "Press button for downloading",
                style: TextStyle(fontSize: 29)),
          ),
        ),
        floatingActionButton: FloatingActionButton(
          onPressed: () {
            setState(() {
              _loading = !_loading;
            });
          },
          tooltip: 'Download',
          child: Icon(Icons.cloud_download),
        ),
      );
  }
}
```

Sometimes we want to create a fixed progress bar that shows how long it will take to complete the task. In such instance, we can simulate a download that will take some time to complete the task and update the LinearProgressIndicator value as follows:

```
import 'dart:async';
import 'package:flutter/material.dart';
void main() => runApp(App());
class App extends StatelessWidget {
  @override
  Widget build(BuildContext context) {
    return MaterialApp(
      home: LinearProgressIndicatorApp(),
    );
  }
}
class LinearProgressIndicatorApp extends
StatefulWidget {
  @override
  State<StatefulWidget> createState() {
    return LinearProgressIndicatorAppState();
  }
}
class LinearProgressIndicatorAppState extends Stat
e<LinearProgressIndicatorApp> {
  bool _loading;
  double _progressValue;
  @override
  void initState() {
    super.initState();
    _loading = false;
    _progressValue = 0.1;
  }
  @override
  Widget build(BuildContext context) {
    return Scaffold(
      appBar: AppBar(
        title: Text("Linear Progress Bar"),
      ),
      body: Center(
        child: Container(
```

```
                padding: EdgeInsets.all(14.0),
                child: _loading
?                       Column(
                    mainAxisAlignment: MainAxisAlignment.
center,
                    children: <Widget>[
                      LinearProgressIndicator(
                        backgroundColor: Colors.
cyanAccent,
                        valueColor: new AlwaysStoppedAnima
tion<Color>(Colors.blue),
                        value: _progressValue,
                      ),
                      Text('${(_progressValue * 100).
round()}%'),
                    ],
                  )
                    : Text("Press button for
downloading", style: TextStyle(fontSize: 28)),
            ),
          ),
        floatingActionButton: FloatingActionButton(
          onPressed: () {
            setState(() {
              _loading = !_loading;
              _updateProgress();
            });
          },
          tooltip: 'Download',
          child: Icon(Icons.cloud_download),
        ),
      );
  }
  // this function updates progress value
  void _updateProgress() {
    const oneSec = const Duration(seconds: 3);
    new Timer.periodic(oneSec, (Timer t) {
      setState(() {
        _progressValue += 0.1;
        // we "finish" downloading here
        if (_progressValue.toStringAsFixed(1) ==
'1.0') {
```

```
                _loading = false;
                t.cancel();
                return;
            }
        });
    });
  }
}
```

CircularProgressIndicator

It is a spinning widget that indicates the waiting process in your application. It depicts the progress of a task in the form of a circle. It also shows the progress bar in two modes: determined and indeterminate.

We utilize a fixed progress bar when we wish to represent the status of ongoing tasks such as the percentage of downloading or uploading files. We may display the progress by entering a number between 0.0 and 1.0.

We utilize an indefinite progress bar when we don't want to know the proportion of a running process. CircularProgressIndicator displays an indefinite progress indicator by default.

In the following example, we will see the circular progress indicator in an indeterminate mode, which does not reflect the progress of any work. It repeatedly displays the circles, indicating that something is being worked out and that we must wait for its completion. There is no need to specify any value to the CircularProgressIndicator() constructor for this. Look at the following code:

```
import 'package:flutter/material.dart';
void main() => runApp(App());
class App extends StatelessWidget {
  @override
  Widget build(BuildContext context) {
    return MaterialApp(
      home: Scaffold(
        appBar: AppBar(
          title: Text('Progress Bar Example'),
        ),
        body: Center(
            child: CircularProgressIndicatorApp()
        ),
```

```
        ),
      );
  }
}


/// This is stateless widget that the main application
instantiates.
class CircularProgressIndicatorApp extends
StatelessWidget {
  @override
  Widget build(BuildContext context) {
    return CircularProgressIndicator(
      backgroundColor: Colors.blue,
      strokeWidth: 9,);
  }
}
```

FLUTTER SLIDER

In Flutter, a slider is a material design widget used to choose a range of values. An input widget allows us to specify a range of values by dragging or pushing on the desired position. In this post, we will demonstrate how to utilize the slider widget in Flutter to configure the range of values and how to alter the style of a slider.

We usually utilize the slider widget to change a value. As a result, the value must be stored in a variable. The slider class in this widget requires the onChanged() method. This function will be called anytime when the slider position is changed.

A slider can choose a value from a set of continuous or discrete values. It employs a continuous range of numbers by default. If we wish to use discrete values, we must supply a non-null value for divisions. This discrete division shows the number of discrete intervals. Before acquiring the value, we must first specify the minimum and maximum values. The slider has min and max parameters for set the minimum and maximum limits. For example, if we had a range of values ranging from 0.0 to 50.0 with divisions of 10, the slider would accept values such as 0.0, 10.0, 20.0, 30.0, 40.0, and 50.0.

Properties of Slider

There are just two mandatory arguments, and the others are optional.

Attributes	Type	Descriptions
Value	double	It is a mandatory input that specifies the current value of the slider.
onChanged	double	It is a necessary parameter that is called when the user drags the slider to a new value. The slider is disabled if it is null.
onChangedStart	double	It is an optional parameter called when we begin to choose a new value.
onChangedStart	double	A non-mandatory parameter is called whenever we have finished picking a new value for the slider.
Max	double	It is an optional input that specifies the maximum value the user may use. It is set to 1.0 by default. It must be more than or equal to the minimum.
Min	double	It is an optional input that specifies the smallest value that the user can use. It is set to 0.0 by default. It must be less than or equal to the maximum.
Divisions	int	It is responsible for determining the number of discrete divisions. If it is not present, the slider is continuous.
Label	string	It defines the text label that will appear above the slider. It shows the position of a separate slider.
activeColor	class Color	It determines the color of the slider track's active area.
inactiveColor	class Color	It determines the color of the slider track's inactive part.
SemanticFormatterCallback		A callback is used to generate a semantic value. It is set to a percentage by default.

Flutter's slider uses the following terms:

- **Thumb:** A circular object that glides horizontally when we adjust values by dragging.

- **Track:** This is a horizontal line down which we may glide our thumb.

- **Overlay:** While dragging, an overlay appears around the thumb.

- **Tick marks:** These are used to indicate the discrete values of a slider.

- **Value indicators:** When we define the labels, it will display the labels for the thumb values.

- **Active:** It is the side of the slider between the thumb and the minimum active value.

- **Inactive:** It is the side of the slider between the thumb and the maximum value that is inactive.

How Does the Slider Widget Work in Flutter?

Here's a simple example of how to use a slider widget in Flutter.

```
Slider(
      min: 0,
      max: 99,
      value: _value,
      onChanged: (value) {
        setState(() {
          _value = value;
        });
      },
    ),
```

With the aid of an example, let us understand how to utilize the slider in Flutter. The value was saved as an integer in the following code, which had to be converted to double when passed as a value parameter and then rounded to integer inside the onChanged function. We've also made the active section of the slider blue and the inactive portion orange.

```
import 'package:flutter/material.dart';
void main() => runApp(App());
// This Widget is main application widget.
class App extends StatelessWidget {
  @override
  Widget build(BuildContext context) {
    return MaterialApp(
      home: MySliderApp(),
    );
  }
```

```
}
class MySliderApp extends StatefulWidget {
  MySliderApp({Key key}) : super(key: key);
  @override
  _MySliderAppState createState() =>
_MySliderAppState();
}
class _MySliderAppState extends State<MySliderApp> {
  int _value =7;
  @override
  Widget build(BuildContext context) {
    return Scaffold(
      appBar: AppBar(
        title: Text('Slider Demo'),
        ),
        body: Padding(
          padding: EdgeInsets.all(16.0),
            child: Center(
              child: Row(
                mainAxisAlignment:
MainAxisAlignment.spaceEvenly,
                mainAxisSize: MainAxisSize.max,
                children: [
                  Icon(
                    Icons.volume_up,
                    size: 44,
                  ),
                  new Expanded(
                    child: Slider(
                      value: _value.toDouble(),
                      min: 1.0,
                      max: 22.0,
                      divisions: 10,
                      activeColor: Colors.blue,
                      inactiveColor: Colors.
yellow,
                      label: 'Set volume value',
                      onChanged: (double
newValue) {
                        setState(() {
                          _value = newValue.
round();
```

```
                                   });
                                 },

semanticFormatterCallback: (double newValue) {
                                 return '${newValue.
round()} dollars';
                               }
                             )
                           ),
                         ]
                       )
                     ),
                   )
                 );
             }
}
```

FLUTTER SWITCH

A switch is a two-state UI element that allows you to toggle between the ON (Checked) and OFF (Unchecked) states. Typically, a button with a thumb slider allows the user to move back and forth to select an ON or OFF choice. It works in the same way as a house's electrical switches.

In Flutter, a switch is a widget that allows you to choose between two options: ON or OFF. It does not keep the condition alive. It will use the onChanged property to keep the states updated. If the value returned by this property is true, the switch is ON; otherwise, it is false. When this attribute is set to null, the switch widget is turned off. This post will learn how to use a switch widget in a Flutter application.

Properties of the Switch Widget

The following are some of the most essential characteristics of a switch widget:

Attributes	Descriptions
onChanged	It will be triggered anytime the user presses the switch.
Value	It has a Boolean value of true or false that controls whether the switch functionality is ON or OFF.
activeColor	It specifies the color of the switch round ball when it is turned on.

(Continued)

Attributes	Descriptions
activeTrackColor	It determines the color of the switch track bar.
inactiveThubmColor	It specifies the color of the switch round ball when it is turned off.
inactiveTrackColor	When the switch is turned off, it defines the color of the switch track bar.
dragStartBehavior	It deals with the drag start behavior. When we set it to DragStartBehavior.start, the drag changes the state of the switch from ON to OFF.

Example: We have defined a switch widget in this application. When we toggle the switch widget, the onChanged property is called with the switch's new state as the value. As shown in the following code, we have defined a Boolean variable is Switched to hold the switch status.

Create a Flutter application in the IDE you're using. Then, in the lib folder, replace main.dart with the following code:

```
import 'package:flutter/material.dart';
void main() => runApp(App());
class App extends StatelessWidget {
  @override
  Widget build(BuildContext context) {
    return MaterialApp(
        home: Scaffold(
            appBar: AppBar(
              backgroundColor: Colors.red
              title: Text("Switch Example"),
            ),
            body: Center(
                child: SwitchScreen()
            ),
        )
    );
  }
}
class SwitchScreen extends StatefulWidget {
  @override
  SwitchClass createState() => new SwitchClass();
}
```

```
class SwitchClass extends State {
  bool isSwitched = false;
  var textValue = 'Switch is OFF';
  void toggleSwitch(bool value) {
    if(isSwitched == false)
    {
      setState(() {
        isSwitched = true;
        textValue = 'Switch Button ON';
      });
      print('Switch Button ON');
    }
    else
    {
      setState(() {
        isSwitched = false;
        textValue = 'Switch Button OFF';
      });
      print('Switch Button OFF');
    }
  }
  @override
  Widget build(BuildContext context) {
    return Column(
        mainAxisAlignment: MainAxisAlignment.left,
        children:[ Transform.scale(
            scale: 2,
            child: Switch(
              onChanged: toggleSwitch,
              value: isSwitched,
              activeColor: Colors.blue,
              activeTrackColor: Colors.green,
              inactiveThumbColor: Colors.redAccent,
              inactiveTrackColor: Colors.yellow,
            )
          ),
          Text('$textValue', style:
TextStyle(fontSize: 22),)
        ]);
  }
}
```

CHARTS IN FLUTTER

A chart is a graphical depiction of data that uses symbols such as a line, bar, pie, and so on to represent the data. The chart operates just like a standard chart in Flutter. In Flutter, we use a chart to convey the data in a graphical format that helps the user to grasp it quickly. We may also draw a graph to show the rise and fall of our values. The graphic makes it simple to understand the data and allows us to see the results monthly or yearly whenever we need it.

Flutter Supported Chart Types

Flutter primarily supports three types of charts, each with several configuration options. The chart utilized in the Flutter application is as follows:

- Line Chart
- Bar Chart
- Pie and Donut Chart

Line Chart

It is a graph that connects individual data points with lines. It displays the information as a sequence of data points. It is mainly used to track changes across short and extended periods.

Example:

```
LineChart(
  LineChartData(
    // write logic
  ),
);
```

Bar Chart

It is a graph that uses rectangular bars to represent categorical data. It can be both horizontal and vertical.

Example:

```
BarChart(
  BarChartData(
    // write logic
  ),
);
```

Pie or Donut Chart

It is a graph that presents information in the shape of a circular graph. The circle in this graph is divided into sectors, each displaying percentage or proportional data.

Example:

```
PieChart(
  PieChartData(
    // write logic
  ),
);
```

Let's look at an example to help us understand.

For instance, open the IDE and start a new Flutter project. After that, open the project, go to the lib folder, and open the pubspec.yaml file. We must include the chart dependence in this file. Flutter has numerous chart dependencies, and we will utilize the fl_chart dependence in this example. As a result, add it as follows:

```
dependencies:
  flutter:
    sdk: Flutter
  fl_chart: ^0.10.1
```

After we've added the dependency, click the get packages link in the top left corner of the screen. Now, open the main.dart file and replace the following code:

```
import 'package:flutter/material.dart';
import 'package:fl_chart/fl_chart.dart';
void main() => runApp(App());
/// This Widget is main application widget.
class App extends StatelessWidget {
  @override
  Widget build(BuildContext context) {
    return MaterialApp(
      home: HomePage(),
    );
  }
}
```

```
class HomePage extends StatelessWidget {
  @override
  Widget build(BuildContext context) {
    return Scaffold(
      appBar: AppBar(
        title: const Text('Chart Example'),
          backgroundColor: Colors.yellow
      ),
      body: Center(
        child: Column(
          mainAxisAlignment: MainAxisAlignment.center,
          children: <Widget>[
            LineCharts(),
            Padding(
              padding: const EdgeInsets.all(17.0),
              child: Text(
                "Traffic Source Chart",
                  style: TextStyle(
                      fontSize: 22,
                      color: Colors.grey,
                      fontWeight: FontWeight.w710,
                      fontStyle: FontStyle.italic
                  )
              )
            ),
          ],
        ),
      ),
    );
  }
}

class LineCharts extends StatelessWidget {
  @override
  Widget build(BuildContext context) {
    const cutOffYValue = 0.0;
    const yearTextStyle =
    TextStyle(fontSize: 13, color: Colors.white);
    return SizedBox(
      width: 370,
      height: 290,
      child: LineChart(
```

```
        LineChartData(
          lineTouchData: LineTouchData(enabled:
false),
          lineBarsData: [
            LineChartBarData(
              spots: [
                FlSpot(0, 2),
                FlSpot(1, 2),
                FlSpot(2, 4),
                FlSpot(3, 5),
                FlSpot(2, 5),
                FlSpot(4, 3)
              ],
              isCurved: true,
              barWidth: 2,
              colors: [
                Colors.black,
              ],
              belowBarData: BarAreaData(
                show: true,
                colors: [Colors.lightred.
withOpacity(0.5)],
                cutOffY: cutOffYValue,
                applyCutOffY: true,
              ),
              aboveBarData: BarAreaData(
                show: true,
                colors: [Colors.lightYellow.
withOpacity(0.5)],
                cutOffY: cutOffYValue,
                applyCutOffY: true,
              ),
              dotData: FlDotData(
                show: false,
              ),
            ),
          ],
          minY: 0,
          titlesData: FlTitlesData(
            bottomTitles: SideTitles(
                showTitles: true,
                reservedSize: 5,
```

```
                  textStyle: yearTextStyle,
                  getTitles: (value) {
                    switch (value.toInt()) {
                      case 0:
                        return '2018';
                      case 1:
                        return '2019';
                      case 2:
                        return '2020';
                      case 3:
                        return '2021';
                      case 4:
                        return '2022';
                      default:
                        return '';
                  }
                }),
            leftTitles: SideTitles(
              showTitles: true,
              getTitles: (value) {
                return '\$ ${value + 100}';
              },
            ),
          ),
        axisTitleData: FlAxisTitleData(
              leftTitle: AxisTitle(showTitle: true,
titleText: 'Value', margin: 12),
              bottomTitle: AxisTitle(
                  showTitle: true,
                  margin: 12,
                  titleText: 'Year',
                  textStyle: yearTextStyle,
                  textAlign: TextAlign.left)),
        gridData: FlGridData(
            show: true,
            checkToShowHorizontalLine: (double value)
{
                return value == 1 || value == 2 || value
== 3 || value == 4;
            },
          ),
        ),
```

```
    ),
  );
 }
}
```

FLUTTER TABLE

A table enables the user to organize data into rows and columns. It is used to store and present our data in an organized fashion, allowing us to compare pairs of related variables readily.

Flutter also lets the user design a table layout in the mobile application. In Flutter, we may make a table by utilizing the Table widget, which employs the table layout method for its children. This widget contains numerous settings to improve or adjust the table arrangement. These are the properties: border, children, columnWidths, textDirection, textBaseline, etc.

What Happens When We Utilize the Table Widget?

We may use a table widget to store numerous rows with the same column width and each column (table) has equal data. Flutter offers a different solution to the same problem by utilizing the GridView widget.

To make a table, we'll need the following items:

- First, insert a Table widget inside the body.

- Following that, we must include TableRow(s) in the table widget's children. Because the table widget contains several rows, we use children rather than the child.

- Finally, we must include TableCell(s) as children of the TableRow widget. We may now write any widget in this location such as a Text widget.

```
TableRow(children: [
  TableCell(child: Text('dartpoint')),
  TableCell(
    child: Text('Flutter App'),
  ),
  TableCell(child: Text('Android App')),
  TableCell(child: Text('My-SQL')),
]),
```

We must follow the following requirements while utilizing this widget:

- This widget determined the column width, which is evenly shared amongst TableCells. If it is not equal, we will receive an error message stating that every TableRow in a table must have the same number of children for every column to be filled. Otherwise, the table will have holes in it.

- Each row has the same height, equals to the tallest TableCell.

- A table's children can only have TableRow widgets.

Let us attempt to explain it with the aid of an example presented below, in which we will try to cover everything relevant to this widget:

```
import 'package:flutter/material.dart';
void main() {runApp(App());}
class App extends StatefulWidget {
  @override
  _TableExample createState() => _TableExample();
}
class _TableExample extends State<MyApp> {
  @override
  Widget build(BuildContext context) {
    return MaterialApp(
      home: Scaffold(
          appBar: AppBar(
            title: Text('Table Example'),
          ),
          body: Center(
              child: Column(children: <Widget>[
                Container(
                  margin: EdgeInsets.all(22),
                  child: Table(
                    defaultColumnWidth:
FixedColumnWidth(130.0),
                      border: TableBorder.all(
                          color: Colors.yellow,
                          style: BorderStyle.solid,
                          width: 3),
                      children: [
                        TableRow( children: [
                        Column(children: [Text('Webs
ite', style: TextStyle(fontSize: 21.0))]),
```

```
                            Column(children:[Text('Tutor
ial', style: TextStyle(fontSize: 21.0))]),

Column(children:[Text('Review', style:
TextStyle(fontSize: 21.0))]),
                    ]),
                    TableRow( children: [

Column(children:[Text('Javapoint')]),
                        Column(children:[Text('Flut
ter')]),
                        Column(children:[Text('5*')]),
                    ]),
                    TableRow( children: [

Column(children:[Text('Dartpoint')]),

Column(children:[Text('My-SQL')]),
                        Column(children:[Text('5*')]),
                    ]),
                    TableRow( children: [

Column(children:[Text('Dartpoint')]),
                        Column(children:[Text('Flut
ter')]),
                        Column(children:[Text('5*')]),
                    ]),
                  ],
                ),
              ),
            ])
        )),
      );
  }
}
```

FLUTTER CALENDAR

It is a system for organizing days, weeks, or months for business, religious, social, or administrative purposes. It maintains track of which events occur on which dates and when the special events occur. This part goes through how to show and use the calendar widget in our Flutter app.

Flutter provides a simple widget called table calendar to display the calendar in our app. The table calendar is very customizable and has many features like gesture, animation, and numerous formats.

The table calendar has several characteristics, which are listed below:

- API is simple to use.

- Custom Builders are available for UI control.

- Vertical auto-sizing is available.

- It has lovely animations.

- It is capable of handling gestures.

- It supports various calendar formats, including month, week, year, and so on.

- We can also utilize several weekday forms.

Let's go over how to make and show a calendar step by step.

- **Step 1:** In the IDE you're using, create a new Flutter project and name it Flutter Calendar Example.

- **Step 2:** Run the project, browse the lib folder, and double-click the pubspec.yaml file. The table calendar dependent must be added to this file as follows:

```
dependencies:
  flutter:
    sdk: Flutter
  table_calendar: ^2.1.0
```

- **Step 3:** After adding the dependency above, we must execute the following command to obtain the necessary packages:

```
$ flutter pub get
```

- **Step 4:** Next, in the dart file, import the dependency as follows:

```
import 'package:syncfusion_flutter_calendar/
calendar.dart';
```

- **Step 5:** Next, we need to create a calendar controller and set the calendar to CalendarController.

```
CalendarController _controller;
@override
void initState() {
  super.initState();
  _controller = CalendarController();
}
```

- **Step 6:** The calendar widget must now be added as a child of any widget. Here, we'll make the calendar widget a child of the scaffold widget.

```
@override
Widget build(BuildContext context) {
  return Scaffold(
    body: SingleChildScrollView(
      child: Column(
        children: <Widget>[
          TableCalendar()
        ],
      ),
    ),
  );
```

- **Step 7:** We can now write our logic and style the calendar to display it.

Example:

```
import 'package:flutter/material.dart';
import 'package:table_calendar/table_calendar.
dart';
void main() => runApp(App());
class App extends StatelessWidget {
  @override
  Widget build(BuildContext context) {
    return MaterialApp(
      theme: ThemeData(
        primarySwatch: Colors.yellow,
      ),
```

```dart
      home: HomeCalendarPage(),
    );
  }
}
class HomeCalendarPage extends StatefulWidget {
  @override
  _HomeCalendarPageState createState() =>
_HomeCalendarPageState();
}
class _HomeCalendarPageState extends
State<HomeCalendarPage> {
  CalendarController _controller;
  @override
  void initState() {
    super.initState();
    _controller = CalendarController();
  }

  @override
  Widget build(BuildContext context) {
    return Scaffold(
      appBar: AppBar(
        title: Text('Flutter Calendar Example'),
      ),
      body: SingleChildScrollView(
        child: Column(
          crossAxisAlignment: CrossAxisAlignment.
start,
          children: <Widget>[
            TableCalendar(
              initialCalendarFormat:
CalendarFormat.month,
              calendarStyle: CalendarStyle(
                todayColor: Colors.green,
                selectedColor: Theme.
of(context).primaryColor,
                todayStyle: TextStyle(
                  fontWeight: FontWeight.bold,
                  fontSize: 23.0,
                  color: Colors.grey)
              ),
```

```
                    headerStyle: HeaderStyle(
                      centerHeaderTitle: true,
                      formatButtonDecoration:
BoxDecoration(
                        color: Colors.brown,
                        borderRadius: BorderRadius.
circular(23.0),
                      ),
                      formatButtonTextStyle:
TextStyle(color: Colors.red),
                      formatButtonShowsNext: false,
                    ),
                    startingDayOfWeek:
StartingDayOfWeek.monday,
                    onDaySelected: (date, events) {
                      print(date.toUtc());
                    },
                    builders: CalendarBuilders(
                      selectedDayBuilder: (context,
date, events) => Container(
                        margin: const EdgeInsets.
all(6.0),
                        alignment: Alignment.center,
                        decoration: BoxDecoration(
                          color: Theme.of(context).
primaryColor,
                          borderRadius:
BorderRadius.circular(9.0)),
                        child: Text(
                          date.day.toString(),
                          style: TextStyle(color:
Colors.black),
                        )),
                      todayDayBuilder: (context, date,
events) => Container(
                        margin: const EdgeInsets.
all(6.0),
                        alignment: Alignment.center,
                        decoration: BoxDecoration(
                          color: Colors.blue,
                          borderRadius:
BorderRadius.circular(9.0)),
```

```
                      child: Text(
                        date.day.toString(),
                        style: TextStyle(color:
Colors.yellow),
                      )),
                  ),
                calendarController: _controller,
              )
            ],
          ),
        ),
      );
    }
}
```

CHAPTER SUMMARY

This chapter covered Flutter widgets, where we discussed layouts, gestures, state management, and Flutter IDE. Moreover, we covered icons, buttons, calendar, lists, checkboxes, and tables.

Appraisal

Flutter is a free and open-source mobile user interface (UI) framework released in May 2017. It enables us to create a native mobile application with a single codebase. This means that we can design two different apps using a single programming language and codebase (for iOS and Android).

Flutter is made up of two major components:

- **A Software Development Kit (SDK):** A collection of tools that will assist us in developing our apps. This comprises compilers and tools for compiling our code into native machine code (iOS and Android).

- **A framework (a widget-based UI library):** A set of reusable UI components (buttons, text inputs, sliders, and so on) that we may customize to meet our specific needs.

Dart is a programming language that is used to create Flutter applications. Google invented the language in October 2011, although it has evolved significantly over the years.

Dart is a front-end development language that may use to construct mobile and online apps.

Dart is a typed object programming language that we should be familiar with if we know some programming. Dart's syntax is comparable to JavaScript's.

EASY TO UNDERSTAND AND IMPLEMENT

Flutter is a cutting-edge framework, and we can tell! It makes it much easier to design mobile applications. If we've used Java, Swift, or React Native, we'll see how different Flutter is.

DOI: 10.1201/9781003299363-6

A QUICK RUNDOWN: HIGHEST POSSIBLE OUTPUT

Thanks to Flutter, we may alter our code and view the consequences in real-time. It's known as Hot-Reload. It takes a few mere seconds after we save to update the program.

Significant changes necessitate reloading the app. However, if we conduct design work, for example, and modify the size of an element, it is done in real-time.

SUPPORTED BY ANDROID STUDIO AND VS CODE

Android Studio and VS Code support Flutter, and are available on a variety of IDEs. Android Studio (IntelliJ) and VS Code are the two primary code editors for creating with this technology.

Android Studio is a complete software package that includes everything. To begin, we must first download the Flutter and Dart plugins.

VS Code is a lightweight tool, and everything can be customized with plugins from the marketplace.

HOW DART STARTED

Dart was created by two Google engineers on October 10, 2011, at the GOTO conference, as a completely new programming language aimed to assist developers in constructing online apps. On November 14, 2013, Dart 1.0 was released.

And, as is usual in the IT industry, anything that comes from Google is met with enormous enthusiasm. The original Dart project has been in limbo from its start (because its developers initially wanted the Dartlang to replace JavaScript or act like CoffeeScript). But so much has changed in the interim years. Dart's primary focus has moved, and the language is now being used in many applications.

Dart is a highly versatile programming language in that it allows us to write code and then execute it anywhere without any restrictions.

Mobile apps created in Dart using Flutter are cross-platform native apps, which means they can operate on Android, iOS, and Windows (like React Native, Xamarin, etc.). We may even create web applications that run in any browser.

Open-source is popular among developers. The whole IT sector is smitten with open-source solutions. Dart earned the hearts of many developers worldwide by embracing the open-source environment from the beginning.

Dart appears to be a direct rival to Java, a proprietary language Google is now experiencing troubles with. In many aspects, Dart is a thousand times better than Java.

If there is an idea for the Dart SDK, you may develop it yourself or submit a proposal. We may report it right away or repair it ourselves if we find an issue. This is something that a proprietary language cannot accomplish.

It takes time, effort, and patience to learn a language. It's not just about learning the language but also understanding its ecosystem, terminology, acquiring the right tools and SDKs for the language, and then going to the popular frameworks and libraries. Despite having learned a plethora of popular languages such as C, Python, Javascript (including Typescript), Go, PHP, and so on.

To begin with, getting started with Dart is simple. We don't even need to install anything if we're trying it out. We enter the Dartpad URL into our browser.

The syntax is easy, the community is already fantastic, and more and more people are flocking to Dart. Also, because Dart is so compatible with JavaScript, more and more JavaScript developers are making the switch.

Dart offers a plethora of tooling support options. Dart is well supported by almost every primary text editor and IDE. We may use powerful IDEs such as Webstorm, IntelliJ IDEA, Android Studio, or basic editors such as VS Code, Sublime Text, VIM, Emacs, Atom, etc.

Dart is a powerful language. Google built it with the primary goal of using C-based Object-Oriented Programming languages such as C# and Java. It compiles quickly and is compact since it is also a general-purpose programming language.

There are advanced aspects in Flutter that we will go through one by one below.

NAVIGATION AND ROUTING

Navigation and routing are two fundamental elements in mobile applications that allow users to travel between various pages. We all know that every mobile application has many screens showing multiple sorts of information. An app, for example, may feature a screen with a variety of items; when the consumer taps on a certain item, complete information about that product is displayed immediately.

In Flutter, screens and pages are referred to as routes, which are just widgets. In Android, a route is analogous to an Activity, but in iOS, it is similar to a ViewController.

Navigating to various pages determines the workflow of any mobile app, and the method used to handle the navigation is known as routing. Flutter includes a basic routing class MaterialPageRoute and two methods Navigator.push() and Navigator.pop(), for navigating between two routes.

FLUTTER PACKAGES

A package is a namespace that holds a collection of classes, interfaces, and sub-packages that are all of the same kind. Packages are analogous to different directories on our computers, where we could have videos in one folder, photographs in another, software in another, and so on. Dart organizes and distributes a bundle of functionality in Flutter via a package. Flutter always supports shared packages provided to the Flutter and Dart ecosystem by other developers. The packages enable us to construct the app without starting from scratch.

The following is the general structure of the package (assume a demo package as mycustom package):

- **lib/src/*:** This directory includes private Dart code files.

- **lib/mydemo package.dart:** It is the primary Dart code file.

FLUTTER SPLASH SCREEN

It is a graphical control element that contains the image, logo, and current version of the software. It is also known as a launch screen, start screen, or boot screen. It is the app's initial screen that appears when the app is loaded. The app's welcome screen might also give a simple first experience when a mobile game or program is launched. The splash screen is just a display panel that allows users to look at something while loading applications to deliver to the user.

A splash screen often includes a firm name, logo, or title. The most popular type of splash screen is the Flutter logo when you launch the Flutter application or the Microsoft logo when launching the Microsoft operating system.

Splash Screen Features

The following are the critical splash screen characteristics:

- It is mainly used for application branding or identity identification, and it conveys the branding impression to users.

- It may also display some loading status indication while the hardware is loading to provide software to the user.

- When the splash screen finishes loading, the user is sent to another functional screen, such as the home screen or dashboard, and then forgotten. We can't return to the splash screen when the loading is finished since we can't use the back button.

FLUTTER GOOGLE MAPS

A map is used to obtain information about the world visibly and straightforwardly. It depicts world locations by displaying their shapes and sizes and their positions and distances from one another. Using the Google Maps Flutter plugin, we can include a map in our application. This plugin can automatically connect to Google Maps servers, display maps, and respond to user gestures. It also enables us to place marks on our map.

Why Should We Utilize Google Maps with Flutter?

Flutter developers use Google Maps because it provides native performance for both Android and iOS. It enables us to implement the code once and run it on both devices (Android and iOS). The Google Map widget includes a Google Maps Flutter plugin that supports initialCameraPosition, maptype, and onMapCreated. We can position the camera and marker anywhere on the earth. We may customize the marker to our liking. It also includes a zoom attribute in a camera position to enable zooming in Google Maps view on the first page.

FLUTTER SLIVERS

Sliver is a scrollable area section used to create a custom scrolling effect. Put another way; the sliver widget is a slice of the viewport. We can use slivers to implement all scrollable views such as ListView and GridView. It is a lower-level interface that gives you complete freedom to construct a scrollable area. It comes in handy when scrolling through a significant number of child widgets in a scrollable area. Because they are dependent on the viewport, they can alter shape, size, and extent based on various events and offsets.

Flutter offers a variety of slivers, some of which are listed below:

- SliverAppBar
- SliverList
- SliverGrid

How Do We Utilize Slivers?

It should note that all sliver components should always contain within a CustomScrollView. Then we can mix the slivers to create a unique scrollable area.

What Exactly Is CustomScrollView?

CustomScrollView is a scroll view in Flutter that allows us to design scrolling effects such as grids, lists, and expanding headers. It features a sliver property via which we may send a list of widgets such as SliverAppBar, SliverToBoxAdapter, SliverList, and SliverGrid, among others.

FLUTTER REST API

Today, the majority of apps make use of distant data via APIs. As a result, this section will be crucial for developers who want to create a carrier in Flutter.

Flutter includes an http package for accessing http sites. The http package employs await and async capabilities. It has many high-level methods for transmitting and receiving data from distant places, including read, get, post, put, head, and delete. These approaches make it easier to create REST-based mobile apps.

The explanation of the core methods of the http package are as follows:

- **Read:** This technique is used to read or retrieve resource representations. It uses the get function to request the supplied URL and delivers the response as a Future.

- **Get:** This method asks the get function for the supplied URL and returns a Future answer. In this case, the response is a class that contains the response information.

- **Post:** This method is used to send data to the specified resources. It sends a request to the provided URL by publishing the given data and returns a Future response.

- **Put:** This function is used to update capabilities. It refreshes the target resource's current representation with the request payloads. This method requests the supplied URL and returns a Future response.

- **Head:** Head is identical to the Get method, except it does not include the response body.

- **Delete:** This technique is used to delete all of the resources specified.

DATABASE CONCEPTS IN FLUTTER

A database is a structured collection of data that can be accessed electronically from a computer system and allows storing and manipulating data. Data can organize into rows, columns, tables, and indexes. It simplifies data administration. We may store numerous items in the database such as a person's name, age, photo, image, file, pdf, and so on.

Flutter has a plethora of tools for interacting with databases. The following are the most commonly used and popular packages:

- **sqflite database:** It enables access to and manipulation of SQLite databases.

- **Firebase database:** The Firebase database allows you to access and alter the cloud database.

SQLite Database

SQLite is a well-known database software library that offers a relational database management system for local and client storage. It is a lightweight and tried-and-true database engine with characteristics such as self-contained, server-less, zero-configuration, transactional SQL database engine.

The Flutter SDK does not natively support SQLite. Instead, it includes the sqflite plugin, which handles all database operations in a manner comparable to the SQLite library.

TESTING IN FLUTTER

Testing is a process used to ensure that a program or application is bug-free and fits the user's needs. It assures that the actual outcome is consistent with the predicted result. It also aids in enhancing software or applications in terms of efficiency, usability, and correctness.

Testing is a critical part of the application development life cycle for ensuring the application's quality. It is the most time-consuming stage of the application or software development process.

The Flutter framework is a wonderful tool for automating application testing. To thoroughly test an application, automated testing is divided into three forms. These are their names:

- Unit Testing

- Widget Testing

- Integration Testing

Dart only became popular among developers once the Flutter project gained traction. Even if Dart was a fantastic language with great productivity tools and documentation from its inception, who cares about the language when large corporations aren't utilized in production? But now we've gotten to the stage where, after learning Dart, we can perform valuable things with it. Companies are now utilizing Flutter, and developers use Dart by default in production. Furthermore, a sizable developer community is willing to share their expertise, experiences, and Dart learning process. We feel now is a wonderful moment to begin studying Dart if we haven't already.

When you spend so much time learning a new technology, you want to be especially cautious about its past, present, and future. After months of learning something new, the last thing you want is for that technology to become outdated, deprecated, or fall out of industry standards.

You can be concerned about everything else regarding the Dart language, but you should never be concerned about the language's development and preservation. Dart is one of Google's fastest-growing languages, and it is utilized by several of its products, including Adwords, Flutter, Fuchsia, AngularDart, and others. Outside of Google, this language is used in Alibaba, Adobe, MailChimp, and JetBrains production.

Dart may be compiled by AOT or JIT. Flutter uses this reality because JIT compilation speeds up development (through Hot Reloading and other such features), but AOT compilation provides superior optimization during release time. Hot Reloading is enabled by default in Flutter, which helps developers be more productive.

Reasons Why Flutter App Development Will Be Important in the Future of Cross-Platform Development

1. A unified codebase for all platforms

2. Widgets that is entirely customizable

3. Quicker application development

4. Access to a large number of open-source packages

5. It has excellent learning resources

6. Offers an excellent development experience

7. Low development cost

8. Ideal for MVP

What Effect Will Flutter Play in Mobile Development?
Continue to Improve in 2021 and Beyond

- The null safety of Dart will implement. The package ecosystem and plugin will be shepherded to zero-risk in Flutter.

- The ergonomics and performance of integrating Flutter in current iOS and Android apps will enhance.

- MacOS, Web, Linux, and Windows will all receive production-quality support.

- The overall quality of the Flutter app will be enhanced by concentrated work on runtime performance, application download size overhead, memory utilization, battery usage, and so on.

Bibliography

@cleveroad. (n.d.). *Why Use Flutter for Building Cross-Platform Apps?* Cleveroad Inc. – Web and App Development Company; www.cleveroad.com. Retrieved July 11, 2022, from https://www.cleveroad.com/blog/why-use-flutter/#:~:text=Flutter%20is%20an%20open%2Dsource,)%2C%20and%20even%20Wear%20OS

An Introduction to Flutter: The Basics. (2018, December 7). freeCodeCamp. Org; www.freecodecamp.org. https://www.freecodecamp.org/news/an-introduction-to-flutter-the-basics-9fe541fd39e2/

Bodnar, J. (2020, December 19). *Dart function – working with functions in Dart.* Dart Function – Working with Functions in Dart; zetcode.com. https://zetcode.com/dart/function/

Callable Classes in Dart. (2022, March 25). Callable Classes in Dart; www.tutorialandexample.com. https://www.tutorialandexample.com/callable-classes-in-dart

Control Flow Statements in DART. (2020, March 9). OpenGenus IQ: Computing Expertise & Legacy; iq.opengenus.org. https://iq.opengenus.org/control-flow-statements-in-dart/

Dart – Control Flow Statements. (2022, April 15). Dart – Control Flow Statements; www.tutorialandexample.com. https://www.tutorialandexample.com/dart-control-flow-statements

Dart – Data Types – GeeksforGeeks. (2020, July 11). GeeksforGeeks; www.geeksforgeeks.org. https://www.geeksforgeeks.org/dart-data-types/

Dart Exceptions – Javatpoint. (n.d.). Www.Javatpoint.Com; www.javatpoint.com. Retrieved July 11, 2022, from https://www.javatpoint.com/dart-exceptions

Dart Features – Javatpoint. (n.d.). Www.Javatpoint.Com; www.javatpoint.com. Retrieved July 11, 2022, from https://www.javatpoint.com/dart-features

Dart Hello World Program – W3Adda. (2019, May 15). W3Adda; www.w3adda.com. https://www.w3adda.com/dart-tutorial/dart-hello-world-program

Dart Interfaces. (n.d.). Dart Interfaces; linuxhint.com. Retrieved July 11, 2022, from https://linuxhint.com/dart-interfaces/

Dart Method Overriding – Javatpoint. (n.d.). Www.Javatpoint.Com; www.javatpoint.com. Retrieved July 11, 2022, from https://www.javatpoint.com/dart-method-overriding

Exception Handling in Dart – GeeksforGeeks. (2020, July 17). GeeksforGeeks; www.geeksforgeeks.org. https://www.geeksforgeeks.org/exception-handling-in-dart/

Fanchi, C. (2021, July 5). *Backend and Real-Time Database For Flutter Web And Mobile.* Backendless; backendless.com. https://backendless.com/best-backend-for-flutter-web/#:~:text=Flutter%20is%20a%20popular%20frontend,maintaining%20a%20consistent%20user%20experience

Flutter – Introduction. (n.d.). Flutter – Introduction; www.tutorialspoint.com. Retrieved July 11, 2022, from https://www.tutorialspoint.com/flutter/flutter_introduction.htm

Flutter Calendar – Javatpoint. (n.d.). Www.Javatpoint.Com; www.javatpoint.com. Retrieved July 11, 2022, from https://www.javatpoint.com/flutter-calendar

Flutter First Application – Javatpoint. (n.d.). Www.Javatpoint.Com; www.javatpoint.com. Retrieved July 11, 2022, from https://www.javatpoint.com/flutter-first-application

Flutter Installation – Javatpoint. (n.d.). Www.Javatpoint.Com; www.javatpoint.com. Retrieved July 11, 2022, from https://www.javatpoint.com/flutter-installation

Flutter Tutorial. (n.d.). TutorialKart; www.tutorialkart.com. Retrieved July 11, 2022, from https://www.tutorialkart.com/flutter/

Generics in Dart and Flutter. (2020, July 11). Dart Academy; dart.academy. https://dart.academy/generics-in-dart-and-flutter/

How to Install Flutter on Windows? – GeeksforGeeks. (2021, September 18). GeeksforGeeks; www.geeksforgeeks.org. https://www.geeksforgeeks.org/how-to-install-flutter-on-windows/

Is Flutter a Programming Language? (n.d.). Is Flutter a Programming Language?; www.netguru.com. Retrieved July 11, 2022, from https://www.netguru.com/blog/is-flutter-a-programming-language#:~:text=However%2C%20Flutter%20is%20not%20a,to%20build%20cross%2Dplatform%20apps

khan, S. (2021, May 11). *Explore Generics In Dart & Flutter | by Shaiq khan | FlutterDevs.* Medium; medium.flutterdevs.com. https://medium.flutterdevs.com/explore-generics-in-dart-flutter-6dd62b6f3ed4?gi=117b1b8e5bb3

Method Overriding in Dart – GeeksforGeeks. (2020, July 17). GeeksforGeeks; www.geeksforgeeks.org. https://www.geeksforgeeks.org/method-overriding-in-dart/

TILLU, J. (2019, September 16). *Interface in Dart. Interface defines the syntax that any... | by JAY TILLU | Jay Tillu | Medium.* Medium; medium.com. https://medium.com/jay-tillu/interface-in-dart-5da3b139a3ea

Top 5 BaaS, You Can Opt for Your Flutter Application | Rlogical Techsoft Pvt Ltd. (2021, August 25). Rlogical; www.rlogical.com. https://www.rlogical.com/blog/top-5-baas-you-can-opt-for-your-flutter-application/

Top 8 Flutter Advantages. (2021, May 8). Relevant Software; relevant.software. https://relevant.software/blog/top-8-flutter-advantages-and-why-you-should-try-flutter-on-your-next-project/

Tutorials | Flutter. (n.d.). Tutorials | Flutter; docs.flutter.dev. Retrieved July 11, 2022, from https://docs.flutter.dev/reference/tutorials

What Is Flutter? Complex Guide for 2022. (n.d.). What Is Flutter? Complex Guide for 2022; www.netguru.com. Retrieved July 11, 2022, from https://www.net-guru.com/glossary/flutter

Write your first Flutter app, part 1 | Flutter. (n.d.). Write Your First Flutter App, Part 1 | Flutter; docs.flutter.dev. Retrieved July 11, 2022, from https://docs.flutter.dev/get-started/codelab

Index